· Mother Teresa ·

· *Mother Teresa* ·

NAVIN CHAWLA

ELEMENT
Rockport, Massachusetts ● Shaftesbury, Dorset
Brisbane, Queensland

Navin Chawla is a senior civil servant who works for the Indian Government. Educated both in India and in England at London University and the London School of Economicas, he has enjoyed a varied and challenging career.

Text © Navin Chawla 1992

First published in the UK by Sinclair-Stevenson in 1992

Published in the USA in 1996 by
Element Books, Inc.
PO Box 830, Rockport, MA 01966

Typeset by Rowland Phototypesetting Limited
Bury St. Edmonds, Suffolk
Printed and bound in the USA by
Edwards Brothers, Inc.

Library of Congress Cataloging in Publication
data available

ISBN 1–85230–911–3

· Contents ·

Acknowledgements		vii
Foreword by Mother Teresa		ix
Prologue		xi
1	*Childhood*	1
2	*'The Bengali Teresa'*	6
3	*An Inner Command*	17
4	*Motijhil*	30
5	*14 Creek Lane*	45
6	*Motherhouse*	64
7	*Brothers and Co-Workers*	87
8	*Shishu Bhawan*	115
9	*Titagarh*	135
10	*Kalighat*	155
11	*'The Most Powerful Woman in the World'*	173
12	*Epilogue*	192
	Appendix I	199
	II	211
	III	217
	Index	221

Acknowledgements

I would not have attempted this book had Mother Teresa not blessed the idea. Throughout the five years that I have taken to research and write it, she has given me her complete support and trust, answered innumerable questions and always made time for me, although our views have not always coincided. I have been enriched by the experience and, in a way, am rather sad that it has achieved finality in the covers of a book. I know that the Sisters and Brothers of the Missionaries of Charity do not relish being named, and most have particularly stressed that I should not do so. I have deferred to their wishes except where I believe their names are essential to the narrative. To Father van Exem I owe much; his help was invaluable. I am in the debt of several friends who have helped in different ways and who have, I believe, made the book more endurable. Tejeshwar Singh in New Delhi and Dr Clive Wing in Singapore were particularly patient and helpful. I would like to mention my publisher, Christopher Sinclair-Stevenson, for his faith in an unknown author. To my family a special word of thanks: Rupika, my wife, 'polished' the first draft and helped with ideas, while my daughters, Rukmini and Mrinalini, prodded me along and fended off telephone calls. My uncle, Dr Shiv Gandhi was an excellent sounding board and also helped in the selection of photographs, while my nephew Arjun Soota painstakingly transcribed the tapes. My cousin Meenakshi and her husband Liaquat Ahamed in London facilitated my research at their end. Finally, I acknowledge, alphabetically, other friends and well-wishers: Manjit Bawa, Joya Challiah, Mr & Mrs Adrien Deckers, Jacqueline de Decker, Maud Franken-Spens, Gopal Gandhi, Sonia Gandhi, Lady Goodall, Bunny Gupta, Professor Nurul Hasan, Sunita

Kumar, Sir Michael and Lady Marshall, Amita Mitter, Sunil Sethi, Dr Karan Singh and Dr Anil Wilson. The photographs are courtesy of the following: Raghu Rai; S. Tarafdar and Associates; Chitrabani EMRC and my friend Amarjeet of Cine India International, who was involved in the project from the very start. Some rare photographs were most kindly presented to me by Jacqueline de Decker, Michael Gomes and Brother Mariadas. My acknowledgements would be incomplete without mentioning Valsala Vijayan and Surender Kumar, who generously typed the text in their spare time, as well as the Librarian and Staff of the India International Centre Library (New Delhi), the facilities of which I availed throughout.

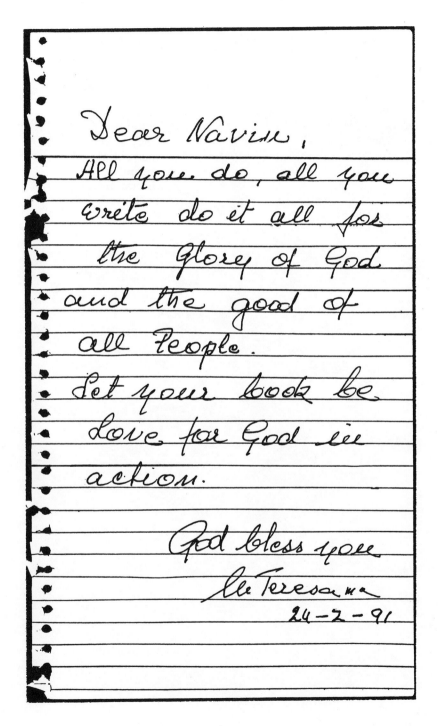

Dear Navin,

All you do, all you write do it all for the Glory of God and the good of all People.

Let your book be Love for God in action.

God bless you
Mc Teresa mc
24-2-91

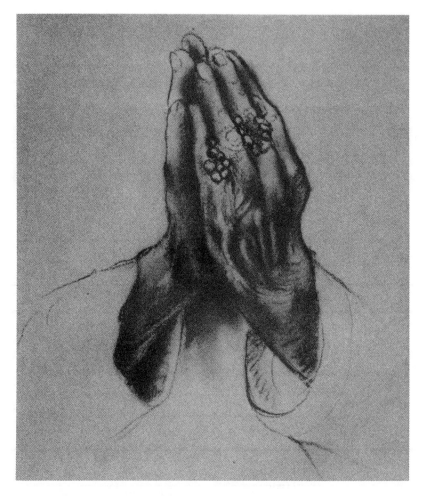

Drawing of Mother Teresa's hands by Manjit Bawa, 1992.

· *Prologue* ·

It was seventeen years ago, at a brief ceremony held in Nirmal Hriday – the Home for the Pure Heart – in Delhi, that I first met Mother Teresa. She had invited the Lieutenant Governor to inaugurate a small rehabilitation centre for elderly inmates as she was eager for Delhi hospitals to place an order for linen and gauze bandages from her tiny two-room unit. She knew that the approval of the head of the city's administration would go a long way to ensure employment for the dozen old people working on the looms. Although I seldom accompanied him on such occasions, I was curious to meet Mother Teresa, and so I went along.

As part of my official functions, I had prepared a speech for the Lieutenant Governor to read out on the occasion. But after being taken around the rehabilitation centre and the two dormitories for homeless old people, who sat up in their cots and greeted us with such warmth and enthusiasm, I was all too glad that my stiff little speech remained in the Lieutenant Governor's pocket.

For it was not a morning for prepared speeches. Mother Teresa spoke about simple things: about love, caring and sharing. She spoke about the new centre and little drops that in the end make the ocean. The Lieutenant Governor responded to her appeal with equal simplicity. He assured Mother Teresa that the hospitals would purchase every last bedsheet, towel and bandage. He also invited Mother Teresa and her Sisters to see him whenever they wished, even without an appointment.

Mother Teresa was prompt in accepting the invitation. One morning not quite two weeks later, there was a knock on my door and Mother Teresa walked into my office. I was so taken aback that it took me a few moments to recover my equilibrium and to respond to this sari-clad nun's 'namaste', her hands folded in traditional Indian greeting. The problem that had brought Mother Teresa from Calcutta was one that most people shudder even to think about: leprosy. This was the meeting which marked the beginning of my involvement with her work.

Mother Teresa, with what I was to soon discover was her usual manner, came straight to the point. I remember her words well. 'There are a number of persons affected by leprosy who migrate to the big cities seeking work or treatment. Many are not able to get help and have no alternative but to beg. If we could be given four or five acres of land, we would start a treatment and rehabilitation centre for them.' I requested Mother Teresa to wait a few moments and informed the Lieutenant Governor of her presence. He immediately received her and the two Sisters who accompanied her. Customary cups of tea were brought in, but these Mother Teresa gently refused, explaining that the Sisters accepted no refreshments, from rich or poor. She spoke to the Lieutenant Governor about the special problems of those afflicted by leprosy. 'Their greatest suffering is that they are feared by all and wanted by none. My Sisters and I try to give them another life, a second life as it were. We have opened many treatment and rehabilitation centres in India. There they work in dignity. They do not have to beg. We are in very close touch with them, and give them tender loving care. We want them to feel that they are also loved.' The Lieutenant Governor was deeply moved. He asked Mother Teresa how much land she required. Mother Teresa, never a person to look a gift horse in the mouth, immediately sensed that victory was hers. With a delightfully childlike smile she promptly doubled the original estimate and asked for ten acres. The Lieutenant Governor instructed me to ensure that at least ten acres of land be handed over to the Missionaries of Charity for a leprosy centre in Delhi.

In the half-hour that Mother Teresa sat in the Lieutenant Governor's chamber, I was able to observe her closely. She was as diminutive then as now, her face deeply lined, even a little shrunken. Her brown eyes twinkled constantly. She appeared to be perceptive and remarkably practical. She could hardly be oblivious of the emotion she aroused in others, but she herself was cheerfully unsentimental. Her vocabulary was limited. She also said 'Thank God' a lot, not in any especially religious sense but as a kind of punctuation mark: 'It's a hot day, thank God', and 'I am glad I came, thank God'. I observed that she wore her sari with grace, something few European women are able to do. Mother Teresa, however, was hardly Albanian any longer. I knew that she had taken Indian citizenship soon after Independence in 1947 and that she spoke Bengali fluently. Long years of working in the slums of Calcutta and elsewhere in India had rendered her as Indian as anyone in her adopted country. It was her hands and her feet, however, that betrayed her arduous life. Her fingers were gnarled and twisted and her feet, encased in rough, ungainly sandals, were misshapen.

Over the years I have often cast my mind back to that morning. What was it that had made it so special? Was it that her self-effacing presence had scaled down the grand chamber in which we sat to her kind of ordinariness? Was it the sari, darned neatly in several places, or the old cloth bag with wooden handles which she carried that contributed to her sense of humility? Perhaps it was all this, as well as the enchantment that clung to her because she had lived so closely with her God.

Gradually I began to understand how deep and whole-hearted is her faith in Christ, whom she sees in every person she ministers to. The first woman she picked up many years ago, lying on a Calcutta street, her face half-eaten by ants and rats, could only be the abandoned Christ. Each emaciated body in her Home for the Dying is the suffering or the dying Christ. For her and for her community it is He whom they tend in every leprous ulcer they clean, child they feed or urine-soaked body they bathe. As Mother Teresa was herself to explain, 'Otherwise I would be able to look after only a few loved ones at the most. People sometimes ask me how I can clean the stinking wound of a leprosy patient. They say to me, "We cannot do it for love of all the money in the world." I tell them, "Nor can we. But we do it for love of Him."'

It was this realisation that enabled me to grasp the acceptance of situations and the ease with which the Sisters smile. Slowly, too, I understood the depth of meaning behind their vows. The vow of chastity consists of giving their hearts to Christ. 'I am married to Him, so to speak, as you are to your wife,' Mother Teresa once casually explained. The vow of obedience is one by which the Sisters dedicate to Him their free will. By their vow of poverty they undertake to live like the poor in order to understand them as equals. They accept no money, not even a cup of tea in gratitude. How can gratitude be material when the service is to God, upon God and for God? Their fourth vow is unique to their Order: to serve only the poorest of the poor. In the process, Mother Teresa gladly offers the rich and powerful a chance to join in the work. When I once observed two American senators and an affluent matron from Nigeria on their hands and knees, scrubbing the floors in the Home of the Dying at

Kalighat, she nodded and said, 'That is the beauty of God's work, it has involved so many people.' She added softly, 'I give them the opportunity to touch the poor.'

When I asked Mother Teresa if poverty was her strength, she replied that poverty was actually her freedom. When she stepped out of Calcutta's Loreto Convent at Entally, her worldly possessions were three saris and a five-rupee note. The only thing she had in abundance was faith: faith in her mission, that He would guide her and that He would provide. When she set foot in Motijhil, she did not feel that it was necessary to carry out a survey or to make a plan or raise funds. She simply saw that there was need for a school. The fact that there was no building, no chairs or tables did not deter her. On a small open patch among the shanties, she began to scratch the Bengali alphabet with a stick on the ground. A few children appeared and with each passing day, more and more children joined. In a spirit of community participation someone donated a chair or two, a bench and a blackboard. Within a few days, the little school had become a reality.

The poor of Motijhil also needed medical help. Mother Teresa had a little training but no medicines. In the time-honoured tradition of mendicants, she taught herself to beg. What medicines she collected were dispensed all too easily, for the need was great. Many needed urgent hospitalisation. When a hospital refused to take in a dying woman for want of space, she sat obstinately at its entrance until the hospital relented. Gradually they not only learned to say 'yes' to her, they sent their ambulance whenever she asked for it. Soon she opened her first dispensary. Over the next forty-three years the institutional ventures of the Missionaries of Charity encompassed not just schools and dispensaries, but homes for abandoned children, for the leprosy-afflicted and for the destitute and dying. More recently they have opened centres for those suffering from AIDS.

By 1990, 456 centres were established in more than one hundred countries. During that year 500,000 families were fed, 20,000 slum children were taught in 124 schools, 90,000 leprosy patients were treated and 17,048 'shut-ins' were visited in their homes. Six AIDS shelters admitted 661 patients, of whom eighty-eight died during the year. From catechism classes to prison visiting, from homes for abandoned children to houses for alcoholics and drug abusers, the Missionaries of Charity have created a multinational organisation that reaches out to the helpless and the poor. The Sisters are in the most unlikely places on every continent. I once asked Mother Teresa if there was any place she had not reached. She replied with a laugh, 'If there are poor on the moon, we shall go there too!'

At a time when dwindling attendances are a matter of concern to the church, the Missionaries of Charity now number almost 4,000. Several hundred girls anxiously await acceptance into a life of almost absurd hardship. Cheerfulness, commonsense and sturdy health are prerequisites. The training of the Sisters and the administration of this global outfit is carried out largely from Motherhouse, as Mother Teresa's headquarters at 54A Lower Circular Road are known. It is to a small office, manned during the day by three Sisters who sit at rickety typewriters, that Mother Teresa, herself, retreats after 10 p.m. She deals with messages, pressing demands and her correspondence until the early hours of the morning. Many of the letters and notes that I have received over the years have been written during those hours of solitude. Sometimes, when I have seen her looking heavy-lidded and asked why she does not sleep at least six hours a night, she has laughingly said that there is enough time for that in the hereafter.

During the early years of our acquaintance I met Mother Teresa almost every time she was in Delhi. I became a frequent visitor to her Delhi 'ashram'. Sometimes she would

> Dear Rukmini,
> May God's blessing
> be with you during
> this time of examina-
> tions. God bless you
> 23-2-91   Mc Teresa mc

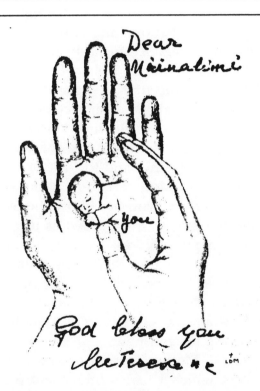

> Dear
> Mainalimi
>
> you
>
> God bless you
> Mc Teresa mc

See! I will not forget you . . . I have carved
you on the palm of My hand . . . I have
called you by your name . . . You are mine
. . . You are precious to Me . . . I love you.

Isaiah

surprise me, as she did the very first day, by opening the door of my office and asking with a disarming smile, 'May I come in?' On other occasions when she was passing through Delhi, I would go to the airport to meet her. I began to welcome her occasionally delayed flights, for this gave me the opportunity for longer talks with her.

One day I asked her if I could help with my hands in some way. She understood my need. The Lieutenant Governor, too, permitted me to take Friday afternoons off, which were spent away from the heat of the Emergency with the leprosy patients and the elderly destitutes of Nirmal Hriday.

It was only natural that over the years Mother Teresa and her community of Sisters became a special part of my family life. She visited our home and blessed our family, friends and neighbours. On the first of these visits, word of her presence spread through the neighbourhood like wildfire and soon our house was overflowing. I asked her to address us and she did so, speaking from her heart about the need for families to pray together and to stay together.

During those years Mother Teresa wrote us letters and notes of encouragement with her blessings. She sometimes sent just a written prayer. She guided us through our difficult times. When my children were nervous before their examinations, she prayed for them. She even held a special mass for me when she believed it to be necessary. Once, after one of life's storms, when she asked me how I was, and I replied I was well, she said with a laugh, 'In that case I can stop praying for you now.'

In October 1988, Mother Teresa came specially to Delhi to release a report which I had written on leprosy in India. Such is her charisma that the lawns where the function was being held were packed well in advance. When her turn came to speak, Mother Teresa asked the audience to join her in reading aloud St Francis of Assisi's prayer for peace, copies of which she had asked me to distribute beforehand.

She spoke simply, without a trace of rhetoric. She told the audience about the work of the Missionaries of Charity in the field of leprosy, enjoining them to help in little ways. She spoke about the 'leprosy of the West', people abandoned to lonely lives, whom she called the 'shut-ins'. She emphasised the need for families to bring prayer back into their lives and also to reach out to neighbours in need. She gave the example of a family of six in Calcutta which, when she had chanced upon them, had not eaten for two days. The children's eyes were shining with hunger. When she brought them some rice, the family divided the portion in two, so that they could share it with a family in their neighbourhood who had also gone without food. The poor, she said, always share. What surprised her was that they *knew* of a need as great as their own. She spoke of simple truths: of love beginning at home and of the sharing of joy, especially with one's own family.

Mother Teresa is not a particularly eloquent speaker at the best of times. That evening, she did not say anything that she had not said many times before. But after she finished speaking, a hush descended on the listeners. It was a spell that no-one wished to be the first to break. For a few seconds, the only sound I heard was from a wealthy, self-obsessed woman sitting near me. Mother Teresa had touched some remote chord in her and she was weeping. Suddenly, a small child ran from her chair and requested Mother Teresa for an autograph. She was followed by her mother. Others plucked up their courage until Mother Teresa found herself surrounded by practically the entire audience, most of whom were holding copies of the report, which had been distributed to them. On these she wrote these twenty letters of the alphabet, slowly and painstakingly, over and over again, 'God bless you, M. Teresa M.C.' When the last guest had departed, it was dark. She sat back, exhausted, with a tired smile. Reaching out, she clasped my hands in hers and

Mother M. Teresa, MC
Missionaries of Charity
54 A Lower Circular Rd.
Calcutta 700016 India

J.D.G.M.

11-12-87

My dear Sisters,

Mr. + Mrs. Chawla — are coming to your place, allow them to take photos of the work and the Poor you serve — and also if they put any questions regarding the work answer.

God bless you
bc Teresa me.

whispered to herself, 'Jesus, I am doing this for you. These twenty letters are for you.'

It was soon after this occasion that I asked Mother Teresa whether I might attempt to write a book about her. Her first reaction was that she did not want yet another summing-up of her life in the nature of a biography. Then, after a moment's thought, she nodded and said, 'Write about the work.' That I did not share her faith was not a matter of any concern to her.

Over the next four years she reposed her trust in me and gave me a letter addressed to all her Sisters, permitting them to show me their work and answer my questions; I used this letter frequently on my travels. I went often to Calcutta, where Mother Teresa would invariably ask when she saw me, 'Is the book ready?' Three years later, as a result of a combination of preoccupation and nervousness, I had not yet written a word and said to Mother Teresa that, being a civil servant, I wanted to do my research thoroughly. She agreed, and never repeated her question. From then on, whenever I arrived in Motherhouse, she would say, 'Achha, so you have come?', and proceed to help me with the odd letter of introduction or answer my latest volley of queries. The only area she remained reticent about was her personal life, which she invariably shrugged off as of no consequence.

Mother Teresa does not lend herself easily to would-be biographers. Her constant refrain is that she, herself, is nothing, merely a pencil in the hands of God. In any event, the biographical details of Mother Teresa's early life are as slight as they are well-known. To inquiries about her life in Skopje, the influence of her mother and her separation from her family when she was only eighteen, her answers were desultory, her heart not in the conversation, her smile leading one away to the work of her community and to her current occupations. As for her twenty years as a Loreto nun, she pointed the way to her contemporaries, who in turn spoke to me about their days as her fellow teachers or students. Father Celeste van Exem, her spiritual confessor during the crucial time she received her Call and the years thereafter, shared with me the developments in those important years of formation. It was mainly in talking about her work that Mother Teresa's enthusiasm was infectious and at its height when she spoke of her faith in God, the incarnate Christ and the Mass which sustained her.

While I was conscious that Mother Teresa had requested me to write about 'the work', I found that it was not altogether easy to separate her from the Mission that she had founded. Her inspiration, humility and grace were like invisible threads that bound the whole together. In the course of my constant examination of the Sisters wherever I went, I was often told to 'ask Mother'. Her teachings, everyday examples and faith are deeply reflected in the work of the community. Even when I spoke with Sisters in countries far from India, it was always 'Mother this' and 'Mother that'. It was almost as if she were present in the next room and would walk in at any moment to rescue them from my enquiries and enable them to get back to the 'real work'.

Her work itself has had a profound effect in the most unlikely places and often at the highest levels. When the Soviet Union failed to respond to her request to open a convent, she reminded President Gorbachov by sending him a greeting on St Michael's Day! She implored President Bush and President Saddam Hussein to desist from a war which was wrecking millions of innocent lives and, after the cessation of hostilities, obtained the Iraqi President's permission to open six centres in that war-ravaged country. Many countries have showered their highest honours on her. With no constituency save that of the poor and least powerful, she has regular entrée into the halls of power. Whether she acknowledges it or not, this eighty-two-year-old nun is a tremendous force in the Church. Mother Teresa would probably be appalled to know that the prelate of Calcutta is referred to in

the Vatican as 'Mother Teresa's Archbishop'. Cardinals vie to
be seen with her. The Pope receives her when she visits Rome
as he might receive his child. Yet she remains humility itself.

It has not been easy to encapsulate Mother Teresa within
the confines of a mere book. For each meeting with this ordi-
nary-looking woman has left behind something memorable.
I can vividly remember her emerging joyfully from an international flight, clutching two heavy plastic bags full of biscuits, soap and other leftovers, a gift from the Captain for the
children of Shishu Bhavan. There was the time when she sat
consoling a woman terribly deformed by leprosy, who had
been abandoned by her sons. I also recall her hugging and
being photographed with a six-year-old child, whose parents
later told me that the doctors in Calcutta had given up their
battle with a malignant disease. The child was dying. Then
one day, Mother Teresa arrived without warning. She knelt
down to pray in this middle-class Hindu home, and somewhere a miracle seemed to have worked: for the last two years
the child has been well and gaining weight. My wife and I
once missed receiving her at Delhi's domestic airport because,
unknown to us, a car had met her at the aircraft itself and
whisked her away; she later joked that there had to be some
advantage to being Mother Teresa! Almost as if it happened
yesterday, I remember the surprise and happiness on her face
when, clutching a tiny premature baby found abandoned on
her doorstep, she exclaimed, 'She's still alive! God willing,
she will pull through.' I reminded her of her early days, when
she walked miles each day in order to find a room from where
she could start her work, and she said that that, too, was the
sacrifice; there has never been any doubt, or anything but a
special happiness in serving God.

As a Hindu, armed only with a certain eclecticism, it took
me longer than most to understand that Mother Teresa is with
Christ in each conscious hour, whether at Mass or with each
of those whom she tends. It is not a different Christ on her

crucifix and a different one which lies dying at Kalighat. Neither exists without the other; they are both one. There can be no contradiction in her frequently repeated words that one must reach out to one's neighbour. For Mother Teresa, to love one's neighbour is to love God; if one is unable to love one's neighbour, one is unable to love God. This is what is essential to her, not the size of her Mission, nor the power others may perceive in her. In a recent meeting, she explained this to me simply but meaningfully when she said, 'We are called upon not to be successful, but to be faithful.' In her life she has exemplified that faith: faith in prayer, in love, in service and in peace.

1

· *Childhood* ·

According to Mother Teresa's Indian Diplomatic passport, Mary Teresa Bojaxhiu was born on 26 August 1910 in Skopje, Yugoslavia. In 1910, Skopje was a small town with a population of about 25,000. It was then part of the kingdom of Albania, itself a part of the Ottoman Empire. Albania had experienced several centuries of Islamic rule under Turkish domination, and Catholics comprised only a small fraction of the population. Albania, itself, was at that time at the crossroads of divergent cultural and religious forces.

Her family were townsmen engaged in business. They were not of peasant stock, as is sometimes believed. Her father, Nicholas Bojaxhiu, was a building contractor. His firm was a well-known one and constructed the first Skopje Theatre. He was a member of the Town Council and spoke a number of languages, including, besides his native Albanian, Serbo-Croatian and Turkish. Father Celeste van Exem, Mother Teresa's spiritual director in the early days, was to tell me that she had described her father as a man with a charitable disposition, who never refused the poor. Her mother, Dranafile Bernai, came from nearby Venice. They lived in a large house set in a spacious garden with a number of fruit trees. There were two other children, Age, a sister born in 1904, and Lazar, a brother, in 1907.

Mother Teresa has said often that her family was a joyful one, and that, 'We were very closely united, especially after my father's death.' The children's early education was at the Sacred Heart Church. They moved on to non-Catholic state schools and were taught in the compulsory Serbo-Croatian language. However, their religious training continued to be strengthened, both at the parish as well as at home. In one of her few references to her family, Mother Teresa said, 'I was very close to my mother', and described her as 'very holy'. Father van Exem believed that her mother had a far-reaching influence on young Agnes (as she was christened a day after her birth), particularly in her spiritual life, for her mother was not merely religious in the formal sense; her sense of commitment to her faith had its practical aspects, which caused her never to turn away those in need who reached her door, whether seeking food, shelter, clothing or even money. 'She taught us to love God and to love our neighbour,' said Mother Teresa.

A few fascinating glimpses of her early life were revealed to the world by her brother Lazar when he attended the Nobel Award ceremony in Oslo in December 1979, when Mother Teresa received the Nobel Peace Prize. As a child they called her not Agnes, but Gonxha, 'flower bud' in Albanian, for she was pink and plump. She was neat and tidy and always helpful. Lazar confessed that as a child he had a great weakness for confectionery and desserts, and often made nocturnal visits to the kitchen cupboard. Gonxha was the only one who never stole the jam. She unfailingly reminded her brother that he should touch no food after midnight if they were to attend mass in the morning, but she never complained about these expeditions to their mother.

Gonxha's mother was imbued with a strong sense of values. The children called their mother 'Nana Loke', 'Nana' meaning mother, 'Loke' meaning the soul; 'the mother of my soul'. She disliked waste of any kind. Mother Teresa confirmed a tale I had once read about this sense of frugality. One evening the children were sitting around their mother, engaged in childish chatter. This went on for a considerable length of time, throughout which their mother remained silent. Finally she left the room, only to turn off the power switch, which plunged the house into darkness. It was of no use, she said, to waste electricity on foolish talk.

It could only have been her deep faith that helped her to overcome the tragedy of the untimely death of her husband in 1917, after which she lay in a stupor for several months. When eventually recovered, she turned resolutely to starting a small business of her own, that of selling embroidered cloth, turning adversity into enterprise. With her earnings she was able to bring up her three children; as Nicholas Bojaxhiu's business partner misappropriated the firm's assets, leaving the widow and her family with scarcely more than the roof over their heads, this was imperative. This self-sufficiency in the face of tragedy must have deeply influenced Agnes, who was seven when her father died.

The Church of the Sacred Heart, more than ever before, became an important part of the family's life. Agnes and her sister began to participate in a number of parish activities. Agnes was frequently in the Church library, as she loved books.

'I was only twelve years old and lived at home with my parents in Skopje when I first felt the desire to become a nun,' recalled Mother Teresa. It was natural for her to turn to her mother, who at first opposed the idea, as Agnes was, after all, still a child. In due course Agnes forgot her first impulse, yet was moving inexorably on an almost pre-ordained path. Mother and daughter spent many hours in church, their most fervent prayer the holy rosary recited at the feet of the Lady of Letnice in Skopje, or late at night in their own home. After school hours, Agnes was involved in parish activities. It was here that her family also came into contact with Father Jambrenkovic, who became the pastor in 1925. He started a branch of a society called the Sodality of the Blessed Virgin Mary. This was to have a far-reaching effect on Agnes, for it was the same Sodality that she was to join, years later, in the Entally Convent in Calcutta.

In the Sodality, they learned about the lives of saints and missionaries, and from Father Jambrenkovic about the Yugoslav Jesuits who went on a mission to the province of Bengal in India in 1924. The zeal of these early missionaries was recounted to members of the Sodality, and struck an especially strong chord in Agnes. 'They used to give us the most beautiful descriptions about the experiences they had with the people, and especially the children in India,' recalled Mother Teresa. She learned that there was an order of nuns serving in Bengal whose main work was in the field of education. These Loreto nuns were members of an international order, and Bengal was served by the Irish Province.

Now a young woman, Agnes had developed several other important qualities. According to Lazar, she was a good student, meticulous in her appearance and well-organised. She started giving children religious instruction and grew to love teaching. A cousin also recalled that even in those early days, she was a girl who refused no-one help or assistance, who could be depended upon and who was friendly to all religious persuasions.

It was six years after those first stirrings that Mother Teresa received a Call to leave her family and loved ones behind and become a missionary. In the face of her own doubts as to whether she had, indeed, received a Call, she turned to Father Jambrenkovic. It was he who explained to her that the Call of God had necessarily to be accompanied by a feeling of deep joy, especially where this was an indication of life's vocation.

Recently, sitting on a small bench outside the Chapel at Motherhouse, Mother Teresa said to me, 'At eighteen I decided to leave home to become a nun. By then I realised my vocation was towards the poor. From then on, I have never had the least doubt of my decision.' Pointing a finger towards Heaven, she added, 'He made the choice.' Nor was there any doubt in her mother's mind this time. When Gonxha informed her, *Nana Loke* went to her room where she remained for twenty-four hours. When she emerged, both mother and daughter were aware of the chosen path, and she advised her young daughter, 'Put your hand in His hand and walk all the way with Him.'

In submission to what quite clearly was God's will, Agnes applied to the Loreto order in Bengal. She was informed that the route to Bengal lay via Loreto Abbey in Rathfarman in Ireland, where she first must go to learn some English. On 26 September 1928, Agnes, accompanied by her mother and sister, left Skopje for Zagreb by train. At the Skopje railway station, she wished her relatives, friends and members of the Sodality, who had come to bid her goodbye, a tearful farewell. The few days in Zagreb with her beloved mother and sister went by in a flash. When finally she waved her mother goodbye at the Zagreb station, it was the last time she ever saw her.

2

· 'The Bengali Teresa' ·

Although Mother Teresa spent barely two months as a young postulant at Rathfarman, she remembers clearly the chapel, the community room and Mother Borgia Irwin, who taught her English, which was to be her spoken language from then on. In November 1928, she set sail for India and arrived at Calcutta after seven weeks.

What her first impressions of Calcutta were we shall never know, thanks to her reluctance to talk of such matters. She would certainly have alighted from the 'Bombay Mail' at the Howrah railway station to strange colours, sounds and smells, with coolies jostling for luggage amidst crowds of people who would have come to receive passengers and goods. She spent just a few days in Calcutta for, on 16 January 1929, she was despatched to the Loreto Novitiate in the mountain resort of Darjeeling, 400 miles north of Calcutta. It was here, below snow-clad Mount Kanchenjunga, that she began her life as a novice.

Darjeeling was a fashionable hill resort. Before the capital of the British Raj shifted from Calcutta to New Delhi in 1911, the Viceroy and his entourage would, on the onset of 'general hot weather', repair to Darjeeling. For four months this small town would witness a seemingly endless succession of balls and fêtes. The garden parties on the immaculate lawns of Government House were attended by a galaxy of uniformed British officials, members of the Viceroy's

Council, generals, judges and a sprinkling of Maharajas and their bejewelled Maharanis.

Even when the summer capital of India shifted to Simla in the north of India, life in Darjeeling continued as before, except that the presiding deity was now the Governor of Bengal. Darjeeling, at this time, was also the principal centre of British education in India. It boasted several schools run by missionaries, which were attended mainly by British children as well as a few from wealthy Indian families. The Loreto Convent, to which young Agnes was sent, was one such school.

Sister Marie-Thérèse Breen was one of Mother Teresa's contemporaries in the Novitiate in Darjeeling. Life in the Novitiate sixty years ago was 'an age apart'. The Mistress of Novices was Sister Murphy, who believed that the novices should be given a thorough grounding in the habits of prayer and the works of the apostolate. For two hours each day the novices also taught poor children, an on-the-job training, as it were. Once a week they went to their Confessor. Sister Breen told me that Agnes was immersed in English lessons from the very beginning. They also had to learn an Indian language: Agnes began to learn Bengali, and picked up a smattering of Hindi as well. So completely absorbed were they in their daily activities behind the Convent's walls that the two years went by quickly indeed.

On 24 March 1931, Agnes took her first vows, those of poverty, chastity and obedience as a sister of Loreto. She felt inspired to take her name in religious life from a French nun called Thérèse Martin, who prayed for missionaries and their success and died of tuberculosis at the early age of twenty-four. Her exceptional goodness in executing the humblest and most ordinary of tasks fired the imagination of Catholics everywhere. In 1927, the Vatican canonised her with the title St Thérèse of Lisieux.

There was, however, a slight problem about the name,

since Sister Breen, who completed her novitiate the year before, had already taken the name of Marie-Thérèse. In order to obviate confusion, Agnes decided to spell it in the Spanish way, 'Teresa', invariably leading people to ask whether she had taken the name of the great Spanish Carmelite nun. 'Not the big St Teresa of Avila,' she explained to me patiently, as she had to hundreds of others before, 'but the little one,' meaning, of course, St Thérèse of Lisieux. In Loreto Entally, however, the community soon found a more novel way of distinguishing the two. She soon came to be called the 'Bengali Teresa', probably because she spoke the language so well.

*   *   *

Her novitiate completed, Sister Teresa, as she was now called, was sent to teach at St Mary's School, a part of Loreto Convent in the Calcutta suburb of Entally. She was to remain there for seventeen happy years, first as a teacher and then, from 1937, as principal of the school. These were years of deep spiritual formation, which she was to acknowledge generously over the years with the words, 'In my heart, I am Loreto'.

My journey into the 'Bengali Teresa's' years as an ordinary Loreto nun began, appropriately enough, at her headquarters at 54A Lower Circular Road in Calcutta. Over the years I had come to accept that Mother Teresa is loath to talk about herself. 'I am not important,' she has often said, and has invariably added, 'write about the work.' I therefore decided to talk to Sister Joseph Michael, whom Mother Teresa had herself assigned to help me with information and direction, to assist me now in reconstructing her life at St. Mary's. As a first step, Sister Joseph Michael, a Calcutta girl herself, arranged for me to meet Father van Exem.

I found Father Celeste van Exem living in retirement in Calcutta's prestigious St Xavier's College. Well over eighty years of age, and unable to walk without support, he now rarely leaves his room. A member of the Society of Jesus, he came to Calcutta from his native Belgium during the Second World War. He had earlier spent several years in the Middle East and spoke fluent Arabic. In Calcutta, he soon made many Muslim friends.

During the war he was asked to perform Mass at St Mary's School in its temporary abode in Convent Street, and there he met Mother Teresa for the first time, on 12 July 1944. It was not long before he was appointed her spiritual director and, during what was perhaps the most crucial period of her life, guided and advised her.

Father van Exem greeted me politely. It became increasingly evident that he guarded his association with Mother Teresa jealously. Only when convinced of my intentions did he open the floodgates of his prodigious memory of Mother Teresa's early days. 'She has never wanted publicity,' he said. 'I used to say that it is a necessity. Mother Teresa cannot advertise her work, she has no ability and no time.' He paused before adding, 'A book about Mother Teresa is all for the good.'

'Have you been to Entally?' he asked me one afternoon. 'They have a written script which contains a few enlightening details. It has been prepared by Sisters who have lived with Mother Teresa for almost twenty years, first in Darjeeling, where she was a novice, and then as a young professed nun in the Entally Convent. Show the nuns your letter from Mother Teresa, show them the blessing, and tell them that you have been here to see me and that I have sent you to the Entally Convent. And there you will learn more.'

Thus prompted, I headed for Entally. The distance from Calcutta's fashionable Park Street, with its large hotels, airline offices and boutiques, to the Convent was only a few miles, but as we drove past down-at-heel neighbourhoods and large slums, we had clearly entered another world.

It came as a pleasant surprise then to enter through tall iron gates set in high grey walls into a neat complex of playing fields and closely cropped lawns. Here stood several buildings of varying vintage, from a large turn-of-the-century colonial edifice with colonnades and bright green wooden shutters to a more compact grey classroom block clearly of more recent origin. Sharing the grounds is St Mary's School, a separate institution with yellow-washed corridors. I first entered the Convent parlour with its polished teakwood furniture and framed prints, and sent a little note to Mother Superior. A few minutes later, a sprightly Irish nun entered. She informed me in quite a matter-of-fact way that she herself had come to the Entally Convent a few months after Mother Teresa had left it, and therefore had no first-hand knowledge that she could share. She did have a few copies of a written script and would be pleased to give me one. Meanwhile, would I like to look around?

The Loreto Convent at Entally began as an orphanage for children of all denominations. Even today, most of its 300-odd boarders are orphans or homeless children. Almost the same number are Bengali children of middle-class families, who attend the day school. Another 200 poor children attend St Mary's where they are taught in the Bengali language by nuns.

It was to St Mary's Convent that Sister Teresa, having made profession of her First Vows in Darjeeling, was despatched. The Sisters worked at St Mary's with the Daughters of St Anne, a diocesan congregation founded by Loreto in 1898. The nuns, comprised of Bengali women who taught in their language, wore not the European habit but the sari. For the next few years, Sister Teresa taught geography, history and catechism, and performed several other duties besides. At that time, Mother du Cenacle, a Mauritian nun, was Superior at St Mary's. It was not long before Sister Teresa was to become Mother du Cenacle's right arm. 'I don't know whether I was a good teacher,' she once laughingly told me, 'I only know I loved teaching.'

Sister Marie-Thérèse Breen now lives in semi-retirement at Loreto College in Middleton Row, the first women's college opened by the Order in India. She is eighty-four; when I remarked that she did not look a day older than seventy, she laughed delightedly, a pleasant tinkling sound that reverberated in the well-furnished hall of the College where we sat. Her complexion, despite the rigours of the Indian sun, has remained the proverbial peaches-and-cream. She told me in her gentle way that she came out from Rathfarman in 1928, 'a year before Mother Teresa did'. She had spent practically her entire life at Entally, shifting to the upper-class precincts of Middleton Row only three years earlier. She no longer taught. Despite her difficulty in walking, she supports herself with a stick and supervises the College gardens, which seem to be doing rather better than those of Raj Bhavan, the Governor's house, not far away.

'Mother Teresa,' said Sister Breen, 'was always very simple and very nice. As I said, I got to know her in 1929. There was nothing extraordinary about her. Just that she was a very simple, ordinary girl. Very gentle, full of fun. Enjoyed everything that went on. In those early years there was nothing to suggest that she would ever leave Loreto, nothing at all. We never thought for one single moment that this would be where she would end up.'

'We were in the Novitiate together in Darjeeling,' she continued, 'then I came to Calcutta. She was still up there; she had not completed her course. When she finished in 1931, she came down to Entally where I was and there we were together again for about fifteen years. But I was not with her all the time, because she was in adjoining St Mary's and I was over at the Orphanage. So I only met her at meal times, when the community got together, and so on. We did not go out in those days, more cloistered if you like.'

The average day at St Mary's was a long one. Classes were held in steady succession from 9 a.m. to 3 p.m. In the morning and evening there was 'minding', the Loreto term for looking after the smaller children. There was correction of classwork, which followed school hours, and supervision of the children's recreation hour. 'We had to keep a certain amount of discipline. We had a timetable which we followed. We were not forced, but if one was unable to follow it, it showed an inability for the vocation.'

'How did Mother Teresa fit into Loreto?' I asked. 'She was a very hard worker,' answered Sister Breen. 'Very. Up to time on this, up to time on that. She never wanted to shirk anything, she was always ready. Always a very pious person, she was just herself. She did not force it on anybody, if you like, she was just what she felt she had to be.' After a pause she added, 'She fitted in very well; we were all very happy, very happy.'

An engaging vignette of convent life in the thirties was recalled by some of the nuns I met. Sister Francesca, now seventy, continues to be Secretary at St Mary's, long after her formal retirement in 1983. As a pupil at St Mary's she was taught by Mother Teresa and recalled that she laid great store by personal hygiene, even in those days.

'When I came here, on 13 January 1936, she was still Sister Teresa. She was not then perpetually professed. In the morning she used to take us for our baths. She would stand there, ring the bell for us to pour water on ourselves, ring the bell for us to soap ourselves, ring the bell for us to pour water again, and ring the bell for us to come out. She would stand at the door with a bottle of permanganate of potassium. As we emerged, she would put this in our mouths and make sure we gargled!

'In those years, between 1936 and 1937, Sister Teresa was put in charge of St Teresa's Primary School, "Bengali Medium" in Lower Circular Road. Before she left in the morning, she took our catechism class. Upon her return at about 4 p.m. she would take us for study and sometimes evening prayers.

'But what I enjoyed the most as a child was Sunday school,' continued Sister Francesca with an impish smile. 'There Sister Teresa organised classes for primary school children. We were all very happy to have an outing. Lots of poor children attended the school. They all used to have a bath after school, and at the end of the year prizes were awarded. What a big crowd there used to be!'

During the war years, from 1939 to 1945, a number of families fled Calcutta. Sister Francesca told me that her family moved to Chittagong in East Pakistan. When she returned to Calcutta seven years later, she found many changes at Entally. Sister Teresa had taken Final Vows on 24 May 1939 in Darjeeling, and was back at St Mary's as Superior. She was now known as Mother Teresa. A year later when Mother du Cenacle became ill, it was quite natural for Mother Teresa to be made Principal, but she continued taking her classes as before.

A number of her pupils testified that Mother Teresa made her classes very interesting. 'She taught catechism well, with many examples from her own life,' said Sister Francesca. Geography was her main subject. A pupil called Magdalena Gomes, later to become Sister Gertrude, recalled that she made the subject 'come alive'. It is not a little ironic that Mother Teresa, who taught world geography for seventeen years, never left the province of Bengal for over thirty years. It would have seemed inconceivable in 1965, when she opened her first house overseas, in Venezuela, that one day the mission she founded would spread to more than one hundred countries encircling the globe.

It was Father van Exem who revealed another secret of Loreto Entally, that of the existence of Sister Rozario O'Reilly. Sister Rozario, a shy, retiring person, was difficult to find, but after several abortive visits, I was finally able to make an appointment to meet her. My first impression was of a kindly face, deeply lined, tanned by the Calcutta sun. She had a pronounced Irish lilt, all too clearly marking her as a 'Rathfarman girl'. She said she was over eighty, but there is something about these nuns that makes most of them look at least ten years younger, and Sister Rozario was no exception.

When Sister Rozario 'came out' in 1938, Mother Teresa had already been in India a decade. 'From 1931 to 1944, Mother Teresa was a teacher. After Mother du Cenacle became ill in 1944, Mother Teresa became Principal. She taught various subjects, presided at meals and at the morning assembly.

'Our day began at half past five in the morning,' said Sister Rozario. 'Mother Teresa was always very punctual. We had meditation first, then Mass daily at six in the morning, after that prayers, then morning duties of the children. I think she used to supervise the children's meals in the morning. She also had her classes. She had office work besides. She helped Mother du Cenacle; they worked very well together. There were classes till three in the afternoon. Then tea. Correction of class work was followed by evening prayers. I know she had evening supervision of the boarders and she supervised the evening meal, certainly.'

Sister Francesca said, 'She is an utterly selfless creature. She is extraordinary in her sacrifice. She can do anything for the love of God, endure any humiliation or suffering. She was always free of personal bias and did not hesitate to speak out when there was something wrong.'

There were other facets to her personality that came across vividly in the accounts of her early contemporaries. She was a dedicated person who did not spare herself. She was charitable but would not easily tolerate uncharitableness in others. Then, as now, she had a ready sense of humour. She enjoyed witty remarks and jokes, and would hold her waist in both hands and bend double with laughter.

She exemplified obedience, then as much as now. 'The only people she is not obedient to are her poor doctors,' said Sister Marie-Thérèse Breen, with a laugh. 'I expect she finds she has so much to do she has not the time to listen to them.' She continued, 'She has always been very steady. Very humble. She has never lost that humility. She has always remained that simple, humble person, she's just herself.'

When I asked Sister Breen what influences could have shaped Mother Teresa in those long Loreto years, she answered without a moment's hesitation. 'Her life of prayer, her closeness to God.' She added, 'She was very ordinary. We just looked upon her as one of our Sisters who was very devoted and dedicated, but I could never envision this large institute around the world, nobody envisioned this.'

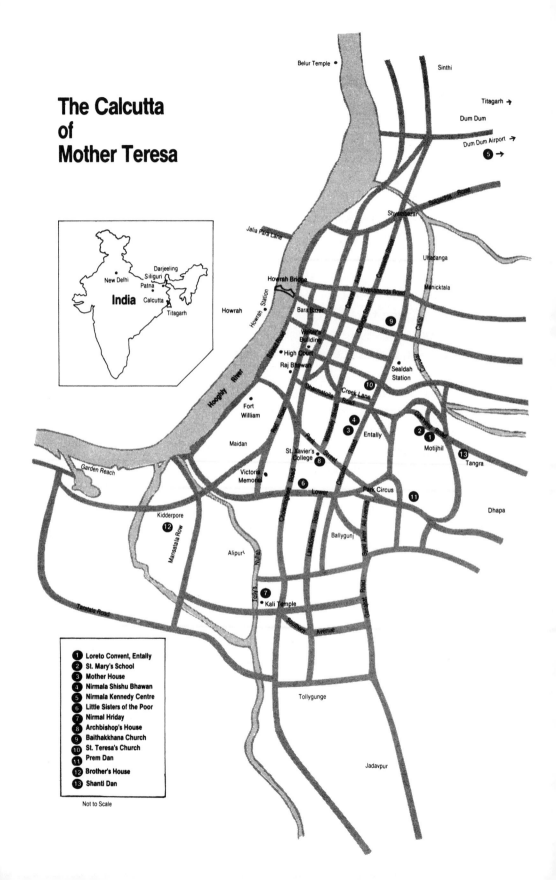

The Calcutta
of
Mother Teresa

India

New Delhi
Darjeeling
Siliguri
Patna
Calcutta
Titagarh

Belur Temple
Sinthi
Titagarh →
Dum Dum
Dum Dum Airport →
⑤ →

Shyambazar
Ultadanga
Manicktala
Jalia Para Lane
Howrah Bridge
Howrah Station
Howrah
Bara Bazar
⑨
Writers Building
High Court
Raj Bhawan
Sealdah Station
⑩
Dharmotola Road
Creek Lane
Fort William
④
③ Entally
② ①
Maidan
Motijhil
⑬
St. Xavier's College
⑧
Tangra
Victoria Memorial
⑥
Lower
Park Circus
⑪
Dhapa
Kidderpore
⑫
Mansatala Row
Ballygunj
Alipur
Nullah
Tangra Road
Kali Temple
⑦
Tollygunge
Garden Reach

Hooghly River

Jadavpur

1 Loreto Convent, Entally
2 St. Mary's School
3 Mother House
4 Nirmala Shishu Bhawan
5 Nirmala Kennedy Centre
6 Little Sisters of the Poor
7 Nirmal Hriday
8 Archbishop's House
9 Baithakkhana Church
10 St. Teresa's Church
11 Prem Dan
12 Brother's House
13 Shanti Dan

Not to Scale

3

· *An Inner Command* ·

The even pace of the Sisters' lives was soon to be disrupted
by the turbulent events around them. Japan's entry into the
Second World War and occupation of neighbouring Burma
intensified the war effort in the Eastern theatre, of which
Calcutta was the operational centre. There were occasional
air raids on Calcutta. Scores of buildings were requisitioned
by the military authorities and had to be evacuated. In 1942,
the Loreto complex at Entally was converted into a makeshift
military hospital, and St Mary's School was shifted to a building on Convent Road.

Close on the heels of the outbreak of war came the Great
Famine of 1942–43. The dislocation brought about by the war
was now to extract an even heavier toll. The transportation
system had already been taken over by the military authorities; even the river craft which could have been used to bring
much needed rice from up-country to Calcutta were requisitioned. Burmese rice was cut off because of the Japanese
invasion, and this alone led to an overall food loss of almost
10 per cent. Prices started to rise. Black marketeers and
moneylenders mushroomed. In the hinterland, the peasants'
meagre savings evaporated rapidly. They began to sell their
land and, in a final bid to avoid starvation, started to flock to
Calcutta. The Bengal Government proved tragically unequal
to the task. There is no exact record of the numbers who perished from starvation: the Bengal Government admitted the

figure of 2,000,000; other accounts put it at twice that, if not
more. So great was the tragedy that its horror has not yet been
forgotten. In any event, hundreds upon thousands thronged
the city. They had no place to live except on the pavements.
Dependent on woefully inadequate soup kitchens, they died
on the streets.

As the war progressed, the Indian National Congress continued to prepare India for freedom from British rule.
Mohandas Karamchand Gandhi spearheaded the movement, which was largely peaceful, Gandhi being the apostle
of non-violence. Alongside the Congress Party had grown
the Muslim League under Mohammed Ali Jinnah, also a
barrister. The League demanded of Britain the partition of
India and a separate homeland for the Muslims, to be called
Pakistan. On 16 August 1946, a mass meeting was called by
the Muslim League in Calcutta's Maidan.* Passions, already
roused to fever pitch, sparked bloody riots between Hindus
and Muslims. For four days and nights, communal frenzy
added a tragic dimension to this hapless and beleaguered
city. Meanwhile, the already scarce food supplies went
underground and for the first time, Mother Teresa was faced
with the prospect of 200 starving children on her hands.

With Independence came Partition and the creation of two
Muslim enclaves that became Pakistan. It meant the division
of the Provinces of Punjab and Bengal, 1000 miles apart from
one another. The largest human migration in history was to
follow. 6,000,000 people travelled each way, and well over
1,000,000 moved from East Pakistan to West Bengal. The
misery was worsened by the massacres that followed, the
result again of communal madness. Calcutta continued to be
inundated by wave after wave of refugees from East Pakistan, until it seemed that there was no space left unoccupied.

* A large open space. The reference is to Calcutta's Great Park near Raj
Bhavan.

Shanty towns sprang up on all sides. Municipal services broke down. Even the most intrepid social workers were aghast at the enormity of it all. Calcutta had truly become Kipling's City of Dreadful Night.

How far did these cataclysmic events permeate the cloister and affect Mother Teresa? Accounts that her room in St Mary's overlooked the burgeoning nightmare of the Moti Ijhil slum, and that this affected her profoundly, are clearly misplaced. This now vastly improved settlement still exists, but can only be viewed from the classroom block, while her room in St Mary's was situated at the opposite end of the complex, from where the slums could not be seen.

In any event, she was certainly no stranger to the poverty of the city. Many of her pupils belonged to impoverished families, and through the Sodality at St Mary's she had encountered even poorer people. Father Henry, who worked closely in the slums and who believed that prayer without action was not enough, was also an important influence on her. Indeed, it is probable that she shared this vision. On the other hand, she was thoroughly happy as a Loretto nun, first as a teacher and then Principal. I asked Mother Teresa what influenced her to leave Loreto.

'It was an inner command,' she said, 'to renounce Loreto, where I was very happy, to go to serve the poor in the streets.' She heard the call on 10 September 1946 on the train to Darjeeling to make her retreat. The Call continued in Darjeeling throughout her retreat. 'The message was quite clear,' she explained, 'it was an order. I was to leave the Convent. I felt God wanted something more from me. He wanted me to be poor and to love Him in the distressing disguise of the poorest of the poor.'

Father van Exem explained this further. 'For Mother,' he said, 'it was not a vision, it was a communication that came as a form of inspiration. She felt distinctly that she had to leave Loreto and start her own work. Mother has never doubted, not for a moment. She was absolutely sure from the beginning that this was her vocation.'

I remembered too, the words of Michael Gomes, with whose family at 14 Creek Lane Mother stayed soon after she left the Entally Convent. Mother Teresa had once said to him: 'I feel it very deeply that I should be snug in my bed and that on the road there should be those who have no cover. I think it is wrong not to share.'

Father van Exem explained it differently. 'Mother had met poverty well before 1946. This was especially so in 1942 and 1943, when the Great Bengal Famine stalked the land. People were starving, people were lying on the road. The girls in Entally were poor girls. But the Call had not come at that time, so Mother never thought of leaving the Convent. She knew the poverty of Calcutta and its people and she wanted to work for them, but she thought only of working through the Convent, as a Loreto nun. That was the ideal.

'Some accounts have tried to make a connection between her life behind convent walls and the poverty and communal killings in Calcutta in those days, but these accounts are completely wrong, only a hypothesis. This was not the inspiration for her vocation. The inspiration came from Heaven. She was very sure from the beginning, and I must say that I was very sure as well.'

Mother Teresa has often explained this as a 'Call within a Call', a second vocation as it were. She would remain a nun; only the work would change. 'I did not have to give up anything: my vocation, my belonging to Christ didn't change. I was only changing the means to serve the poorest of the poor.' Yet leaving Loreto was a big sacrifice. She was to admit, 'It was the most difficult thing I have ever done, it was a greater sacrifice than to leave my family and country to enter religious life.'

Father van Exem shared a secret with me. With excitement bubbling in him, he recalled the eventful day in October 1946 when Mother Teresa came to see him. 'The day she came back from Darjeeling she showed me two sheets where she had written down the Inspiration. I took these with me to Baithak Khana Church. I was very impressed. From the beginning I had a feeling that it was a real vocation, a real Call, and subsequently all that has happened is difficult to explain in a natural way. Mother was not an exceptional person, she was an ordinary Loreto nun, a very ordinary person, but with great love for her Lord. So she was very happy to offer a second sacrifice. She made her first sacrifice when she left her mother. Then she made another sacrifice, perhaps as big as the first, when she left Loreto.'

'The message was clear,' Mother Teresa related, 'I knew where I belonged, but I did not know how to get there.' Several complex permissions were required. She was, after all, a simple person, principal of a school certainly, but nonetheless a comparatively small functionary in the hierarchy of the Church. Moreover, she needed permission from the Vatican itself to work directly with the poor, not as a laywoman but as a vowed nun, by the indent of exclaustration.

'I had the blessing of obedience,' Mother Teresa once remarked. It was with this spirit that she turned to her spiritual director for guidance and advice. He placed before her the choices. She could write directly to Rome and seek the authority of the Vatican, which would be final and binding on Loreto. Or she could take up the question with the Archbishop of Calcutta, head of the Archdiocese. She would also need the permission of the Mother General at Rathfarman, the head of the Loreto Order. Father van Exem, in his wisdom, advised the latter course. Mother Teresa, ever obedient, agreed. Meanwhile, he would take up the matter with Archbishop Perier at an opportune time.

If Father van Exem thought that the Archbishop would readily agree, he was mistaken. When, two months later, Father van Exem broached the subject, the Archbishop was actually quite upset about the idea. A cautious man, the idea of a lone European nun on Calcutta's streets at a time of political and communal strife filled him with alarm. Shortly after Father van Exem had spoken to the Archbishop, Mother Teresa was transferred to Asansol, a city about 175 miles north-west of Calcutta.

While Mother Teresa was away, Archbishop Perier made several discreet enquiries regarding this most unusual occurrence, without, of course, revealing her identity. He asked Father Julien Henry of St Teresa's Church, and Father Sanders, the pastor of St Mary's Church in Kurseong (a hill resort not far from Darjeeling), for their views. Father Sanders, who belonged to the Faculty of Theology, 'the other Gate' as Father van Exem was to put it, was of the opinion that it was theoretically possible to erect such a congregation. Father Henry, who was only an assistant vicar in the parish church, was consulted by the Archbishop because he was familiar with Calcutta's slums. Father Henry, in fact, became so excited about the prospect that he asked his parishioners to pray for a special intention.

Like Father van Exem, Father Henry was Belgian. One day, when he was a young man in Dampremy, he was on his way to attend mass when he heard the Call. He was to leave Dampremy and go to India, never to return home. In October 1938 he arrived in Calcutta, and from 1941 to 1947 worked closely with Mother Teresa at St Mary's, where Mother was in charge of the school. Father Henry taught catechism to some classes and was, in effect, the priest in the convent chapel. Mother Teresa had great confidence in him. They also worked together in the Sodality at St Mary's.

'Father Henry was all for it from the very beginning,' said Father van Exem. 'I have proof of that. Father Henry was my guru. A little older than I, we came out on the same boat from Belgium. Every morning on my way back from Entally I would pay him a visit in his church at St Teresa's. One day he was very excited. He said there was great news. His Grace had confided in him that a mother was coming for the poor. She would work, not in a convent, nor in big schools, colleges or hospitals but among slum people and in the streets. Father Henry asked me whether I knew who this person might be.

'I could not reveal the secret to Father Henry,' continued Father van Exem, enjoying this hugely, 'but I do know that the very next day he started prayers for the mother of the poor, who was desperately needed to start work in Calcutta. He was later to confess to me that he could never have dreamt that it was Mother Teresa!' After a pause, a wistful smile returned to Father van Exem's face. 'He died in the very next room, you know,' he added. 'He was not only my guru, he was like my older brother.'

Archbishop Perier was still unsure whether Mother Teresa's plan was workable. Before he left on a tour of Europe, he informed Father van Exem that she would have to wait. He intended to consult two other very knowledgeable persons, the Father General of the Society of Jesus, Father John Baptist Jansen, and also Father Joseph Creusen, a specialist in the canon law of nuns. When Father van Exem revealed that he knew both men well, the Archbishop was alarmed. 'I forbid you to write to them!' he said.

Father van Exem chuckled loudly as he continued his tale. The Archbishop was very strict with him, but nonetheless he ventured to submit to His Grace that the Call had manifested itself as the will of God. 'Your Grace,' Father van Exem remonstrated, 'it is the will of God. You cannot change the will of God.' Whereon Archbishop Perier said with a snort, 'I am the Archbishop, and I do not know the will of God, and you, a young priest in Calcutta, you know the will of God the whole time.' The 'young priest' lay back on his pillows and laughed.

Father van Exem's confidence in Archbishop Perier's

judgement never wavered. He knew his superior to be a very prudent person, and was well aware that the Archbishop was the most important prelate in India at that time, with experience both of administration and of dealing with people. I understood Father van Exem to mean that if the Archbishop recommended the case to Rome, it would have stood a good chance of being favourably received. He appreciated, too, that it was a very important and possibly far-reaching decision for the Church, and that Archbishop Perier could not be hurried. 'Mother Teresa waited the whole year of Indian Independence. In the meantime, His Grace considered the complexities of the issue. He rarely spoke to Mother Teresa.' The Archbishop conveyed to her that her intention must remain secret and that she was not even to mention it to her own superiors.

At the end of 1947, Archbishop Perier finally permitted Mother Teresa to write to her own Superior, the Mother General of Loreto at Rathfarman, asking for permission to be released from the Loreto Order. He insisted, however, that the letter first be shown to him. Mother Teresa wrote the letter in her simple way and Father van Exem typed it for her. She explained her call to Mother General and sought permission to work in the slums as a nun, by an indent of exclaustration. The Archbishop, however, refused to accept the word 'exclaustration'. In its place, he desired that the word 'secularisation' be substituted. This came to both Mother Teresa and Father van Exem as a shock, for secularisation meant that Mother Teresa would no longer be a vowed nun. She would be a laywoman; in effect a social worker. Father van Exem appealed in vain to the Archbishop.

Mother Teresa made the change desired by the Archbishop and applied to her Mother General for the indent of secularisation. Mother General Gertrude's reply, sent through the Archbishop, followed almost immediately. Father van Exem repeated the reply verbatim.

'My dear Mother Teresa,

Since this is manifested as the will of God, I hereby give you permission to write to Rome. Do not speak to your own Superior, do not speak to your own Provincial. I do not speak to my own Counsellors. My consent is sufficient. However, when you write to Rome do not ask for the indent of secularisation, but exclaustration.'

Mother General of Loreto could not have offered stronger support. Father van Exem and Mother Teresa were over-joyed that their prayers had been answered; she now had permission to write to Rome. She wrote the application per-sonally, but as instructed by her own senior-most authority, asked for the indent of exclaustration. Although Mother General Gertrude had also given her permission to write to Rome directly, she nonetheless obeyed Father van Exem and gave the letter to him to take again to Archbishop Perier.

When Archbishop Perier read the brief letter, he again stopped short at the key word 'exclaustration' and ordered Mother Teresa to replace it with the word 'secularisation'. Without this change, he said, he felt unable to forward her letter. However, he informed Father van Exem that since Mother Teresa had been permitted by her own Superior to write to Rome, she was free to do so and could ask for the indent of exclaustration directly from the Vatican, if she wished. Even though the choice had been left to her, in implicit obedience Mother Teresa once again made the change Archbishop Perier required and gave her letter to Father van Exem to give to the Archbishop for its trans-mission.

'The Archbishop sent the letter to Rome with his own remarks,' continued Father van Exem. 'What he wrote I do not know. This is the Archbishop's secret. She could have sent it directly to the Holy Congregation (in Rome), but I had advised Mother to send it to the Archbishop.' The letter went first to the Apostolic Nuncio in Delhi in February 1948. Weeks went by, then months. Mother Teresa waited and prayed. Often she asked Father van Exem if a reply had been received. But there was none.

Finally, at the end of July 1948, Archbishop Perier summoned Father van Exem. He had received the Vatican decree that very afternoon. It had been conveyed by the Apostolic Nuncio in New Delhi. Mother Teresa had been granted the Indent of Exclaustration! She would remain a nun, but was permitted to work outside the convent. The permission denied to Mary Ward* 300 years ago was now given to Mother Teresa. There was, however, a caveat: she would remain outside cloister for one year, at the end of which, Archbishop Perier had been authorised to decide whether her work should continue or whether she would return to Loretto.

It was on 8 August 1948 that Father van Exem was permitted by the Archbishop to break the news to Mother Teresa. He had gone, as usual, to celebrate Sunday mass. After the mass, he asked Mother Teresa to stay behind, as he had something to tell her. Mother Teresa sensed that the reply from Rome had been received, and for a moment she froze. Then, recovering her composure, she said, 'Excuse me, Father, I will pray first.' When hearing the news, her very first question was, 'Father, can I go to the slums now?' Father van Exem completed the remaining formality by obtaining her signature on three copies of the Vatican decree: one for Rome, the second for the Archbishop's records and the third for Mother Teresa herself.

There was now no withholding the secret. Word spread

* An Englishwoman who lived in the seventeenth century, her life's aspiration was to work with and for the very poor. She founded the Institute of Mary, from which the Loreto Sisters were descended. In 1690 the Vatican suppressed the Institute's activities by imposing the rule of enclosure.

like wildfire, not only in Entally but also among the Catholic missionaries in Calcutta. Said Sister Marie-Thérèse Breen, 'It came as a shock to us when we heard, because it had never been discussed between us as these things are private, so we never knew until she left.'

Sister Rozario, too, got to know only a few days before Mother Teresa actually left Entally on 17 August. 'We began to feel there was something about,' she chuckled, 'but we did not really know. It had to be a secret. Father van Exem, who was her spiritual director, had asked her not to speak about it for a year, to let it mature in her mind, as it were. If she still continued to feel the same after the year (1947) was over, it would be real. When news finally came that Mother Teresa was to leave the Order, I felt very happy and said, "Well, it's a challenge, I hope she will have the health."' Meanwhile, letters went out to every Loreto institution in India. They were asked neither to criticise nor to praise, but only that they should pray for her.

That evening, Mother Teresa came to the sacristy of the Convent Chapel and asked Father van Exem to bless the dress that she would wear from then on. Placed in the sacristy were three white saris with blue borders, and on them a small cross and a rosary. Father van Exem recalled the scene. 'Mother Teresa stood behind me. Standing next to her was Mother du Cenacle, her Superior, who was sobbing. I blessed the saris because they would be a religious habit for her.'

Father van Exem had already given some very sound advice. Since she wished to work in the slums, some medical training was essential, to which Mother Teresa readily agreed. He then wrote to the Medical Mission Sisters in Patna in the neighbouring state of Bihar, who had no hesitation in inviting her to take training in their hospital.

Mother Teresa turned to Father van Exem to perform a particularly delicate task. She had already written to her mother in Skopje to inform her that she was leaving Loreto. In order that there should be no lingering doubt in her mind, she asked that her spiritual adviser also write to her mother to assure her that it was in pursuance of the Call, and with the permission of the Vatican itself, that she was leaving Loreto, her religious vows intact.

On 17 August, Mother Teresa wore for the very first time one of the saris that Father van Exem had blessed. Her pupils were especially curious to see her and tried unsuccessfully to get a glimpse of her, but it was already quite dark when she slipped out of the Convent at Entally. 'The Bengali Teresa' had started on her 'little way'.

* * *

The care and providence of her Loreto superiors followed Mother Teresa for several years thereafter. 'Loreto offered her a certain allowance, the exact amount I don't know. According to canon law, that should be done. They helped her with furniture, tables and beds when she was starting, as well as utensils,' said Sister Rozario.

If she carried little money with her, it was her own wish. The Sisters from whom she went out were bound by church law to provide for her needs, and they certainly did so. She opened her first dispensary at St Teresa's School and started a sewing class on the verandah. On Sundays she took a meeting of the Sodalists, many of whom were day scholars from St Mary's. Some of these were her earliest postulants and are now pillars of her congregation. On 7 October 1950, when the congregation was canonically erected, it was Mother du Cenacle who fittingly represented Loreto at the simple ceremony held at 14 Creek Lane.

Her contacts with Loreto continued and initially, her young Sisters received free education at Loreto schools. 'We gave her four sisters,' Sister Rozario told me, 'four of the very best.' Among them was Mother Bernard, who joined her in 1950, taking the name of Sister Francis Xavier. She was destined to work in the various leprosaria. Others followed and today many Loreto past pupils are numbered among the Missionaries of Charity. The present apostolate of the Missionaries of Charity would certainly have provided deep satisfaction to Mother Teresa Ball, who first sent sisters from Rathfarman to India in 1891. When I remarked to her friend and companion in Entally that Mother Teresa had brought glory to Loreto, Sister Rozario said softly, 'Not just glory to Loreto, glory to God!'

4

· *Motijhil* ·

On a morning in February 1991, I was sitting with Mother Teresa on a bench outside the office in Motherhouse. She had unexpectedly returned a day earlier from an overseas visit. Because people were not aware that she was back, there were few visitors. Her doctors, whom I suspect had long since given up expecting her to heed their advice to cut down on travel, would have been surprised to see how well she looked that morning. While talking to her, I remembered reading a story about the early days, when she had just returned to Calcutta after undergoing a few months of training with the Medical Mission Sisters in Patna. According to this tale, she found a man lying on the street suffering from a gangrenous thumb, which needed immediate amputation. Thereupon, she said a prayer, took a pair of scissors and cut it off. The patient promptly fainted, falling in one direction while Mother Teresa fainted in the other! When I delivered the punchline, Mother Teresa bent double with laughter. 'A made-up story,' she said, but she thoroughly enjoyed the joke. It pleased me enormously that I had been able to make her laugh so much that day.

One thing led to another, and we were soon on the subject of her Patna days, where she had undertaken some months of training in nursing, dispensary and hospital work in 1948. She said she had assisted in midwifery, accident and surgical cases. She was called to be present and eventually to assist, with as many emergencies, operations and deliveries as possible, and she learned to administer injections and to prescribe medicines. She became familiar with maintaining a hospital ward. By all accounts, a more enthusiastic student would have been difficult to find. The Patna Sisters had recalled that she seemed to be everywhere at once. Mother Teresa acknowledged that it was a most useful training, and has often commended the generosity of the Sisters.

Apart from medical instruction and the experience she gained, the recreational hours gave Mother Teresa an opportunity to discuss her ideas with the Sisters, who acted not merely as sounding boards, but provided several practical suggestions. These exchanges led her to discard some of her early notions: with their wide experience of health and disease, the nuns dissuaded her from her view that members of her Order would eat what the poor ate, plain rice sprinkled with salt. If she and her Sisters were themselves not to succumb to the very diseases that they hoped to cure, they would need a nutritious and balanced diet, however simple. There was also need for adequate rest. To rise before 5 a.m. and work for eight hours and more, required some rest in the afternoons. A weekly day off was necessary and an annual change from the workplace desirable. For anyone who had to work in the streets, personal hygiene was fundamental. For this reason, each of them would need to have at least three saris: one to wear, one to wash, and one for emergencies and special occasions. They further advised that it would be practical for them to cover their heads as protection from the sun, for on an Indian summer's day temperatures can reach over 40° celsius in the shade.

After she had been in Patna just a few weeks, Mother Teresa was impatient to return to Calcutta. In letter after letter to Father van Exem, she requested him to permit her to start the 'real' work. 'It was always that she wanted to come back, that she had studied enough, that she had seen all the diseases; that the diseases in Calcutta were different from those in Patna, and that the diseases which she would find in the slums of Calcutta, she didn't find in the hospital,' he recounted to me with amusement.

Father van Exem went to make his retreat in Patna in November 1948. Upon arrival, he went straight to the hospital. 'At the hospital I saw a group of sisters and nurses chatting, and went up to them. I said to the group, "I have come to see Sister Teresa. Where is she?" "But Father, I am here," said a voice from the back. Mother Teresa was standing there all along, but I had failed to recognise her, for she was in a sari. Although I had blessed the three saris, I had never seen her wear one. That was the very first time.'

At the hospital, he spoke to her Superior, Sister Stephanie, an American, and told her that Sister Teresa wanted to return. He added that, in his view, it was doubtful that she could have learned much about medicine or nursing in so short a time, and admitted to being nervous about the prospect of allowing her to return prematurely, fearing that she might make some mistakes. 'And that would be the end of the work,' he remembered saying. To his surprise, Sister Stephanie said, 'Yes, Father, Sister Teresa can go to Calcutta. She is very prudent and will not make a mistake. There will be plenty of people who will come to help and advise her. They will undertake their own responsibilities in the sharing of the work.' The doctor-in-charge, a Dutch woman called Elise, confirmed this when she said, 'Sister Teresa is ready. She can go today.'

'From Calcutta, I wrote to her that the Archbishop had granted his permission for her return, and that I had found her a place to stay with the Little Sisters of the Poor. I did not want her to come during their retreat, which was from the first to the eighth of December. She arrived on the ninth morning, after almost four months in Patna,' he recalled. It must have felt strange for her not to head directly for the

Loreto Convent at Entally. The St Joseph's Home, which was run by the Little Sisters, accommodated about 200 elderly people with little or no means. It was, and continues to be, located at 2 Lower Circular Road, the same road where Mother Teresa would establish her own headquarters barely five years later.

In several respects, the St Joseph's Home was an appropriate sanctuary, for the Little Sisters of the Poor were vowed to poverty. Although they worked through institutions, they had no regular sources of income and were entirely dependent on providence. For the first few days Mother Teresa spent a few hours each day helping the Sisters in their work. From 10 to 18 December Father van Exem also directed her in a short retreat. On the morning of 19 December, she was ready to begin her work. 'I suggested that she should first go to Taltolla. In this middle-class suburb lived many of her old students from Entally. I believed it would be useful for them to see Mother Teresa in her new dress. They would also know that she was beginning her work.' This was Father van Exem's way of 'introducing' her to the difficult work in the 'bustees' (slums) and the streets. But that very evening she told Father van Exem that she would not return to Taltolla. It was not where the 'real work' lay. On the morning of 20 December, according to Father van Exem, she stepped out, for the first time, into the 'bustee' of Motijhil.

Motijhil, literally translated, means 'pearl lake'. It is nothing of the kind. It is actually a largish tank in the middle of the locality. Today, its residents would be outraged if one were to attempt to call their habitation a 'bustee'. For Motijhil boasts paved roads, electricity, a proper drinking water supply and sewage. The houses may be small, but most of them are well-built. TV aerials sprout from many a roof. But forty-four years ago, when Mother Teresa first entered into her work, there was no sign of well-being. The sump was the sole source of water for drinking and washing. Sewage flowed into open drains, and rubbish piled up for days before it was removed. There was no clinic or dispensary. There was no school.

It was not unexpected for Mother Teresa to begin her work in Motijhil. It was already a familiar sight from the windows of the classroom block of the Entally Convent. Moreover, the members of the Sodality at St Mary's had worked there. Father Henry, the parish priest, knew the 'bustee' well, and was anxious to help her. It was from him that she obtained the addresses of several poor families who lived there and whose children attended St Teresa's parish school.

It was these parents whom Mother Teresa met on the very first day. They were delighted at the prospect of a little school in their midst and promised to send their children to her. That there was neither a building nor even a room available did not deter her. She had no money for even a blackboard and chalk, or for the slates used commonly by village children. On her second morning in Motijhil she found five little children waiting for her. The only open spot was under a tree near the sump. 'I took a stick and used it as a marker on the ground where the children sat. We began right on the ground,' she said.

It did not matter to Mother Teresa that her new workplace was a considerable distance from the Convent of the Little Sisters of the Poor. She began to carry her 'tiffin' or midday meal with her. The principal of the parish school at the time was Sister Rozario, who recalled those days quite clearly. 'When she came back (from Patna) in mid-December, she first came to me,' she said. 'We were good friends. Her work day began very early, and by 12.30 p.m. she was often still in Motijhil. On her way back she would stop and have her little lunch in the school. In the evening she would return to the Convent by tram or bus, but there were times when she would offer her tram fare, which was sometimes all the money that she possessed, to some needy person. She would then walk the entire distance, which often took her an hour.'

It was only a matter of time before the word spread in St Mary's that Sister Teresa was back from Patna and that she had started a small school in Motijhil. One afternoon some of her former students went there to meet her. Used to seeing her in a nun's habit, they got a shock seeing her wearing a sari of the cheapest kind. In the Calcutta of 1948, she must have presented a strange sight indeed: a European, and yet not one. True, there were plenty of European women married to Indians, but they wore fine silk and cotton saris. Nor were their feet ever exposed: Mother Teresa's bare feet were encased in rough leather sandals, a parting gift from the Patna Sisters. As if all this were not enough, the group found it difficult to reconcile themselves to her 'school'. Until a few months ago, she had been their principal. Now she did not have a roof over her head. Without tables and chairs, books and pencils, they found her conducting a 'class' of raggedy children who sat beside the stinking pool.

*   *   *

Mother Teresa kept a brief record, in the form of a 'book' of her work, from 25 December 1948 to 13 June 1949. The idea came from Archbishop Perier, in an attempt to resolve a disagreement between Mother Teresa and Father van Exem over the return of letters Mother Teresa had written to him in the early days of her work. She wanted the letters back, while he wished to keep them to record the genesis of her Congregation. This would serve as an acceptable alternative.

Although she is a prolific correspondent, she has neither time nor space to keep the multitude of letters that she receives, nor has she ever been known to keep a written record of any sort. Therefore this 'book' is unique, and all quotations from it have been reproduced exactly as she wrote them. Father van Exem told me that 'she wrote late at night, after the day's work was done. She was often dead tired and must have fallen asleep many times at her task. I knew she would not have been able to carry on for very long.' He continued, 'There are books which refer to this as a "diary". It was not a diary, nor was it a matter of conscience. It was a record, written for the Archbishop, which described the experiences of the day.'

The 'book' was seen once, about twenty years ago. While a few of the entries have been used in accounts before, the majority are being published for the first time. There are some discrepancies. Sometimes the dates do not tally with known events, and often the entries are brief. Its immense value undoubtedly lies in the recording of her first steps: the doubts she experienced, the failures she encountered, the rebuffs she faced and the happiness she felt in her work. What also comes across vividly is that, in her scheme of things, there was never a preconceived 'grand plan' towards which she worked. As she encountered problems in the slums, she never felt it necessary to travel the usual administrative path: making a survey, drawing up plans, gathering resources, training people. She saw only the immediate need of a particular individual and tried to meet it then and there. If it were an undernourished child, it was not for her to work out a project on malnutrition; she went by the shortest route to get food for that child. This approach has remained unchanged over the years.

Notably, the other aspect to become apparent is that, even then, Mother Teresa could have more than one activity going simultaneously. The Motijhil school was only good for Motijhil; it was no good for the children of Tiljala. So it was essential to have a school in that slum. It did not bother her that there were still problems to sort out at Motijhil. And thus for dispensaries, homes for the dying and so on. Since this was His work, He would ensure that they all took off. Perhaps more than anything else, her notes are testimony to her faith in her Call, her complete self-surrender and her conviction that she herself was nothing, merely an instrument.

When she plunged into Motijhil, she had no money. Had she wanted it, the Loreto Order would certainly have given her a reasonable sum to cover her expenses. She had been given five rupees for her journey to Patna, and presumably was given money to cover her return journey as well. When she returned to Calcutta, it is possible that the Little Sisters gave her a few rupees to cover her tram fare.

Exactly a week later, she unexpectedly came into a comparatively large sum for those days. That morning, she had been to Sealdah to meet the parish priest. Although she said that he was 'glad for the work', he refused to offer help or encouragement. She went next to the parish priest of Park Circus. In marked contrast, he was 'simply delighted' to see her. 'To show his appreciation, he gave me 100 rupees to begin with.' With this sum in hand, she wasted no time in finding a schoolhouse. 'I rented two new rooms for five rupees each per month, to use for the school and dispensary. It is right in front of a big tank,' she wrote. It is noteworthy that she rented the rooms on 27 December, less than twenty-four hours after she received the money.

The rooms needed repairs and cleaning, so the school remained outdoors for some weeks. December, January and February are comparatively cool months in Calcutta, and it is quite comfortable out of doors. It is in June, when the monsoon breaks, that cover becomes vital. Meanwhile, the outdoor school was growing. By 28 December, there were already twenty-one children. A teacher from St Mary's had also volunteered to help. 'The little children were dirty and untidy, but very happy,' wrote Mother Teresa. Once at school, they were not only given lessons but instructed in cleanliness. Reminiscent of the Sunday school at St Mary's, she gave everyone a good bath and awarded cakes of soap as prizes for attendance and cleanliness. On 29 December she noted that the children were 'much cleaner'. 'Those who were not clean, I gave a good wash at the tank.' School began with a lesson in hygiene and was followed by the reading class. 'I laughed a good many times as I had never taught little children before. The *kaw-khaw-gaw* (letters of the Bengali alphabet) did not go so well. We used the ground instead of a blackboard – everybody was delighted.'

The chant of the alphabet being repeated soon became a familiar sound in Motijhil. Although children sat on the ground, the people of the 'bustee' recognised goodness when they saw it. In a spirit of community service, books and slates appeared. People came forward with a little money, a stool, the odd table they could spare. These were small acknowledgements of their appreciation. By 4 January, Mother Teresa had three teachers helping her. They were certainly needed, for by then the attendance had leapt to fifty-six. Mother Teresa soon started Bengali and arithmetic lessons; the needlework class was proving to be very popular with the girls. By 14 January, the schoolroom was ready. In honour of Father Nicaise, who was coming to bless the school the following day, Mother Teresa tried to teach the children to sing a little Bengali hymn. 'I don't think a single voice kept straight!' she wrote with amusement. Mother Teresa gave the school the name of Nirmal Hriday (a name she later transferred to the Home for the Dying). The little school in the shadow of the Loreto Convent had become a reality.

'There are so many joys in the slums,' she observed one day, 'I had a lovely day with the children – they come, some of them, long before the time and run to meet us.' And a few days later: 'The children are really improving. They have taken a special virtue, not to use bad language. [The children] brought a little boy who has been using bad language with his mother. I told him that Nirmal Hriday will not like little boys who abuse their mother. He was very sorry for himself.'

On 14 January 1949, Mother Teresa recorded that a new family came to live in Motijhil, a Bengali lady with her two little children and her sister who was a nurse. They had seen better days and were now in terrible want. While Mother Teresa was taking a class, one of the children said, '"You know, Sister, Zena and her brother have had nothing to eat since yesterday morning and will have nothing tonight also." Poor children. They could not say it themselves. I had only three annas. Well I can walk from St Teresa's easily. So I brought some *muri* (puffed rice) and the two eggs I had, and made a little meal for the poor children.'

It was while she was walking home that very day that she received her 'first rude shock'. She had stopped at a church on the way back, hoping to receive a donation for the work. 'Coming home, I was surprised how quickly I was at Park Street. I thought and went to try [a priest's] generosity. What surprise. He treated me as if I was doing something very wrong. He advised me to ask the parish priest to finance me. Great was his surprise when I said I shall finance myself by begging. He went off saying he did not understand, and did not [say goodbye]. It was the first good blow and a hard one. Coming up Camac Street, tears often filled my eyes,' she recorded. It is likely that she gave way to her emotions because she was tired or lonely or both. What is interesting is that the brush-off did not weaken her resolve or deflect her from her mission. On the contrary, it brought to the fore her inner resilience. If the ultimate humiliation was for her to beg, so be it.

In India, mendicancy has formed part of an ancient and honourable tradition. Through the ages priests, holy men and teachers have depended for their livelihood upon the support of rulers and the community. Mother Teresa fitted into this mould easily enough. Soon there were frequent references to 'begging letters' and 'begging expeditions' for medicine, food and old clothes. This was a logical outcome of her avowed poverty and dependence on providence for all things. What, however, filled her with a strange unease was when an extremely rich and socially prominent Calcutta couple visited the Motijhil school and promised all possible help. 'From my heart I prayed fervently that nothing may spoil our absolute poverty and union with Him. I never understood better than now how very nothing I am.'

Mother Teresa's reluctance to accept a Government grant for her school crystallised gradually. As soon as she started the Motijhil school, she went to meet the local Inspectress of Schools to seek a grant. From her she learned that in the normal course of events, the Government could not offer a grant until the school had been going for a year. Some weeks later, Mother Teresa recorded: 'I went with Sabitri to see Miss Roy, the Inspectress of Schools. She was ready to give a grant for the School. I told her I wanted to teach the children the things they need most and I wanted to be free.' Yet it was not until she had moved to Creek Lane that she took a final decision; not only would a regular grant, from Government or Church, run counter to her vow of absolute poverty, it would also bring in its wake a host of conditions that would affect her freedom.

No sooner had Mother Teresa got the little school underway than she gave her attention to the opening of a dispensary. She had already begun to visit the sick. Tuberculosis and leprosy were rampant. 'I met a leper woman,' she observed on 14 January. 'What a terrible sight. She was thrown [out] by her people on account of her disease. As her fingers are all gone she finds cooking most difficult. She spends her time playing with the cat.'

An old and sick Muslim lady to whom she gave some medicine felt that a miracle had taken place. She said to Mother Teresa, 'After so many years of suffering, this was the first day [that] I am feeling no pain. Allah sent you to me.' And at the end of March, Mother Teresa noted: 'At Motijhil an old Muslim woman came to me. "I want you to promise me something," she said. "When you hear that I am sick and dying, please come. I want to die with God."'

'At Motijhil, lots of sickness among the children and people. Everywhere they call. Thank God, Campbell [Hospital] takes every patient I send – tetanus, cholera, meningitis, plague. All kinds. They send an ambulance at a minute's notice,' she recorded. Not everyone needed to be admitted to hospital. She needed more and more medicine for her increasing number of house calls, which led her to start making regular rounds of the chemists' shops. She prevailed on some of them to give to her whatever they could spare. There are frequent references in her notes to such visits. For example: 'I went to Smith Stani Street to beg. They gave me some medicine.' Perhaps it was on one such visit that she received, not medicine, but a volley of abuse. She was not discouraged. She wrote: 'At Tiljala I got a first-class *gali* (abuse), but the poor man was so ashamed of his speech, I came to forgive him. And I really did forgive him from the bottom of my heart.'

As it happened, the first dispensary that she opened was not in Motijhil, but in a classroom offered to her by Sister Rozario in the parish school. After school hours, a large room that opened onto a verandah was converted into a makeshift screening centre for tuberculosis patients. Before long, lengthy queues began to form before opening time. Many of them were rickshaw pullers and 'coolies' who carried heavy weights on their heads in the bazaars. Mother Teresa managed to obtain a screening apparatus; whether this, too, was in response to a 'begging letter' or if it was donated by an early benefactor, she does not say.

It is a measure of how rapidly she organised herself that within a fortnight, Mother Teresa had opened both a school and a dispensary. On 4 January 1949, she decided to open a second school, this time in Tiljala. She observed: 'I begged the parents to get the children to school. I shall do everything in my power to help these poor creatures. Their misery is much more terrible than at Motijhil.' On 19 January, she wrote: 'At Tiljala the children were excited about going to school. For the boys, all is ready. The girls will be all right also. Please God, I will be happy to see them in school.' A week later she observed: 'The children are great. At Tiljala we had only six. . . . At least six little children kept away from idleness and mischief. The place does not suit, so I have to make other arrangements. The old woman wants five rupees for the little room. The place outside is more suitable, so I think I will take it.' And three days later: 'At Tiljala I got a room for four rupees per month. The people came forward and were very pleased to get a place for their children. This will also do for a dispensary as the children can have their class outside.'

The simple little school did not take long to get organised. On 2 February, she noted: 'Our Lady's day. Last year on this day, Mother General's letter arrived. . . . At Tiljala, I had twenty-three children. The children are very nice and so very respectful. They love their games – Nirmal Hriday is growing, God be praised for it all.' Then, in a poignant reference to being alone in her work, she added, 'When Our Lady thinks it fit to give me a few children of my own, then only, Nirmal Hriday will spread its love everywhere in Calcutta. I keep on telling Her, "I have no children," just as many years ago she told Jesus, "They have no vine." I put all trust in her Heart. She is sure to give to me in Her own way.'

An essential trait of Mother Teresa's make-up is her very practical nature. From the very beginning she never had time nor inclination to engage in unnecessary talk, yet at the same time she has a ready and engaging wit. An entry made after she had met the Education Officer at the end of February 1949, in the context of the Motijhil school, reflected this to some measure: ' "Sister," he said, "I admire you and envy you. Your love for these destitute classes is great and here we are of [this] country doing nothing for our own. Go to the Prime Minister and tell him what you are doing. He should do this work with his Government, not you. A little Sister, but you seem determined on doing it, and you will succeed." I wish he gave me something instead of this empty talk.'

Just as the Patna Sisters had predicted, Mother Teresa acquired helpers from the outset. On her first day in the slums she observed, 'Two St Mary's teachers came, anxious to help. Das Gupta, a Hindu family, came to see me. Sabitri, the youngest, wants to help by all means. Mr Vincent and Mr Gasper came. Two good Bengali Catholics. They told me they will do everything in their power to make the work a success.' However, there were days when the volunteers were not able to come. Several times there is a passing mention of a teacher or a doctor who was not able to attend to his or her duties. This would throw things out of gear. It was not long before Mother Teresa came to believe that it was difficult for lay people, who had responsibilities to their families, to devote their undivided attention to work in the slums.

On 14 January, she noted: 'I went to see the sick but there was too little time and the teacher was anxious to get to her [own] children. It shows how necessary it is that we be religious for this work.' This impression was strengthened as the days went by. On 23 January, she again observed: 'To persevere doing this work for a long time you need a greater power to push you from behind. Only religious life can give this power.'

It was within a few weeks after she began work in Motijhil that a few people began to express doubts about her activities. A single nun, working in an unorthodox manner in the slums, made some of the local clergy distinctly uncomfortable. They remarked that she had done well as a teacher, and that her good work was in danger of being lost to an uncertain future. It is likely that these rumblings reached the ears of Mother Provincial in Entally. Mother Provincial, who was very fond of Mother Teresa, pleaded with her to return to Loretto. 'I went to see Mother Provincial,' she wrote. 'Her one desire is for me to go back to Loretto, but I know God wants the work.' To avoid the possible temptation, she practically stopped visiting Entally. The whispers eventually reached Mother Teresa's ears. It was a measure of her faith that she recorded: 'I believe some are saying what use of working among this lowest of the low that [as] the great, the learned and the rich are ready to come, it is better to give full force to them. Yes, let them all do it. If the rich people can have the full service and devotion of so many nuns and priests, surely the poorest of the poor and the lowest of the low can have the love and devotion of us few – "the Slum Sister" they call me, and I am glad to be just that for His love and glory.'

5

· *14 Creek Lane* ·

I once mentioned to Mother Teresa that I wanted to visit Creek Lane, to see the house where it all began. 'What for?' she said. 'Go and see the real work instead.' I should have known better than to ask.

Nevertheless, the urge to explore the inception of this religious order, which had grown so rapidly from a single room in the backwaters of Calcutta into a multinational organisation, was irresistible. On this journey of discovery, it came as a surprise to me that Creek Lane even existed. It was, after all, in 1953 that Mother Teresa had moved out, and since then enough time had elapsed for anything to have happened. The street name could have been changed twice over, the neighbourhood redeveloped, or the house at Number 14 replaced by a block of flats. It would not have been a surprise if the Gomes family had moved elsewhere: Michael Gomes might even have emigrated, as other members of his family had done. Yet none of this had happened. It was as if a crucial piece of the jigsaw had fallen into place when, at the first available opportunity, I found myself in Creek Lane.

True to its name, Creek Lane meanders in an uncertain way. Like most other streets in Calcutta, it seems to be a jumble of houses, shops and small business establishments. Everyone there seemed to know each other, which was just as well because there was no street numbering worth mentioning. 'Gomes Babu,' said a shopkeeper when I asked for directions, 'he lives at Number 14,' and he pointed to a faded archway a short distance down the street.

The bougainvillaea that cascaded over the high wall almost covered the small marble plaque that proclaimed this to be 'The Retreat'. I was directed by one of the members of the extended family living on the ground floor to two floors above, where Michael Gomes now lives with his wife. As I climbed the wooden staircase with its charming cast iron balustrade, I could not but reflect that it was these very stairs that Mother Teresa and her small band had swept each day during the four years they had made this their home.

Upon her return from Patna on 9 December 1948, Mother Teresa initially stayed with the Little Sisters of the Poor. Father van Exem soon realised that she needed to be closer to the Motijhil slum where she had begun to work, so both Father Henry and he started to search for a more convenient place for her to live. 'I did not know what to do with Mother Teresa,' said Father van Exem. 'Father Henry and I went about on our cycles to East Calcutta and other places, trying to find a suitable house. Then it struck me all of a sudden that Alfred and Michael Gomes, two brothers whom I knew, were living in a nice, three-storeyed house. I knew that the top floor was vacant. Mother could begin there, and then slowly things would improve.'

That morning Father van Exem contacted Alfred Gomes who did some secretarial work for him. 'I found him as usual in the sacristy of my church at Baithak Khana. He had already heard about Mother's work, and she had been seen everywhere. I said to Alfred, "You have a house, and nobody lives on the top floor. Could you not give it to Mother Teresa?"' Alfred responded positively, but said that he would have to ask his brothers, two of whom lived in East Pakistan, as the house belonged to them jointly. Their affirmation was not long in coming, and on 28 February

1949, Mother Teresa moved into an empty room on the top floor of the Gomes' residence.

Mother Teresa's own notes revealed that things did not work out quite as smoothly. As soon as she was back from Patna she began to search for premises for a convent, but on more than one occasion, the arrangements fell through at the last moment. She found 'an ideal place for the Missionaries of Charity, far from the world and yet close to everything', at 46 Park Circus Avenue. When everything was practically settled, the landlord appeared to have changed his mind. On 16 February she wrote,

'I went to meet the landlord of 46 Park Circus. The man never turned up. I am afraid I liked the place too much – and our Lord just wants me to be a "Free Nun", covered with the poverty of the Cross. But today I learned a good lesson – the poverty of the poor must be often so hard for them. When I went round looking for a home, I walked and walked till my legs and arms ached. I thought how they must also ache in body and soul looking for home, food, help. Then the temptation grew strong. The palace buildings of Loreto came rushing into my mind. All the beautiful things and comforts – in a word everything. "You have only to say a word and all that will be yours again," the tempter kept on saying. Of free choice, My God, and out of love for you, I desire to remain and do whatever be Your Holy Will in my regard. I did not let a single tear come, even if I suffer more than now. I still want to do your Holy Will. This is the dark night of the birth of the Society. My God give me courage now, this moment, to persevere in following your Will.'

Understandably, she could barely contain her excitement in a note of 21 February:

'Good news of the house at Creek Lane. How strange
and wonderful are the works of God. In all its
poverty, the place is still rich. I must take what you
have given, not what I prefer.'

There was enthusiasm again on 25 February:

'The new place is getting ready, I am longing to be
there.'

Yet on the day that she actually moved into Creek Lane, she
was overcome by loneliness occasioned, doubtless, because
she was entirely alone. In the preceding weeks she had
shared the companionship of the Little Sisters of the Poor.
They had prayed together and had shared their supper with
her. In one of her rare references to the early days, she had
once said to me, 'I was on the street, with no company, no
helper, no money, no guarantee and no security.' This might
help to explain the touching entry of that first evening in
Creek Lane:

'28 February – Today, my God, what tortures of
loneliness. I wonder how long my heart will suffer
this. Tears rolled and rolled. Everyone see my
weakness. My God give me courage now to fight self
and the tempter. Let me not draw back from the
Sacrifice I have made of my free choice and conviction.
Immaculate Heart of my Mother, have pity on Thy
poor child. For love of Thee I want to live and die a
Missionary of Charity.'

It was into that very room which the parish priest had
blessed, that Michael Gomes now invited a stranger armed
with notebooks, camera and tape recorder. I remembered
that Mother Teresa had called him 'a holy man'. I was drawn

by his gentle and shy manner. Slim and in his sixties, he sat and listened as I proceeded to explain my mission. He answered a few questions in a desultory fashion, even, it seemed, a little grudgingly. After a while, he suggested that I return the following day. I wondered whether this was because Sister Joseph Michael had been unable to send him a message about my visit and its purpose. The following evening Michael Gomes was much more communicative; Mother Teresa's message system had worked its magic.

Mother Teresa had moved into a single room, he told me. 'She had nothing, except a black box which she placed there,' said Michael, pointing to a space near the entrance. 'It served both as a bench and a desk.' On the wall Father van Exem had placed an image of the Immaculate Heart of Mary, which was originally her gift to him. Mother Teresa was not quite alone, but was accompanied by Charu Ma, a widow who was the cook at St Mary's. In accord with Bengali custom, she was referred to by the name of her son as Charu Ma, the mother of Charu. Devoted to Mother Teresa, she had decided to leave the Convent to cook for her and be her companion. Michael remembered offering Mother Teresa some furniture. 'After all, my brothers' furniture was available in the adjoining room, but she was reluctant to use it.' She did, however, accept a chair and a few packing cases, and these served as seats as well as tables.

'I admire the way it all grew,' said Michael, lost in thought. 'How did she do it?' he asked, as if to himself. 'We would share food with her whenever we could, but I knew there were occasions when she would give her own morsels away and ate nothing. Sometimes I would get a note from her saying, "Michael, let me have six mugs of rice. I will pay you back." More often than not she would give it to a starving family waiting at the gate. She never tried to pay us back, because she knew it would hurt us.' What Michael Gomes did not reveal, but the Sisters did, was that the family refused to accept either rent or money for food and numerous things they provided in those early days. 'We gave nothing,' said Michael Gomes, 'we only received.'

As we conversed, I was all too conscious of the fact that it was in this very room that Mother Teresa began her work forty-two years ago. It was a fairly large room, opening out on both sides to comfortable-sized verandahs. On the clean uncarpeted floor, there was an ordinary wooden settee on which I sat, and a set of matching chairs, one of which Michael occupied. At one end stood a large desk. Were these the pieces of furniture that she had declined to use, I wondered? On the walls were several photographs, including one of a niece of Michael Gomes who wanted to join the Missionaries of Charity. She had died a young, untimely death. There was a wedding portrait of the Gomes' daughter, Mabel, now living in the USA. A child of seven or eight when Mother Teresa had moved in, she had frequently accompanied Mother on visits to the slums. She was in every sense one of Mother Teresa's first co-workers.

Mother Teresa had recorded in her 'book' that Father Henry had given her a 'beautiful' statue of our Lady of Fatima for the altar. I assumed that this must have found a place in the adjoining room which eventually became the little chapel. Curiosity got the better of me, and I enquired whether I could peep in. 'There was no furniture here in those days,' Michael said, pointing to the four-poster bed and a large cupboard that dominated the small room. 'There was only a small altar. When the congregation was erected, this room became their chapel. After a few years, there were almost thirty girls up here. The whole house used to resound with their laughter during their hour of recreation,' he recalled with a smile.

'Slowly people started coming for help and for medicine. There were early tuberculosis cases. One day Mother Teresa said, "Michael, can you come out with me, I want to go on a begging expedition.'' We went to the house of someone known to us. She was an inspectress of schools. Mother Teresa spoke to her about the work and of those needing medicine and help. She spoke and spoke. The Inspectress listened and gave nothing, but her sister, partly blind, was moved and gave five rupees.' He fell silent for a while. 'She had many disappointments in life,' he added. Then after a long pause he smiled again and said gently, 'You know, she used to scrub these floors herself each day.'

It was interesting to learn from Michael Gomes that Mother Teresa was systematic and methodical from the earliest days. From the outset she had a clear idea how to proceed. According to their Constitution, the Sisters are to go out as Jesus' disciples did, in pairs, to hospitals, to the lepers, to pick up people from the streets, even if they are drunk. 'In the beginning, she would take the children of the house with her, or my wife or I would accompany her. One day Mother Teresa had taken our little daughter to the slums. Normally, they were back by noon or so, but on that day it was past one and my wife began to worry, especially as there was a real downpour that afternoon. At about two in the afternoon, a rickshaw arrived, and Mother Teresa and Mabel alighted. They were soaked to the skin. The first thing she said to my wife was that she was sorry that Mabel was wet. She then recounted that in Motijhil they had entered a house with a low circular wall which was filled with water. Holding a child on her shoulders and protecting it against the rain with a broken enamel bowl stood a woman in water up to her knees. The child was burning with fever. The landlord had not received two months' rent, only four rupees per month, and despite the rain, had sent his employees to remove the roof of the house. Just for eight rupees! Having brought Mabel back, Mother Teresa returned to see what she could do for them. While it made her very sad, at the same time, it redoubled her resolve to do something for the destitute. She was convinced that if she could help even one woman and child, it would reduce the total suffering, if only by a fraction.'

If Michael Gomes was sometimes embarrassed to accompany an unknown, unorthodoxly dressed nun on her 'begging' expeditions, he gave no hint of it. One day they set out on one of these visits to the manager of a pharmaceutical firm. He was only slightly known to Michael Gomes, and had promised to donate some medicines. It was one of those Bengal monsoon days, when the rain comes down in sheets, and even animals scurry for cover. While riding in the tram on their journey out, Mother Teresa noticed a man, sodden to the skin, slumped under a tree. She pointed him out to Michael. As the tram was between stops, they were unable to alight. Mother decided to look for him on the way back and perhaps find him some shelter. They collected the medicines and hurried back to find him still there, but his head had fallen into a pool of water. He was dead. Mother was in anguish. Perhaps he had wanted to say something before he died so tragically alone, but there was no-one even to hear his last words. 'If only we could find a place where people can die in dignity,' said Mother. 'This was the beginning of her search which led to Kalighat,' recalled Michael.

While he reminisced, it was almost as if he had forgotten I was there. With eyes half-closed, he seemed to be talking softly to himself. I rose from the settee and went and sat quietly next to him, lest my movements disturb his train of thought. 'One morning in the early days, we were travelling in a tram to Howrah. Some people sitting across from us began passing remarks about the fair-skinned lady in a sari. One person remarked that she was a nun out to convert Hindus to Christianity. Another said that this foreigner was doing this work not even for the sake of money, but to make more Christians. They did not realise that she understood every word they said. Remember, she taught the students of

St Mary's in Bengali. For a long while she heard them in silence. Finally, she turned to them and said, gently, but in a determined voice, *"Ami Bharater Bharat Amar,"* which means, "I am an Indian and India is mine". They were dumbfounded. It became clear to them that she had understood their every word. There was complete silence till we reached Howrah.'

Recalling this incident seemed to make Michael Gomes fall silent as well. I could hear the clock ticking in the room, while two floors below, the noises of the late evening traffic continued unabated. I had been there almost two hours, and had perhaps overstayed my welcome. As I got up to leave, he said, 'We cannot view her through Catholic eyes, or Hindu eyes, but only through human eyes, for she does not discriminate. She respects all religions and all people. It is not as if she is not a good Catholic. She is, but she does not make it exclusive. There lies the great appeal in her work. She is something not so tangible as we imagine.' I could not quite grasp the meaning of this, but because it sounded faintly mystical these words remained in my mind. By not making her religion 'exclusive', Michael Gomes probably meant that Mother Teresa's compassion encompassed all religious persuasions and the irreligious and disbelievers as well. I also recalled what Father van Exem had once written in a letter to me in this context: 'For Mother Teresa, her religion is not only the main thing, it is everything. It is this religion that makes her love every human being. Her life is love for God, whom she sees in the poor.'

About three weeks after Mother Teresa had moved into Creek Lane, she was joined by her first postulant, Subashini Das, the future Sister Agnes. Subashini was, perhaps, the only one of Mother Teresa's former pupils at St Mary's who had some inkling that their Principal would leave them to start an order of her own. A pupil of Mother Teresa's from Class Seven onwards, she was one of the group whom

Mother had motivated to render practical help to the poor, especially on Saturday afternoons after school. Unable to leave the Convent herself, Mother Teresa had encouraged the older children of St Mary's to visit needy patients in the city hospitals and also to teach poor children in the slums. 'She asked us to gather them around us, teach them the alphabet and some songs, and to make them happy,' recalled Sister Agnes.

'One day,' said Sister Agnes, 'I told Mother Teresa, "You have often spoken about the need to start this kind of work. We are ready to help, but we need a leader. Why can't you be our leader?" It just came out spontaneously. Mother smiled, but hushed me into silence. It was then that I first realised that something was already going on in her mind. When she finally left Loreto, it did not come to me as a surprise. When she moved to Creek Lane, she sent me a note asking me to meet her. I remember clearly that it was on 1 March that I went to see her. She asked me if I were ready. I replied that I was waiting only for a date and time. Mother Teresa suggested 19 March, which was St Joseph's feast day. I could hardly wait. On that day, I entered into my new life, which has brought me only happiness in serving God.'

In her notes, Mother Teresa was to record the following entry:

'19th March: A great day. Subashini Das joined the little Society. We went to Baithak Khana for her consecration to Our Lady. May the Immaculate Heart, cause of our Joy, guide and help, bless and perfect the beginnings of this Her least Society. She is beautifully simple. God keep her like this.'

A short while later, another former student of St Mary's, Magdalena Gomes, appeared outside the door. While

Subashini was short and quiet, Magdalena was tall and communicative. She became the second postulant, and took the name of Sister Gertrude. On 26 March, Mother Teresa wrote jubilantly:

'Great day. Magdalena Pattin [Gomes] joined the little Society. She is a fine, strong soul. She will do well with the poor. We went to Baithak Khana for the consecration. She must smile down on us, trying to give Our Queen all our love and devotion.'

And two days later:

'In our Convent we are so very happy. Silence is beautifully observed. The young postulants are so fervent that I am forced to follow them.'

Just as Subashini was encouraged to complete the last few months of her teacher training course, Magdalena was encouraged to further her education. Realising how useful it would be to have a doctor in their band, Magdalena was put to studying medicine. Michael Gomes (no relation of Magdalena) recalled that Mother requested him to coach Magdalena in mathematics. 'She did very well in her final examination,' he said. 'She came home very excited and showed Mother the gold medal that she had been awarded for having achieved third place. Mother Teresa surprised her by asking what she would do with it. Magdalena said she had not thought about that. Mother said she was happy that she had done well, but added that she did not need gold medals to treat poor people. It could instead be awarded to the person who had got fourth place, which is, in fact, what happened.'

I asked Sister Agnes whether the early days were difficult ones. She shook her head, and with a smile she said, 'The young are so enthusiastic. We did not think of difficulties, and always felt God would provide. We had simple things, but they were enough. Perhaps Mother Teresa was sometimes anxious about food for us, but we were not bothered at all. There were times when we had no rice. Then Mother would write Michael a note, and he would buy some for us. Our tuberculosis patients needed nourishment far more than we did. Father van Exem and Father Henry made an announcement at Sunday mass for *musti bhikkha*. This is a Bengali custom, whereby any family that could afford to, would put aside a ''handful of rice for a beggar''. A religious group called the Legion of Mary went from door to door to collect these portions. Often the leftovers were all mixed up together, but it was nonetheless nourishment for those on the verge of starvation. These leftovers were the beginning of our feeding programme.'

Within the next few months a growing number of young women came to join Mother Teresa. Not surprisingly, most of them had been her students at St Mary's. These included the future Sister Dorothy and Sister Margaret Mary. From four they grew to ten in the space of a few months. Soon the room and verandahs became overcrowded. 'One day, Mother sent me a note that one of the girls had come down with chicken-pox and needed to be segregated. Could she have another room?' recalled Michael Gomes. 'Then it was this and then it was that, and soon they had occupied the entire floor! They were regulated by a bell system. According to the ringing of the bell they had to eat, go out to work, pray, or rest. During their recreation time, they played games such as tug-of-war. You could hear their laughter down the street. They had to study a great deal as well. They were not allowed to give up their studies, and, in fact, Mother Teresa would tutor them in the evenings.' 'We lived as nuns,' recalled Sister Agnes, 'but we had not yet been recognised as a separate congregation.

The Archbishop had yet to approve our way, and there was no Constitution yet. But we were convinced that approval would come.'

Michael Gomes was conscious of the criticism against Mother Teresa. He referred to it in an oblique manner. 'There was the day she had gone on one of her "begging expeditions". She left early that morning, well before eight, and returned at about five in the evening. I was surprised to find that she was sitting in the back of a truck on top of some bags of flour and rice. She had gone to the railway station to receive these consignments. There was no clearing agent to do this for her, she went herself. She had not eaten or drunk since the morning. I sometimes hear criticism that Mother Teresa has not organised her work properly, that she does not answer letters, nor immediately acknowledge donations, and that she has little business sense. When they criticise her, I cannot but remember her sitting on those bags of flour and rice to make sure that nothing was stolen and that her girls had something to eat.'

The young women, dressed in distinctive white saris with blue bands, were soon to become a familiar sight, not only in Creek Lane, but in the poor areas they served, such as Motijhil and other slums, where the inhabitants were 'very warm and very welcoming', recalled Sister Agnes. The Sisters ran the school in the mornings and the dispensary in the afternoons, every day except Sunday. They regularly visited sick families and tried their best to admit the sick into city hospitals, but often had no choice but to tend to the dying where they found them, on the streets.

Meanwhile, Archbishop Perier had kept himself abreast of Mother Teresa's work. He would soon have to make a decision, whether the group was to be disbanded and Mother Teresa asked to return to the Loreto Order, or whether he would accept them as a congregation for the diocese of Calcutta. Father van Exem, who continued to be

Mother's spiritual adviser, remained in close touch with the Archbishop throughout.

'Did I tell you that I put in an advertisement in *The Statesman*?' Father van Exem asked me one day. 'I could not support Mother Teresa's work from my church or orphanage funds, as these were earmarked. Although news of her work in Motijhil had spread quickly, they had almost no financial means. There were days when the Sisters had only rice to eat. So I wrote to *The Statesman* with an advertisement seeking support for Mother Teresa's work in Motijhil, and received a very nice answer immediately. It said they very much appreciated the work of Mother Teresa and had decided to follow it in their paper. They said, "Do not put the address of Mother Teresa as 14 Creek Lane, as it would not inspire confidence, but put instead, the address of your church."

'It may have been the second or third day after the advertisement was published, I don't remember precisely, when a car drew up outside my church and an officer stepped out. He had been sent by the Chief Minister of Bengal, B. C. Roy, to make a donation to the work of Mother Teresa. This was the very first response. You know, I don't remember if I paid for the advertisement,' he reminisced.

By the beginning of 1950, just a few months after Mother Teresa began her work in Motijhil, Archbishop Perier had decided conclusively in favour of the path that the young nun had embarked on. In fact, he had only one condition left, and that was for Father van Exem to place on his table, before 1 April, a Constitution for the new congregation! Since he, himself, was travelling to Rome in April, he wished to carry five copies and present them to Cardinal Petrus Fumascni-Biondi, head of the Office for the Propagation of the Faith, who would have to give the final recognition.

Archbishop Perier played an important role in Mother Teresa's development in more ways than are widely recognised. Originally from Antwerp in Belgium, he came to India as a young priest in 1906. It was due largely to his efforts that the Yugoslav Jesuits initially agreed to enter Bengal, and it was the letters which these earliest Jesuits from Yugoslavia wrote home that aroused the desire in the young Agnes to become a missionary in Bengal. Although cautious and conservative in his approach to all matters, once convinced that Mother Teresa's work was motivated by the will of God, Archbishop Perier gave her his unstinted support throughout the rest of his life.

The Archbishop charged Father van Exem with the task of writing out the Constitution. This presently comprises 275 rules, and is called 'The Constitutions* of the Missionaries of Charity'. 'I took into account the existing canon law, and the constitutions of some other congregations, but most important of all, the Inspiration that Mother had received on the train journey to Darjeeling and which recurred throughout her retreat. I had read the Inspiration sheets only once, but I knew what was in them. She had to leave her convent and live like the poor, she should not have a big house or big institutions, her work would be in the slums and on the pavements of Calcutta. If they acquired large houses and institutions, it would only be for the helpless, such as abandoned infants and children, or lepers and dying destitutes. Theirs was to be a religious society, not social work. It was charity for Christ in the poor.'

If one had to choose two words to sum up Mother Teresa's underlying concept of the congregation, then these might very easily be the words 'I thirst'. Inscribed above every crucifix in every chapel and centre of the Missionaries of Charity, these words represent Christ's symbolic cry of spiritual love and acceptance. They also serve as a reminder for each Missionary of Charity of the general aim of the Society,

* invariably referred to in the plural.

which is to quench the infinite thirst of Jesus on the Cross by a life of prayer, contemplation and penance. As a means to better understand the special call 'to love and serve Christ in the distressing disguise of the poor', the Missionaries of Charity are prepared to accept suffering, renunciation and even death.

For Mother Teresa, in her religious development and in her response to her environment, it could no longer be wholly sufficient to observe the three vows of 'chastity, poverty and obedience', which were common to other congregations as well. While fully endorsing these, she took an additional fourth vow of 'wholehearted and free service to the poorest of the poor'. This vow would bind the Missionaries of Charity, without counting the cost of the hard labour involved, joyfully and without expectation, actually and spiritually to feed, clothe, shelter and nurse the sick and dying, the unloved, the outcasts, the lepers and those who had lost all faith and hope in life. The Call and the Inspiration sheets made it abundantly clear that they must reach out to the destitute on the streets, which was clearly not possible from behind convent walls. Invariably, the Sisters refer to this fourth vow as 'our way'.

On 7 October 1950, the Constitutions were approved by the Sacred Congregation in Rome. Father van Exem read the Decree of Erection during a Mass celebrated by Archbishop Perier himself. It began thus:

'For more than two years now, a small group of young women under the guidance of Sister Teresa, a lawfully uncloistered religious* of the Institute of the Blessed Virgin Mary, have devoted themselves . . . to helping the poor, the children, the adults, the aged and the sick, in this, our Metropolitan City.'

* used in the Decree as a noun.

The Decree went on to spell out the fourth vow in greater detail. It spoke of the additional requirement

'to devote themselves out of abnegation to the care of the poor and needy who, crushed by want and destitution, live in conditions unworthy of human dignity. Those who join this Institute, therefore, are resolved to spend themselves unremittingly in seeking out, in towns and villages, even amid squalid surroundings, the poor, the abandoned, the sick, the infirm, the dying . . .'

Unique to the Missionaries of Charity, the fourth vow represents the determination to return God's love and compassion by loving Him in His 'distressing disguise', be it the outcast dying of AIDS at a New York centre, or the leprosy sufferers huddled in their thousands in the Calcutta slum of Dhapa. Mother was to tell me on several occasions, 'If we did not believe that this was the body of Christ, we would never be able to do this work. No amount of money could make us do it. In our wholehearted free service to the poorest of the poor, it is Christ we touch in the broken bodies of the starving and destitute. He said, "What you do to the least of my brethren, you do it to me."' Then, taking my hand in hers, she pressed into my palm first my thumb and then each finger, one at a time, while she counted aloud, 'You – did – it – to – me.'

Michael Gomes recalled that over the next two years, something like thirty young women joined the Order. Not only was the top floor entirely occupied, Mother Teresa had to build a makeshift room on' the roof. It was obvious that they now needed a larger place. Father Henry and Father van Exem, ever concerned for this fledgling congregation, once again got on their bicycles and began to search for a larger place. Meanwhile, the Sisters started special prayers.

One day, recalled Sister Agnes, a man arrived at Creek Lane with news that a suitable building was for sale. He offered to show Mother Teresa the property, located at 54A, Lower Circular Road, and to take her to the vendor. When Mother Teresa met Dr Islam, a magistrate, he was astonished that anyone should have known of his intention to sell, as he had discussed the matter only with his wife. Meanwhile, the man who had led Mother Teresa there had vanished. When Islam heard of their work, he was touched, recalled Sister Agnes. 'Money is not everything,' he said to Mother Teresa.

Finding the property to be centrally located and eminently suitable, Mother Teresa discussed its acquisition with Father van Exem and the Archbishop. 'I went to see the place,' said Father van Exem. 'Islam stood in front of the house and just looked at it. He seemed to be very moved. After some time he asked me if he could step out for a while, as he wished to go to the nearby mosque of Maula Ali to pray. I said I would wait in the little room which was later to become the parlour. When he returned, he stood in front of the house again. There were tears in his eyes. He said, "God gave me this house. I give it back to Him." And then we parted. I never saw him again. He sold the house to the Archbishop, I don't think for very much.'

When the Archbishop was approached by Mother Teresa, he directed the vicar-general of the diocese, Monsignor Eric Barber, to survey the property in question. Since no-one quite knew how much had been paid for the property, I went one evening to meet Monsignor Barber. He confirmed that the church had advanced Mother Teresa an interest-free loan of 125,000 rupees (about £10,000 in 1953). I asked him whether Mother Teresa had repaid the loan. He proceeded to pull out the original register from a nearby shelf, and showed me the figures he had entered in his own hand over the following ten years. These ranged from 1000 rupees to 3000 rupees every month. 'Despite the fact that it was repaid in dribs and drabs,' said Monsignor Barber with a laugh, 'she paid back every penny of the loan.'

In February 1953, the Missionaries of Charity Sisters, twenty-seven in number, moved into Lower Circular Road. It became the headquarters of the Missionaries of Charity, and was henceforth called Motherhouse. At the time it consisted of three small buildings surrounded by a compound wall. Coming from a few rooms in Creek Lane, the Sisters may have wondered at the comparative spaciousness of their new surroundings. Little could they have imagined that in less than forty years this would become the nerve-centre of the most flourishing religious order in Christendom; in modern corporate parlance, it would have grown into an intercontinental organisation with a transnational membership, benefiting the largest constituency of the world's most abject poor. Without the assistance of either an army of executives or a battery of computers, telex and facsimile machines (but only a single telephone, which Mother Teresa was reluctant to install for fear of adding to her costs!), the work of Mother Teresa took root in practically every city and town in India and in over 100 other countries besides.

6

· *Motherhouse* ·

Motherhouse is a nondescript three-storeyed building that stands amidst small pavement shops and food stalls at 54A Lower Circular Road. The street has recently been renamed Acharya J. C. Bose Road, but the people of Calcutta still seem to prefer its old name. Entry is gained from an alley on the side, so narrow that it can at best take a single car. At the door is a small board that announces 'Mother Teresa'. Beneath it is a shutter that can be moved either to 'in' or 'out'. Through a small hole hangs a thin chain which, when pulled, rings a brass bell inside. This is an eminently sensible arrangement, as an electric bell would be of little use during the hours of 'load shedding', when Calcutta sweats without electricity. Upon the sound of the bell, the door is instantly opened by a novice, whose only task seems to be to mind the door. The parlour into which one is ushered is a small room, with a wooden table and five or six chairs that fail to match. The sides are lined with narrow wooden benches. Apart from two hand-painted boards listing the activities of the Missionaries of Charity, there are a few photographs on the walls. One shows Mother Teresa with Pope John Paul II.

The parlour opens into a small courtyard, where there is constant activity. Here novices draw water in old-fashioned metal buckets from an underground tank for *dhobying* their saris. The only time they noticeably stop is to pray. They are frequently seen standing before the statue of the Virgin in the grotto close by, singing hymns in unison.

'Have you ever been to Mass?' Mother Teresa asked me on one of my visits to Calcutta. I did not want to remind her that the last time she had invited me, I had overslept. 'Come by six tomorrow,' she said with a smile. I quite understood that this was Mother Teresa's way of saying that, just as it had been necessary for me to observe the different activities of her work, it was at least as important to be present at the prayer from which Mother Teresa and her Sisters drew their strength and inspiration.

As I stepped into the chapel the next morning, my first thought was that this was the plainest chapel that I had seen. It was a large bare rectangular room, shorn of any decoration, running the length of the building, with windows opening on to Lower Circular Road. There were neither pews nor seats: everyone knelt or sat on simple jute mats that covered the floor. As in any temple or mosque, footwear was left outside. The altar was a plain table. To one side of it was a large statue of the Virgin. The only embellishment was a small bunch of fresh flowers placed in a vase at her feet.

I joined a group of about twenty volunteers. Opposite us sat the novices, as many as 100 young girls, who wore white saris without the distinctive blue band. Facing the altar were the Sisters. Behind them all, her back to the wall, her hands folded, deeply sunk in prayer, was Mother Teresa.

That morning, like any other, Mother Teresa and her Sisters had awakened before 5 a.m. Mass had already been preceded by half an hour of meditation. After Mass they would begin their assigned housework duties, cooking, washing or administration. By 8 a.m., after a breakfast of tea and chapatties, they would fan out in every direction of the city. Some would walk the short distance to Shishu Bhawan, others would climb into a creaking van that would carry them to Kalighat. A few would head for the leprosy clinic. There were teams for the tuberculosis clinics, the general dispensaries, the homes for abandoned children, nursery classes and crèches. About 250 nuns and novices would leave Motherhouse to spread themselves into the city's more deprived sections.

Even as they did so, there were rules to observe. An important everyday rule is that they must go in pairs. I asked Mother Teresa whether this was because she was concerned for their safety. The reply was crisp: 'The Lord in the Gospel sent his apostles two by two.' Father van Exem was to explain this more fully. 'Mother wants them to be careful, especially as they work in difficult and distant areas. There may also be circumstances [in some parts of the world] where there may be physical danger – war, riots and so on. Nuns in some orders go out alone, but because of the particular work of the Missionaries of Charity, in the streets and in the slums, Mother insists on the Rule of Two. I do believe it is a wise policy.'

Yet even in the meanest streets of Calcutta, the Sisters need no protection. They are recognised from afar, and wherever they go they are respected. The underlying reason is that they are as poor as anyone else and treat the poor as their equals. 'Thank God,' said Mother Teresa, 'not one of our Sisters has ever had any trouble anywhere in the world. In India, especially, there is great respect for holiness.'

Another important rule is that they are not permitted to eat or drink outside the convent or workplace. They may not even accept a cup of tea. Knowing how hot an Indian summer day can be, each Sister carries a bottle of water in her cloth bag; these are usually cheap plastic water bottles or recycled medicine bottles. As usual, there are several practical considerations which guided Mother Teresa in her decision. One of the first questions I asked Mother Teresa several years ago was why she had refused a cup of tea offered to her when she visited the Lieutenant Governor in Delhi. She had then replied, 'Wherever my Sisters and I go, people want to say "thank you" in their own way. Sometimes they offer a cup of tea, or a cold drink or something to eat. Often it is something they can ill afford. I cannot refuse them and take from the rich. It is simpler not to accept from anybody. That way, no-one is hurt.'

The Sisters travel as the poor do. They usually walk, or, if the distance is far, use public transport. In Calcutta, I have accompanied them in the city's overcrowded trams. Someone, invariably, offers them a seat. They travel in much the same way in the other cities where they work. In Rome, I had occasion to accompany them on foot. 'It's only a short distance away,' a pair of tertians said disarmingly. We must have covered at least three kilometres in a cold drizzle before we reached our destination, a broken-down room where an AIDS patient lived. Often enough, the Sisters pray as they walk, measuring the distance in a curious way. 'It's five rosaries away,' said the pair in Rome, when they asked me if I wished to accompany them on another house visit. Upon seeing my perplexed face, they burst into peals of laughter and explained that they measured distance in terms of the time taken to pray the rosary.

At about noon, the Sisters are expected back for lunch. At 1 p.m. they rest for half an hour. Having already packed in a full day's work, a thirty-minute nap is vital. Mother Dengal's sound advice given to Mother Teresa in Patna is equally wisely heeded, for, without breaking the day in two, it would be difficult for the Sisters to be as productive in the second shift. At 2 p.m. the Sisters are once again on their feet. Some are assigned different tasks, partly to prevent the work from becoming monotonous. They work continuously till 6 p.m., when they finally return to Motherhouse. This is time for an hour of Adoration, some recreation, supper, followed again by half an hour of prayer. They are in bed by 10 p.m.

Mother Teresa's work routine is, as to be expected, somewhat different. Sometimes as much as half the year is spent visiting her Missions all over India and overseas. It is only natural that every Sister longs for her to visit their house. Hardly is a visit over than the question arises, 'When is Mother coming again?' On these occasions, Sisters bring to her notice problems that they themselves have not been able to resolve. Local issues might necessitate a visit to Calcutta's Writers' Building, to meet her friend the Chief Minister of Bengal ('I can walk into his room without an appointment at any time'). It might mean a visit to a Union Minister in New Delhi, or even a call on the Prime Minister, if she considers the problem to be so pressing. She carries out her routine engagements as well: there is hardly a day when she is not invited to give a talk, attend a religious engagement, or visit the sick. She might inspect a building as a possible site for a new house. There may be a local priest or bishop to meet. While all this goes on, ordinary people continue to pour in, some to offer a donation, request a photograph, to share a problem or to seek her blessing. To as many people as possible she hands out her 'business card', a small yellow card on which five lines are printed:

> The fruit of Silence is Prayer
> The fruit of Prayer is Faith
> The fruit of Faith is Love
> The fruit of Love is Service
> The fruit of Service is Peace

> Mother Teresa

At the end of the day, after her Sisters have gone to bed, she retreats to her small office where she settles down to administration and correspondence. The many handwritten letters and notes that I have received over the years have usually been written during these hours. Each has received her undivided attention. Until her recent illness, this was also the time to speak to her on the telephone. She would invariably lift the receiver on its first or second ring with the words, 'Yes, Mother Teresa speaking.'

While Mother Teresa takes no day off, the Sisters do not attend to their regular schedule of work on Thursdays. It is a day for household chores, for cleaning and scrubbing, or to catch up with their religious studies. It is also a day for contemplation. Occasionally, perhaps once or twice in the year, volunteers are permitted to take them to a quiet spot for a picnic. Their regular work on this day is handled by the novices who are assigned to assist them during the week. This helps to give the novices confidence, and is good training for them.

Thursdays are also meant for mending and darning. The Sisters each possess three saris in all. Considering the arduous nature of their work, these require darning and stitching all too often. In this, as in all other respects, Mother Teresa sets the example. I do not think I have ever seen her wear a sari that is not neatly patched. They are always spotless. Neatness and cleanliness, the saris seem to announce, can certainly go hand-in-hand with poverty.

With the three saris, each novice or Sister is given a small crucifix (which is pinned to the sari), a rosary, a metal-rimmed plate for her food, and a thin palliasse rather like those used by the inmates in the Home for the Dying. The only fan in Motherhouse is in the parlour and is meant for visitors. Strangely enough, whenever I visit Motherhouse, I never seem to need it.

In an age of self-indulgence, where 'quality of life' are words that are constantly used to explain our ever-growing needs, the Sisters live a life which is a study in contrast. It was in this spirit that Mother Teresa refused a gift of a washing machine and, more recently, a generator that could provide for a few lights during the electricity cuts. The telephone is the only concession that she has made in recent years, and that because she was finally persuaded that it has its uses. It has always surprised me that in a city where the telephones work occasionally, the one in Motherhouse is never out of order. There is no television, video, fax machine, even an oven or a toaster. In the kitchen, the food continues to be cooked on a charcoal fire, the fuel of the very poor. What about a radio to know what is happening in the world, I asked. 'No,' replied Mother Teresa, 'we have the reality.'

The reality for the Missionaries of Charity, many of whom are very young, is a hard life, yet one that is surprisingly fulfilling and joyful. The Missionaries of Charity wear their happiness like a badge, wherever they may be assigned to serve. So important is this, that cheerfulness of spirit is an essential qualification, rather like an honours degree. 'Our people deserve the joy of human love as much as dedicated service,' says Mother Teresa. Loving trust, total surrender and cheerfulness form part of their spirit. 'The best way to show our gratitude to God and people is to accept everything with joy,' are words that form part of their Constitution.

One can understand why a cheerful nature is important. The training itself is long and hard. It consists of lectures in catechism and the faith, as well as on-the-job training. Over the years, Mother Teresa has made no attempt to soften this regimen, as who could know better that the reality calls for many qualities, not least of which are quick wittedness and commonsense. The girls who join know that they are expected to sever their links with family and loved ones. They are allowed to return home on very rare occasions, on an average of once in ten years, when a parent is dying, or on the eve of an assignment to some distant country. Yet, astonishingly, the Missionaries of Charity have one of the largest novitiates in the Church. At a time when the Church is viewing its dwindling numbers with concern, Mother Teresa is flooded with requests to join, often from girls of good family, some of whom are well-educated.

I asked Sister Agnes, Mother Teresa's first postulant, what her parents' reaction was when she so bravely joined Mother Teresa in 1949, when neither Mother Teresa nor the work was known. She replied, 'My mother was very upset, and although she lived in Calcutta, she did not come to see me from 1949 to 1953. It took a long time before she could accept it.' Another Sister, who requested anonymity, said that her parents had for many years urged her to leave the order, but when they finally realised how much at peace she was with herself, they accepted her decision. 'The parents are usually very happy to give their own child to God. It is a big thing, a very big sacrifice on their part. Sacrifice does not cause sadness when you give up to God,' said Mother Teresa.

Every once in a while the press comes out with sensational stories about Sisters who leave. Two years ago, a Sunday paper carried a story about a senior nun called Sister Emaques, who cited illtreatment and Mother Teresa's 'dictatorial' ways as her reason for leaving the Society. The paper alleged that several others had left with her. Co-workers in Calcutta brought the article to Mother's attention. Some weeks later, on a visit to Calcutta, I asked her about it. I could see that she was hurt. There never was a Sister by that name, she said. Not only was the story a complete fabrication, but a letter written to the Editor, pointing this out, was not published. 'Out of respect, the paper should have published our co-workers' reply,' said Mother Teresa. 'I feel sorry for those who have written such a story only to sell more papers. How can they misuse our name like that?' she asked.

This is not to suggest that novices and Sisters do not leave. There is ample freedom to do so. Plenty of girls enter the

Order as 'come-and-sees' for a few weeks or months, to see if the vocation is for them. Some find the life difficult, others wish to return to their families or to get married. Yet the number of professed Sisters who have left is comparatively small. Perhaps this has something to do with Mother Teresa's charisma and the way that she has kept her flock together. Whether the Order will continue to grow, only time will tell. For the present, more girls join than leave, with the result that today there are almost 4000 Sisters and novices spread over the world.

The schedule of training consists of aspirancy for six months and postulancy for a year. The qualifications officially required are health of body and mind, ability to acquire knowledge, commonsense in abundance and a cheerful disposition. Those who complete the postulancy undergo a novitiate for two years. The novitiate over, they are permitted to make their first vows. The professed Sisters undergo a juniorate (as it is called) for five years. They renew their vows each year. The sixth year of vows is called the tertianship, after which, they take final vows. Before their final vows, Mother Teresa sends them home for three weeks. Her intention is clear. The life ahead calls for tremendous and unusual dedication; the girls must have a final opportunity to decide carefully whether they wish to remain and serve.

I put this question to a pair of tertians, whom I accompanied on one of their regular house visits to an AIDS sufferer in Rome. One girl was Irish, the other Swiss. They were in their late twenties. They wore rough overcoats over their hand-woven cotton saris, and sensible shoes suitable for their work. On the way, we passed a group of smart young girls dressed in the latest fashion. After the group passed us by, I asked the two whether they were also tempted by nice clothes and make-up. Both laughed delightedly, as if I had cracked some very funny joke. They assured me that they had plenty of opportunities to take that route, had they wished to. They left me in no doubt that spiritually they had evolved much beyond their young ages.

This is not to say that the Sisters are turn-of-the-century evangelists. Italy, of course, is predominantly Roman Catholic, and so no question of conversion would arise. In India, too, a frankly evangelist role that existed from the eighteenth century onwards has gradually been tempered with the attainment of independence in 1947. For Mother Teresa, there is no longer the need for counting of souls, baptism and deathbed conversions. In living with Christ, and in serving him through the poor, she is at one with him. 'I am married to Jesus, so to speak, as you are to your wife,' she explained one day. Her preference is obvious. 'I do convert,' she said to me with a laugh, when I asked her what her reaction was to this criticism. 'I convert you to be a better Hindu, a better Catholic, a better Muslim, or Jain or Buddhist. I would like to help you to find God. When you find Him, it is up to you to do what you want with Him.' I know that the babies of Shishu Bhawan are not baptised unless their parentage is known to be Christian, or unless they are to be sent into adoption into a Christian home. Most of the children, in fact, go into Hindu homes, and for Mother Teresa to baptise such a child would not only be unthinkable, it would be a sin. Similarly, in Kalighat, the dead are invariably sent for cremation, unless specifically known to be Muslim or Christian. In all the years that I have known Mother Teresa, not once, not even obliquely or by inference, has she suggested to me a conversion of faith. Mother Teresa's frequent refrain has always been, 'Have you begun to pray yet?' When I said that once in a while I could say a prayer to her, she laughed and answered, 'In that case it's all right, because I pray for you!' Then, becoming serious, she added, 'You must offer my prayers to God.'

One principle that she has not allowed to see diluted is

that the Missionaries of Charity must go out on to the streets. 'You have seen,' she said to me, 'how difficult it is for our leprosy patients to come to us from Dhapa or Titagarh, or from the slums. We must go to them. We must not stay behind our walls.' The only institutions that she has permitted are those for children, for the mentally retarded (such as Prem Dān in Calcutta), for the leprosy destitute, and for the dying. These are all special categories that need institutional care. It is only a small proportion of the Sisters who run these institutions (with the help of novices and volunteers); most of the Sisters go into the slums and localities where they are most needed. This is fundamental to Mother Teresa's thinking, and forms a part of their Constitution: 'The Missionaries of Charity will remain right on the ground by living Christ's concern for the poorest and lowliest.'

She has invariably declined all offers of a regular income. One day she refused a local millionaire when he offered her a large sum of money on the condition that she could use the interest (which would have been considerable), but without being able to touch the principal. What is the good of that money, she asked, if I can't use it when and where it may be needed. 'I don't want the work to become a business. It must remain a work of love.' She is unshakeable in her conviction that God will provide. 'Money,' she told me, 'I never give it a thought. It always comes. We do all our work for our Lord. He must look after us. If He wants something done, He must provide us with the means. If He does not provide us with the means, then it shows that He does not want that particular work. I forget about it.'

It is easy to understand why Mother Teresa has never accepted Government funding or Church maintenance. Both would involve keeping accounts. This would mean that in the 468 houses of the Missionaries of Charity around the world, at least one Sister would be distracted from her true work of comforting and helping the lonely, the afflicted and despairing. It would also mean an army of accountants. Anyone who has seen the tiny office in Motherhouse, where three Sisters hammer away on antiquated typewriters to keep in touch with the work in over 100 countries, would know that Mother Teresa would grudge every rupee spent away from the 'real work'.

In the days before she received the Nobel Prize, when Mother Teresa was not as famous nor her work quite so well known, there were occasions when it became necessary for Providence to step in. I remember Mother Teresa herself telling me of a day when food ran out at the Shishu Bhawan in Delhi. There was nothing to eat, nor even money to buy the cheapest dāl (lentils). The Sisters were preparing to boil rice, which is all they had, on which they would sprinkle a little salt. Just then a car drew up from Prime Minister Indira Gandhi's house, sent by her daughter-in-law Sonia. It was laden with vegetables, fresh from the garden. 'The children and the Sisters ate well that day,' chuckled Mother Teresa.

In this spirit, Mother Teresa has always refused any effort of fundraising. In fact, she specifically forbids it. No Co-worker is permitted to raise any money for the Society. Donations, wherever they are received, are sent to the Regional Superior, who decides how best to utilise them according to the needs of the houses in that region. There can be no investment of funds. 'I do not need money in the bank,' she said to me, 'I need money to use for my people.' The quite remarkable sums that are donated are spent almost as quickly on medicines (particularly for leprosy and tuberculosis), on food and on milk powder. Some donations are enormous. A single behest last year was almost 3,000,000 Swiss francs! As it happened, the money was quickly spent on much-needed supplies for Eastern Europe. The point, however, is that in Mother Teresa's scheme of things such large sums, while important, are not vital. What she holds dear is 'sacrifice money'.

I learned about this when I once teasingly asked Mother why she had such a dim light leading to her room in Mother-house. Could she not install a couple of brighter lights? She was unusually serious in her reply. 'The money I get is not money for business. It's sacrifice money. The people who give it sacrifice a lot. They buy cheaper clothes, go without meals. Did I tell you about this young Hindu couple?' she asked. When I shook my head, she went on. 'They loved one another so much that they wanted to share this love and joy with me and the poor. They decided not to buy expensive clothes for the wedding. Instead they bought ordinary clothes. No feast, no saris, nothing. They gave me all the money they saved.'

The following day, as I sat talking to Mother Teresa in the parlour, I saw for myself an example of what she meant. Some people entered the room. Among them were a Swiss banker and a senior official of the largest Swiss supermarket chain, Migros, as well as a shy Calcutta lad, about eighteen or nineteen years of age. The two Swiss presented Mother with their visiting cards. Mother promptly offered them her business card. 'Now you will have to pray,' she added with a chuckle, and, turning in my direction, said, 'and why should he be left out? You will also have to learn to pray.' Mother's laughter was infectious, and we laughed de-lightedly. The banker said he had been contributing to Mother Teresa's homes in Europe for many years. 'Thank God,' said Mother. The Manager of Migros said that his chain, as a matter of policy, donates 1 per cent of its profits each year to charity. Could they help Mother Teresa in any way? Mother Teresa replied, 'We have recently opened a home in Romania, where many people are living in poverty and in extreme cold. There is urgent need there for food and clothing. Can these be sent directly to the Sisters in Romania?' The Manager promised to organise this within a short time.

Mother then called the young Bengali, Subroto Mitra. He wanted to say something, but the words did not seem to come easily. Mother spoke to him gently in Bengali. At first he faltered, and then the words came tumbling out. He had been waiting outside for more than an hour, he said. This was his first visit to Motherhouse. He had heard the name of Mother Teresa since he was a child. Yesterday, he received his first salary of 600 rupees. He wished to donate it to the really poor. His mother had advised him to give it to Mother Teresa. Having said that, the young man placed the envelope at Mother's feet. She held his head and pulled him up. She blessed him. She knew how much the pay packet meant to that middle-class family. It represented many years of parental sacrifice. At that moment nothing else seemed more important to Mother Teresa, nor to those of us present.

In the parlour where we sat there is a hand-drawn chart that lists the total range of activities carried out by the Missionaries of Charity. The social activities include child welfare and educational schemes, family visiting, day crèches, feeding programmes and homes for alcoholics, night shelters and natural family planning centres. The medical activities listed are dispensaries, leprosy clinics and rehabilitation centres, homes for abandoned, crippled and mentally retarded children, for unwed mothers, for sick and dying destitutes and AIDS patients. Educational activities include the various schools and sewing, commercial and handicraft classes. Under the Apostolic listing are prison visiting, family contacts, catechism classes, Catholic action groups and Sunday schools.

The growth in activities was gradual. For the first ten years the Society was based in Calcutta. This was strictly in accordance with canon law, which forbids the opening of new houses outside the diocese by an institute less than ten years old. Some accounts I have heard suggest that Mother Teresa was somewhat impatient on this score. Archbishop Perier, ever cautious, refused to compromise on the point. It was only in 1960 that Mother Teresa was permitted to open her first house outside Calcutta. This was in Ranchi, a town in India's tribal belt. The next home, in Delhi, was opened by Prime Minister Jawaharlal Nehru himself. 'He was ill, but got up from his bed and came. I asked him if I could tell him about the work. He said, "No, Mother, you need not tell me about your work, I know about it. That is why I have come."' As Prime Minister, he commended her to the President of India for the prestigious Padma Shri award, which she received in 1962. It was the first time that it was given to someone not born an Indian.

The opening of new houses followed rapidly. In 1960, work began on sites in Jhansi and Agra. In 1961, land was received for the future leprosy settlement of Shantinagar. Houses in Ambala, Bhagalpur, Amravati, Goa, Bombay, Patna and Darjeeling followed in quick succession. Now there was no looking back. By the end of the 1960s there were twenty-five houses in India; by the end of the 1980s the number had grown to eighty-six. By 1991, 168 houses had been established and their number continues to grow.

It was inevitable that Mother Teresa would carry her work overseas. The opening of the first non-Indian house, in Cocorote in Venezuela in 1965, came about in a curious way. The Society was still under the Archdiocese of Calcutta, which meant that Mother Teresa reported to Archbishop Perier. The Archbishop, who was reluctant to allow the work to spread too rapidly in India, was hardly likely to give permission to Mother Teresa to start a house at the other end of the world.

The idea came from Archbishop Knox, the Papal Nuncio in New Delhi. At a conference in Rome, he heard about the plight of the landless people of African descent in Venezuela, and was inspired to suggest that he had the answer to their particular needs – Mother Teresa and her

Missionaries of Charity. Archbishop Perier could hardly refuse the Papal Nuncio. Moreover, in February 1965, the Society was placed directly under the Vatican. It became a congregation of pontifical right.

At the invitation of the Bishop in Venezuela, Mother Teresa went to see the situation herself. This was to become her invariable rule for the opening of all houses: the local bishop would invite her, and she would go to make an assessment. The poverty in Cocorote convinced her of the need to send a mission. Moreover, the number of Sisters had grown to almost 300, which enabled her to respond to this need. The first group of four Sisters sent by Mother Teresa were all Indian. On the way to Venezuela, Mother took them to the Vatican to be blessed by the Pope. This may have had something to do with the opening in 1968 of their second overseas home, in Rome itself. The following year Mother Teresa opened two homes in Australia, one for alcoholics and drug addicts and one for aborigines. In 1970, she opened four new homes: in London, Jordan and two more in Venezuela. Thereafter, she opened several houses in quick succession, in the Bronx in New York, Bangladesh, Northern Ireland, the Gaza Strip, Yemen, Ethiopia, Sicily, Papua New Guinea, the Philippines, Panama, Japan, Portugal, Brazil and Burundi. Additional houses were opened in England, the USA, and in the last few years, she opened houses in the USSR, South Africa and all over Eastern Europe. Finally, after much prayer, came the turn of Albania, the country of her origin.

Setting up houses in many of these countries was not easy. The former Soviet Union was particularly difficult. Mother Teresa told me that she wrote several times to former President Gorbachov. She received no reply, but persisted in her efforts. One day, she told me with a laugh, that as a gentle reminder, she sent Mr Gorbachov a congratulatory telegram on St Michael's day! When permission came, it was in the

MISSIONARIES OF CHARITY
54A ACHARYA J. CHANDRA BOSE
CALCUTTA 700016, INDIA

10/7/90

Dear Mr. N. Chawla,

   Thank you for your kind letter and the article you wrote. I hope it will be all for the glory of God and the good of all who read it I have just returned from Eastern Europe where I have opened a number of houses. In all these houses people are hungry for God. I hope the presence of our Sisters will help them. Let us pray.

              God bless you
              M Teresa MC

wake of tragedy. The devastating earthquake of 7 December 1988 in Armenia created the circumstances which enabled Mother Teresa to fly in a relief mission of Sisters with medicines, clothes and equipment. The rest followed easily enough, and today she has ten houses in the former Soviet Union.

I had a small contribution to make towards the establishment of a Mission in South Africa. India has no diplomatic relations with that country. This meant that Mother Teresa, who holds a diplomatic passport given to her by the Indian Government, could not enter South Africa. She told me that while she also held a passport provided to her by the Vatican, she almost invariably travelled on her Indian passport. Now, if she could not enter South Africa on this, she would rather not go. This also meant her recalling six Sisters who were at that very time waiting in Nairobi for permission to enter South Africa. Four of the six Sisters were also Indian. I arranged for Mother Teresa to meet the then Cabinet Secretary, Mr. B. J. Deshmuk in New Delhi. She discussed her problem with him. As head of the civil service, he found a solution within a few hours: Mother Teresa was offered a non-diplomatic passport in place of her diplomatic one. As this did not involve any question of diplomatic relations, the South African Government was prompt in giving Mother Teresa and her Sisters the necessary visas. When she returned to Delhi, she told me that she had opened her first house in Cape Town.

An interesting tale is attached to the opening of a house in the Vatican in 1988. Although by this time there were already three houses in working-class districts of Rome, Mother Teresa was convinced that there were enough poor in the shadow of St Peter's to merit the opening of a fourth house, in the Vatican itself. One day when she was there, she took up the case with Pope John Paul II, and received a most positive response. The next time that she was at the Vatican, she reminded the Holy Father, who immediately issued instructions that a suitable place be made available. This was not so easy, as the Vatican is small and over-crowded. Some months went by before Mother Teresa's next visit. By this time, the Pope, anticipating Mother Teresa's gentle reminder, enquired about the progress of the house. He is supposed to have said, 'As soon as Mother Teresa sees me, she will ask me about the house.' Before her fourth successive visit, the Vatican was ready. The Pope, knowing that Mother was sure to ask, said he wished the key to be kept ready for her. After she had received his blessing, but before she could ask, the Pope presented her with the key to a brand new house. It had been specially constructed within the ancient structure of the Vatican, and stood immediately adjacent to the Audience Hall itself. Mother Teresa was delighted. More than once she told me, 'Now our poor have a place right in the Vatican. Our people [the poor] are the only ones who can walk into the Vatican with-out buying a ticket.'

Casa Dono di Maria, as the house is called, contains two dining halls, which each seat sixty people. There are also dormitories for old women. People start queuing up for an evening meal from 4 p.m. At 6 p.m. the doors are opened on a first-come, first-served basis. No-one is allowed to go hungry. I asked Sister Bharoti, the Sister in charge, whether they bought the food. She laughed. 'We never have to buy anything. In the beginning, we used to beg for food at the vegetable, fish and meat markets. Now they just give it to us.'

I found plenty of volunteers about the place, including Luciana, aged fifty-two, and her daughter Venturella, aged twenty-five, who were cutting, chopping and washing in the large, well-equipped kitchen. 'What is tiring work at home is not tiring here,' said the daughter. Another volun-teer was Riccardo, thirty-five years old, whom I found help-ing to serve the food. He is a flight attendant with Alitalia.

How did he manage the time, I asked. 'We get two or three days between flights, so I muddle around here,' he answered with a smile.

On the chilly winter afternoon when I was at Casa Dono di Maria, the doorbell rang. I accompanied Sister Bharoti to the door. Standing shivering in the rain was a boy of about sixteen. He had no warm clothing and said that he had come from Mauritius. Did the Sister have something she could give him to keep warm? Near where he was standing, someone had left a large carrier bag full of clothes. On top was a white jacket. Sister pointed to it, and asked him to try it on. His delight in finding that it fit him perfectly was matched only by Sister Bharoti's smile. When I recounted this incident to Mother Teresa, she nodded and said, 'This happens many times a day. It happens all the time.'

While discussing the soup kitchen, I asked Mother Teresa how the Missionaries of Charity succeeded in organising themselves so rapidly in distant countries and how they set up camps for disaster relief overnight. Mother Teresa seemed amused by my question, and replied, 'We have plenty of practice, no? For the last thirty-six years that's what we have been doing.' We both laughed. She went on to say, 'Anytime something happens we are there, and we know what to do. We know what people need, and we start doing it. During floods, the Sisters collect food, while the Government provides helicopters to deliver it. Many organisations come forward to help. People give. They help. If everybody does something then the work is done. I have plenty of Sisters who do wonderful work.'

Yet there is a distinct impression that in the strength of this well-organised Society may well lie its weakness, for authority is concentrated in the hands of Mother Teresa herself. I asked Mother Teresa if she controlled everything. Her measured reply was, 'No, we now have many Sisters. Every house has a Superior, then a number of houses together are placed under a Regional Superior. Each Regional Superior is responsible for a Province, e.g. Western Europe, America and so on. Then we have four Councillors-General. We have Church laws which direct us. We are a religious congregation. The Church has laws and regulations for religious congregations, how to live in spiritual love and at the same time have rules that will guide and lead us, otherwise there would be confusion. If you go to any country where we work you will see exactly the same thing: Sisters sitting on the floor, the same poverty, the cheapest food, and so on. Mother Teresa is not in all the houses at the same time. Yet the work goes on. God's work has to be done properly. If people can do it for money, why can't we do it for the love of God?'

Knowing that many people are anxious about the future of the Missionaries of Charity when Mother Teresa dies, I diffidently asked her about it. Her first reaction was to point a finger heavenwards and say, 'Wait until I go first!' Then, more seriously, she said, 'If we remain wedded to our poverty and do not end up unconsciously serving the rich, all will be well.'

As it happens, this religious Congregation has a detailed Constitution and rules which govern every aspect, including the election to the post of Superior General and the four Councillors-General. It is the General Chapter that is final authority in the Congregation. Every six years, the General Chapter elects the Superior General and the four Councillors-General. It consists of about one hundred members including all Regional Superiors and delegates representing the various Regions amongst others. The General Chapter has met every six years since 1967, and then a last time, after five years, with special permission from Rome. The elections are by secret ballot, and an absolute majority is required.

According to Father van Exem, Mother Teresa tried to

step down more than once; the first time, in 1973, she was sixty-three years old. The second time, when the General Chapter met in 1979, she said to her Sisters, 'I am old and tired. It is difficult for me to do the work. It is better to have a younger Sister now.' In 1983, aged seventy-two, she fell seriously ill for the first time: she was visiting her mission in Rome, when one night she fell out of bed. 'Fortunately, it was an MC [Missionaries of Charity] bed,' she said with ready wit, 'so I didn't fall very far.' She felt a pain in her side and finally, thinking that she may have broken a rib, decided to go for a check-up. The doctors' investigations led them not to the fracture that she suspected, but to a cardiac problem. They promptly hospitalised her. 'They told me that it was lucky that I had come to the hospital, otherwise I would have had a severe heart attack.' Her hospitalisation – the first of several – caused concern the world over. The Salvator Mundi hospital was flooded with letters and telegrams. The President of India, the President of the United States and her friend Jyoti Basu (the Chief Minister of West Bengal) sent telegrams. The King and Queen of Belgium went specially to Rome to see her. She remembers a particularly touching letter she received from a man in Kashmir, who wrote that, as a Hindu, he was praying to the Goddess Kali to take his good health and give it to Mother Teresa, while Mother Teresa's poor health be transferred to him.

In December 1989, Mother Teresa had a dizzy spell and, but for the restraining hand of a Sister, might have fallen down the stairs at Motherhouse. The pacemaker which had been implanted a few years ago had to be replaced. When I visited her in hospital in Calcutta, she looked faded and worn-out. After a long and anxious spell, she recovered. This time she wrote to the Vatican and, in accordance with the Constitution, sought the permission of the Holy See to convene a General Chapter a full year before it was due, so that a successor could be elected. The Vatican agreed to

Mother Teresa's request, and permitted her to step down. The General Chapter was summoned for the first week of September 1990.

The Sisters, including the most senior amongst them, even now resisted a change. Father van Exem told me that immediately prior to the eight-day retreat that precedes the election, he was visited by two very senior Sisters, Sister Agnes and Sister Nirmala. They specifically wanted to know if they were precluded by the Vatican from voting once again for Mother Teresa. 'I know that Rome gave her permission to step down, but I don't think that the Vatican gave an Order to the Sisters not to vote for Mother. They returned and reported this to the Sisters. The result was unanimous to retain Mother Teresa. I know that Mother was not happy with the outcome. She did not want to hang on. She wrote to me to say, "It is better to serve than be served." But, as with everything else, she accepted.'

'I wanted to be free, but God has His own plans,' she said to me one day, referring to the election. She pointed a finger to the heavens. 'This is His work, not mine. As long as we remain wedded to Him and our poverty, the work will prosper. I am not important.'

7

· *Brothers and Co-Workers* ·

One night at the Howrah Railway Station in Calcutta, a group of young hoodlums were rounded up by the police. Amongst them were pickpockets, alcoholics, pimps, drug peddlers and other petty criminals. Without much ado they were taken for the night to the 'lock-up' in the station hall, to be brought before the magistrate the following day. A young Brother was amongst them. He tried to tell the policemen who he was, but his voice was drowned in the general howls of protest and proclamations of blamelessness. Before he knew it, he found that he, too, had been herded into the cell. Through that hot and humid night, he was bitten by mosquitoes and nipped by rats. What was infinitely worse was the way his fellow prisoners taunted him. 'Hey, Brother,' they laughed, 'why do you bother to help us when you can't help yourself? Where is your God now?' He had no answer. As his eyes filled with tears, he fell on to his knees to ask why he had been chosen to be so humiliated. Was this his Cross to bear?

The priest was a Missionary Brother of Charity who had recently entered the Order. Part of his mission lay in helping the hundreds of young vagrants and destitute boys for whom the railway stations of Howrah and Sealdah were the only homes they had ever known. He soon got to know the young kids who eked a living by carrying luggage, polishing shoes or running errands. Since he himself was young and energetic, he sometimes organised a game of football for them in a nearby field. It was difficult to tell who enjoyed these Sunday outings more. Because he worked in the nearby slums and streets, he also came to recognise the petty criminals who operated in and around the railway stations. He tried hard to wean them away from crime by persuading them to learn a trade instead.

It was some of these young hoodlums who had mocked him that night, an experience he could never forget. Had the Brother worn a religious dress, it is most unlikely that such a mistake would have occurred. Yet, unlike their counterparts the Sisters, the Brothers wear no distinctive uniform and hence are not easy to distinguish at a distance or in a crowd. Moreover, the clothes they wear in India, an ordinary shirt and trouser, are unlikely to identify them as Mother Teresa's Missionaries of Charity. Only when one is practically face-to-face with them does one notice a small crucifix pinned on their shirt. To most people in India, used to seeing priests in cassocks, a rosary or a crucifix by itself is hardly suggestive of a religious life, or missionary work.

Although it is not widely known, the need for a distinctive dress was a point of disagreement between Mother Teresa and Brother Andrew, who was the first General Servant (or Superior General) of the Brothers' branch. Brother Andrew, who retired from the Order in 1986, once said to me, 'Mother Teresa believed that the Brothers should be in a religious dress. Many of the Brothers also wanted it. It gave a little bit of status. I believed that without a uniform we were more identified with the poor and underprivileged. I also liked the simplicity of a cross pinned to the shirt.' At the same time he accepted the need for women to wear a special dress, for it offered them a form of protection. And what if the Brothers suffered some humiliation as a result of not being identified, I asked? 'So be it,' said Brother Andrew. Mother Teresa's answer, some months later, was not dissimilar. Her eyes had become pools of sadness, when she said, 'This young Brother had to go through this humiliation for one night only. There are so many of our poor who have to go through this night after night.'

I never did tell Brother Andrew the story about his young Brother, but I did ask him whether he considered the issue of the dress to be quite so important. After a few moments of reflection he replied, 'Possibly I was wrong in this. Even now, Mother Teresa would like to see the Brothers in a uniform. The rule might be changed in the future.'

The Brothers' branch was started in 1963, with the gradual realisation that men were better suited for certain kinds of work. As in many other things, Mother Teresa sought the advice of Father van Exem. He was then parish priest in Asansol. One day in 1961, Mother Teresa unexpectedly paid him a visit. She explained that the boys in Shishu Bhawan were growing up, and the Sisters would soon have difficulty in looking after them. Moreover, in Kalighat and in the leprosy work, men could better handle the heavier work that was involved. For these reasons, she wished to start a congregation of Brothers. Would Father van Exem kindly ask the Archbishop for his permission, she enquired. Father van Exem, who thought this an excellent idea, travelled to Calcutta especially to discuss this with Archbishop Albert Vincent. 'Now this Archbishop was very different from Archbishop Perier, who always opposed a new idea. (You remember all the questions he used to put to me such as "how do you know it is the Will of God", and all that?) I put Mother Teresa's idea to him. For a minute – a very long minute indeed – he was silent. Then he said, "In India we have understood the vocation of a Father and of a Sister, but we have not understood the vocation of a Brother. I understand the vocation of a Brother. I want Brothers. Tell Mother Teresa to begin." It was settled in five minutes.'

Mother Teresa was delighted and requested Father van

Exem to send her some suitable young men as soon as possible. Within a few weeks of his return to Asansol, he located and despatched half a dozen strapping young men to Calcutta to begin the new activity. 'They were put up somewhere in Shishu Bhawan, I remember, amongst all those babies,' he laughed. 'Then Sister Gertrude (the doctor), who knew, of all things, some carpentry, started to give them carpentry lessons. It was very funny.' Father van Exem laughed so much at the recollection that he got hiccups. He drank a glass of water before he settled down again. 'Then Mother Teresa told me, "You see, Father, they are men. They need exercise. I have told them to play volleyball every evening."' The thought of tiny Mother Teresa leading a group of hefty young men into some volleyball field was altogether too much, and this time both of us held on to our sides. Father van Exem needed another glass of water.

There were several teething problems before the Congregation could get properly organised. Men were reluctant to join until it became a recognised Institute, and in turn, recognition from Rome depended on numbers and proper organisation. Another difficulty lay in the fact that the Roman Catholic Church does not permit a woman to be head of a religious congregation of men. These issues took more than a year to settle. Then, Mother Teresa tried to obtain the services of Father Gabrić, a Yugoslav Jesuit whom she knew. The Order of Jesuits was not prepared to release him. She then asked for Father van Antoine, a French priest, but it is possible that he may not have wished to sever his links with his own Order. It was at this juncture that a young man, then undergoing his tertianship, applied and was selected. Mother Teresa did not know him earlier. The Jesuit Order agreed to his release. He was an Australian by the name of Ian Travers-Ball. He took the religious name of Brother Andrew.

Over six feet tall, charismatic and articulate, Brother

Andrew speaks gently but without any trace of hesitation. 'I came to India in 1954, as a young Jesuit,' he said. 'I became interested in the poor when I was working in the Hazaribagh coal mining area of [the State of] Bihar. As part of my training, I thought I would spend a month with Mother Teresa because it would help me in my future work. She had a group of young men whom she was directing, but she was looking for someone to head the Order. I walked in quite by chance.' He was thirty-eight years old at the time.

I spent an evening with Brother Andrew at 7 Mansatala Row, the small building in a grubby locality that serves as the headquarters of the Brothers' branch. There was a terrific amount of noise and laughter and the clapping of hands. It was recreation hour, explained Brother Andrew with a smile, and the Brothers were letting off steam. He spoke to me about the beginning. 'I believed that we had to get away from Shishu Bhawan if we were to develop as an independent group. I don't know whether it was my male chauvinism or my Jesuit training. I felt that the Brothers needed to develop their own leadership and in their own style. We would draw inspiration and support from Mother Teresa, but we needed to function autonomously. Mother entirely agreed.

'We rented a place in Kidderpore before we found this house. Mother bought it for us. There were about fifteen of us when we first moved in.' Significantly, he added, 'The lifestyle of a group of men will necessarily be different from that of women. We could not, for instance, live on top of each other the way the women have managed to do. Men need to go out for a walk, or have a game of football on a Sunday afternoon or watch some wrestling. The Sisters don't go out for anything except their work. Household arrangements, too, could not be the same for us. I did not feel bound to follow all the small details.'

Brother Geoff, the present General Servant, believes that

they are not different in essentials, but the nature of their work leads them to be less regimented and less enclosed, especially in contacts with outsiders and visitors. From the very beginning, they adopted a different route from that of the Sisters. Less sheltered, they needed to adapt themselves to local and cultural conditions, which might vary enormously in the different regions of the same country. Their communities, too, are smaller; there are fewer Brothers per home. The community language used outside India is not necessarily English, although it is English that is most widely used. Finally, said Brother Geoff, as if responding to Father van Exem's comment that they began their activity in Shishu Bhawan, they no longer work with babies!

Amongst the first places where the Brothers began to work was the Howrah railway station. There were, quite literally, hundreds of boys and young men who lived under its cavernous roof. Most of them were orphans, some had run away from home, others had jumped probation. Many suffered from infections and disease. The Brothers began to help them in little ways. Some of them needed urgent medical attention. The Brothers gave them bars of soap to keep themselves clean. Gradually the Brothers organised an evening meal for the station kids, so that they could eat at least one hot and nourishing meal a day. A few of the boys were given temporary refuge in Mansatala Row, until they could be provided with vocational training. Along with the older boys from Shishu Bhawan, they were gradually transferred to other houses that were established in and near Calcutta.

The first of these was a special home for homeless and handicapped boys, called Nabo Jeevan (New Life), which was started in Howrah. An increasing demand for some form of training led initially to the creation of a radio-repair workshop at Dum Dum, where boys were trained to do simple repairs which could get them a little job somewhere.

For the mentally disabled boys and the men who were tubercular, the Brothers acquired a farm at Nurpur, about twenty miles away from Calcutta. Here, some became involved in simple agricultural work.

The Brothers continued their involvement in leprosy work. At first they assisted with the mobile dispensaries. Later, they went regularly to Dhapa, the large leprosy colony in Calcutta, where they tended the sick. In due course, they began to assist the Sisters in Titagarh. The problems in the leprosy colony on the other side of the railway tracks were not tasks that women could be expected to handle. It was not long before the Brothers took over the work completely.

Ten years after their origin in India, Brother Andrew opened the first overseas house in war-ravaged Vietnam, a country in which the Sisters were not working. The Brothers would always choose houses overseas in countries or cities where the Sisters did not have a presence. They began with a small rented house, its first occupants a handful of people, including children orphaned by the war. Two years later a second house was opened, this time in Los Angeles, California, in a seedy, crime-infested Mexican-American neighbourhood known as 'Skid Row'. Here they began a small home for alcoholics and drug addicts.

Gradually Brother Andrew led them to other troubled spots and rough neighbourhoods on every continent. The countries they spread to included Hong Kong, Japan, Taiwan, Korea, Guatemala, the Philippines, El Salvador, the Dominican Republic, Haiti, Brazil, Madagascar, and even France. Some of these areas were constantly erupting into violence, and on one occasion in El Salvador, a brother was kidnapped. He was released after three months upon the intervention of the Archbishop of El Salvador, who himself was critically shot a few months later.

For the most part, the Brothers undertook the tasks that they knew best, like running shelters for homeless boys, alcoholic men and drug addicts. They started a soup kitchen in Paris. In many places they were assisted by groups of people who came to be known as 'Come-and-Sees'. This was an interesting phrase coined by Brother Andrew for the many young people who were interested to try their hand at the work for a few weeks or months. There was no obligation to join the Order or to take vows. This name was soon adopted by Mother Teresa for the young women who wanted to see if they liked or could do the work. Several Missionaries of Charity, Brothers and Sisters alike, working today in places as far apart as Taiwan, Haiti, Burundi and Peru, joined at one time or another as 'Come-and-Sees'.

Before Brother Andrew left the Order in 1987, he was succeeded in 1986 by Brother Geoff, also an Australian. With him came a difference in style, a change of gear, a time for reflection and taking stock. In some ways, he is thought to have brought the Order closer to Mother Teresa's original vision. The Constitution of the Brothers branch is presently being re-cast. It may bring about greater conformity with the Constitutions of the Sisters branch, but that remains to be seen.

Yet the Congregation is growing slowly. The number of new candidates is less than in earlier years. Some of the reasons are that the background from which candidates come is not as 'fertile' as it was before. The effect of materialistic values and smaller families has taken its toll. The Congregation itself is being more selective and encouraging prospective candidates to complete their school education. Regardless of current factors, it is usual for Brothers' Congregations to attract less vocations than Sisters' or Priests' Congregations because there is a preference for the status that goes with them. 'Yes, some do leave,' said Brother Geoff. 'In the year of temporary vows, it is usually part of the normal process of discernment. Departures after final vows are less but, as in any congregation, there are always a few.

There is also the fact, that in the times in which we are living, commitment is less valued and so more easily terminated.' Brother Geoff also believes that rapid expansion in the last decade or so overstretched the Organisation. For these reasons, the total number of houses is down from a peak of ninety-four to eighty-one (in 1991), of which forty-five are in India and thirty-six in twenty-five other countries.

One man who believes deeply in his calling is my friend who spent that tormented night in the station jail. Twenty years later, I was to ask him whether he had any regrets or if he had ever felt tempted to leave. I prefaced it by saying that these were difficult questions which he was at liberty not to answer. His reply was straightforward. 'It is not at all a difficult question to answer,' he said. 'There was a time before I joined the Order that I had many problems, so many fantasies and desires. I was fragile and unhappy. Why God saved a miserable creature like me is a constant source of wonder. He called me to this life. Now, I cannot, not even for a minute, think of leaving my vocation as a Missionary Brother of Charity. The more difficult, the more demanding my life, the closer I feel to Him. I can never leave.'

As I got up to leave the tiny parlour where we sat, my eye chanced on a framed Hindi proverb that hung near the door:

> If you have
>   two loaves of bread
> Give one to the poor,
>   sell the other –
> And buy hyacinths
>   to feed your soul.

*   *   *

Far from sophisticated London, in one of the city's less affluent sections, stands a dilapidated church. Its peeling paint and broken windows stand testimony that it went out of business because it had become too costly to maintain. For years its front door remained locked. Now it is opened at 6 p.m. every evening by a group of women, mostly foreigners in saris. These are Mother Teresa's Missionaries of Charity. By their side are a few volunteers and a handful of Co-Workers. The hundred-odd beneficiaries who shuffle in are largely men, white, some surprisingly young. They seem distanced from reality by alcoholism or drugs. Some of the women are mentally disturbed. There is a wild-eyed man whose face is completely tattooed. They enter in silence and sit at the tables laid out in the hall. After a prayer, a hot meal is served. They eat in total silence and shuffle out again.

The food they eat is not bought with money. Tonight's dinner is unused food from a very expensive London hospital. It has been specially prepared by its chef, who is also a Co-Worker. Food has never been bought. A well-known chain of food stores sends unsold vegetables and fruit. The Co-Workers have also quietly spread the word to butchers and bakers: 'Please don't throw good food away, send it to Mother Teresa.' In the hall, half a dozen volunteers help to serve, and later to clear away and wash up. They are not Co-Workers; they come by occasionally to help. One of them is a young man, fresh from Winchester, one of Britain's leading public schools, who is training to become a lawyer. He comes along once in a while. 'It's a part of life,' he says. 'Besides, I enjoy talking to the people and to the Sisters.'

The two Co-Workers who had taken me to the Quex Road Church were Bridget Eacott, the International Secretary, and Faye Larkins, the National Link for Britain. 'All over Great Britain we first try to see what can be done in our own region and in our own neighbourhoods,' said Faye. 'In the North-East region we channel everything we collect into our own special areas of need. In the inner cities of Manchester, Birmingham and Liverpool, the Co-Workers look after the physically destitute. Other areas are more likely to be emotionally and spiritually deprived. There are thousands of lonely people, living by themselves, not necessarily physically poor, but poor in ways that Mother says are worse than in Calcutta. She says the spiritual poverty of the West is far greater than the physical poverty of the so-called developing countries. She calls these unwanted people the "shut-ins". It is far harder to cure that form of loneliness. These people are "nobody". Nobody notices them. Mother wants the Co-Workers to be "somebody" to "someone".'

Some of the people whom few care to notice live in a veritable township of cardboard boxes, huddled under Waterloo Bridge, in parks such as Lincoln's Inn Fields and near London's underground stations. Home is a cardboard box a little larger than the size of a coffin. It is often their only protection against the icy winds of winter. For most of them, the only genuine smiles they receive are from the Sisters and Co-Workers. On two nights a week, beginning at about 10 p.m., an ambulant soup kitchen brings them a hot meal. With this come words of cheer and sounds of laughter.

The term 'Co-Workers' was borrowed almost half a century ago by Mother Teresa from Mahatma Gandhi, whom she greatly admired, but whom she had never met. (He was assassinated soon after she began her work.) Gandhiji had referred to his helpers as 'Co-Workers'. These were people who joined him in his social programme to uplift the status of women, combat leprosy, promote literacy and eliminate the pernicious practice of 'untouchability', practised by the upper castes against the lowest rungs of Indian society. The expression fitted neatly into what Mother Teresa had in mind: her Co-Workers would be an association of men, women, young people and children from all over the world, belonging to all religions, irrespective of social status. They 'would seek to love God in their fellow men, through wholehearted service to the poorest of the poor of all castes and creeds and would wish to unite themselves in a spirit of prayer and sacrifice with the work of Mother Teresa and the Missionaries of Charity.'

In fact, the first Co-Workers were Michael Gomes and his family. The doctors, dentists and nurses who responded to her early call and gave freely of their professional services were also Co-Workers in that sense. The formal idea of a society of Co-Workers took root gradually. During the 1950s, a group of British wives who were involved in social service in Calcutta found themselves attracted by Mother Teresa's immense 'pull'.

Anne Blaikie, the wife of a British businessman, had read of Mother Teresa's work in *The Statesman*, which was beginning to notice her activities. Curiosity took her, one morning in July 1954, to meet Mother Teresa. She offered to help. Mother Teresa promptly bundled her into a decrepit van and took her to the Home for the Dying in Kalighat. By the time Anne Blaikie returned home that evening, her life had changed. Within the month, on 26 July 1954 to be precise, Anne formed the first Co-Workers' group in Calcutta. For the next few months the group worked hard towards collecting serviceable clothes to be presented to the children of Shishu Bhawan and in the slums at Christmas. They did quite well and, with Christmas over, sat back waiting to be congratulated. Mother Teresa arrived soon to thank them for their effort, but told them that they had little time to waste, for Id and Diwali, the respective main festivals of the Muslim and Hindu communities, were around the corner and these children were looking forward to their share of clothes as well! From then on, there was no looking back for Anne Blaikie.

In 1960, Anne Blaikie returned to live in England. Nearby in Sussex lived John Southworth, who had helped with leprosy work when he was in Calcutta. They soon found several other ex-Calcuttans who had also helped Mother Teresa, all living within a radius of a few miles of each other. Before long, a 'Mother Teresa Committee' was formed, with Southworth as Chairman and Anne Blaikie as Vice-Chairman. Mother Teresa's visit to England in November 1960 gave an impetus to their work.

Having begun in Calcutta in a modest way and taken root in England, smaller groups of Co-Workers began to spring up in other countries where the Missionaries of Charity opened houses. The total numbers are unknown, but it is estimated that in the UK alone, there are altogether about 30,000 Co-Workers and approximately 10,000 in the United States. In some countries in Europe, there are only a few hundred.

In India I have met hundreds of Co-Workers, but their groups are not well organised. The only thing that can be said with any certainty is that for every one Christian, there are at least ten non-Christian (mainly Hindu) Co-workers. The success of the different units depends on the energy and enterprise of those in charge of the different areas, who are called 'Links'. Neighbourhood groups are small, ranging from two to twelve members. When they grow larger another group is formed. At their meetings, only non-alcoholic drinks are served in order that a meeting may take place with equal ease in the homes of rich and poor alike.

The organisation of Co-Workers is not widely known, as they are forbidden to engage in publicity or fund-raising.

The only publicity is in-house, in the form of the *Co-Workers Newsletter*, which is printed on the cheapest possible paper and goes out to all members. Mother Teresa prefers it to be mimeographed, as it is cheaper that way. The Co-Workers responsible for its publication may not hire an office or staff. This applies equally to the collection centres for old clothes, which should not be rented; the room may be a cellar in someone's house, or a garage or a spare room. Said

Faye Larkins with a laugh, 'My husband says that now that every inch of our house is filled with clothes for Mother Teresa, we will have to find another house for ourselves!'

It is remarkable that quite considerable sums are now offered in the name of a woman who began her work without a rupee less than fifty years ago. The International Speakers of the Co-Workers told me that cheques large and small arrive regularly in their post. These sums are spent almost as quickly as they are received.

The Sisters send in periodic requisitions for medicine, milk powder, proteins and clothes, to Co-Workers designated to make bulk purchases. This team is headed by the International Link for Relief Supplies located in Antwerp. This Link is assisted by a Committee of Co-Workers. To give some idea of the size of these shipments, in 1990 alone, 17,000,000 Belgian francs' worth of milk powder and 200,000 Dutch guilders' worth of protein biscuits were purchased and supplied to Africa, South and Central America and Asia. In addition, 3,000,000 Belgian francs' worth of clothes were purchased at one-tenth of their retail value and sent out to nine countries in West Africa. In 1991, twenty-four huge containers of used clothes in good condition, as well as much-needed blankets and bandages, were shipped to several destinations in Asia. These had been collected door-to-door by British Co-Workers.

Yet, in *Newsletter* after *Newsletter* Mother Teresa enjoins her Co-Workers not to drift away from humble works. Nothing is ever too small, not the writing of a letter for a blind person, nor the helping of an elderly neighbour to clean her house or to wash her clothes. Let the big things be done by other people, she has repeated. Acts of neighbourly kindness are as important. There are thousands of 'shut-ins' who receive no visits even from their own families.

In speaking about the poverty of the West, Mother Teresa once mentioned the case of a woman who lived alone in a block of flats in London's bedsitter district. She hardly ever received a visit, or even a letter. Lest her neighbours gain the impression that no-one ever wrote to her, she wrote and mailed letters to herself. It is these sad and lonely lives that Mother Teresa urges her Co-Workers to brighten. A paragraph in the Co-Workers Constitution is reflective, too, of Mother Teresa's inherent philosophy: 'The Co-Workers of Mother Teresa recognise that all the goods of the world, including gifts of mind and body, advantages of birth and education, are the free gifts of God, and that no-one has the right to a superfluity of wealth while others are dying of starvation and suffering from every kind of want. They seek to right this grave injustice by the exercise of voluntary poverty and the sacrifice of luxuries in their way of life.'

Mother Teresa and her Co-Workers are united in the words of St Francis of Assisi, a prayer which Mahatma Gandhi, too, had cherished:

> Lord make me a channel of thy peace . . .
> that where there is despair I may bring hope,
> that where there are shadows, I may bring light,
> that where there is sadness, joy . . .*

* * *

A very special strand of the institution of Co-Workers are the sick and suffering who are unable, due to handicap, illness or old age, to join in active work. Instead they are each linked with a particular Missionary of Charity Sister or Brother. They offer only their pain and agony and prayer for the work. In turn, their active counterparts work with renewed energy and pray for them. One is a 'second self' to the other. It has helped to give meaning to lives in pain,

* The full text of the prayer appears in Appendix II.

for their suffering is accepted as a form of redemption.

The person whom Mother Teresa entrusted with the organisation of the Sick and Suffering Co-Workers, as they came to be known, was Jacqueline de Decker. When the International Association of Co-Workers of Mother Teresa was recognised by the Vatican on 26 March 1969, Jacqueline was named the International Link for the Sick and Suffering, an office she has held ever since. Over the years she has painstakingly 'linked' each Missionary of Charity with someone who is ill and in pain. Despite her own constant agony, she has written thousands of letters in her own hand. As Mother Teresa's 'second self', she was present in Oslo when Mother Teresa received the Nobel Peace Prize in 1979.

'Two weeks ago I met a European lady in sari in the Parochial house of St Joseph's Cathedral, Trivandrum,' wrote a journalist in a magazine in Kerala on 25 August 1948. 'At first I was not impressed by her . . . I thought she was eccentric or peculiar.' He rapidly revised his opinion. 'She is a native of Belgium and belongs to a good Catholic family. She is a graduate of the great Catholic University of Louvain, having done sociology as her special subject. She has also obtained a Diploma in Nursing and First Aid. After completing her studies in the University, she worked as a nurse for six years and rendered valuable service in tending the wounded and prisoners of war. Her great desire, however, was to come out to India and uplift the social condition of the humble and the poor in this land. It is only a year since Miss de Decker came to India. She has adopted the Indian way of dressing and eating. She wears a sari, takes her food sitting on the floor, doing away with spoons, knives, forks etc., and sleeps on the floor, as cots and such comforts are not meant for one who has devoted her life to the cause of the poor.' The writer was touched that she was ready to render service to anybody in need of help and was looking for a home in Madras which offered easy access to the poor.

Jacqueline de Decker was seventeen years old when she felt convinced that her vocation was to become a missionary. Some years later she met a Jesuit priest who inspired her to go to India to start a school for social and medical training, but the war intervened. After the war was over she prepared to voyage out, but no sooner had she boarded the ship than she received a telegram that the priest who had offered to guide and support her had died. Nevertheless, she pressed on, despite having very little money and no back-up. She decided to live very simply and took to Indian ways.

A Jesuit priest whom she met in Madras told her of a nun, then in Patna, who had laid aside her habit, and like herself, wore Indian dress. Although Patna was a long journey by train in those days, Jacqueline was inspired to leave immediately to meet a kindred soul who was equally committed to working with India's poor. 'It was 5 p.m. when I arrived at the Medical Mission in Patna,' said Jacqueline. 'I remember the time well, because when I asked for "Sister Teresa from Loreto", I was told, "It's 5 p.m. That means the work is over and she is in the chapel." Sure enough she was there. Later I joked with her and said, "The first time I met you, you showed your back to me!"'

They soon came to know one another well. There was much they shared in common: a love for the poor, a love for India and a love for their Lord. Sister Teresa invited Jacqueline to be the first to join her in the work that she soon proposed to begin. To Jacqueline this was the answer to her prayers. But first she urgently needed to return to Belgium to be treated for a severe pain that had developed in her spine. As soon as she recovered, she would join her in the work in Calcutta. 'I asked Sister Teresa how she would go about the work. She answered simply, "I will go to Calcutta in December. I will go into the streets and see what I can do. He will lead me."'

The doctors who examined Jacqueline in Belgium

diagnosed a debilitating disease of the spine. To prevent certain paralysis they needed to perform a series of operations to graft a spinal vertebra. After many painful operations, her doctor had said to Jacqueline 'I have never before performed such extensive surgery as I have now done on you,' and told her of the need for yet additional surgery. For Jacqueline, it meant the end of a dream, one that had come so close to realisation. To this day she repeats, 'My life has been a failure.'

Jacqueline de Decker was born into a very old Belgian family. Her father was a wealthy businessman who owned coffee plantations in Brazil and rubber plantations in Indonesia. Her earliest memories are those of life in their villa, located in the grounds of her grandmother's castle. Suddenly, in a reversal of fortune, commodity prices crashed, and her father lost practically everything. Jacqueline became a nurse. She worked selflessly throughout the war, giving invaluable help to British soldiers in Antwerp. Today, Jacqueline lives simply in a small Antwerp flat. She is surrounded by books and papers; her desk piled high with correspondence relating to her work. Behind the desk hangs a full-length portrait of her mother in evening dress, and scattered *objets d'art* in the room are testimony to her affluent past.

Now, however, she wears an orthopaedic collar round her neck, an iron corset encases her body and she needs crutches to help her to walk. She has a beautiful face, and enormous dignity. Not once while I was her guest in Antwerp did the word 'pain' cross her lips, although it keeps her awake most nights.

The story of the formation of the Sick and Suffering strand of the Co-Workers cannot be better described than in Mother Teresa's early letters to Jacqueline. While some portions of the letters are personal and have been omitted, these old and faded letters form a unique and rare record of the formation and development of Mother Teresa's work in India. For this reason they must be permitted, as far as possible, to speak for themselves.

It was on 29 May 1949, that Mother Teresa wrote to Jacqueline for the first time. She addressed her formally:

> 14 Creek Lane
> Calcutta 14
> 29 May 1949

My dear Miss de Decker,

May God bless you for your kind thought and generous gift. You must have deprived yourself of much to be able to help me. But surely He will pay you back.

You will be glad to hear at present I have got three companions, great zealous workers. We have five different slums where we go for a few hours. What suffering, what want of God. You should only see their eager faces how they brighten up when the Sisters come. Dirty and naked though they be, their hearts are full of affection.

My dear Sister, be brave and cheerful and think often of the Missionaries of Charity when you find it hard, so that we may all unite in doing God's Will.

God bless you and keep you always in His Heart.

> Yours affectionately in our Lord,
> Mother M. Teresa

About six months later Mother Teresa wrote again to Jacqueline, who was recovering from an operation:

Missionaries of Charity
14 Creek Lane
Calcutta 14.
19 Nov 1949

My dear Jacqueline,

Your letter of 8 November 1949 I got yesterday. I am so happy to hear you are well again and in such a good place . . .

Yes, there is so much to be done. At present we are five, but please God more will join and then we will be able to make a ring of Charity round Calcutta using our Centres in the different slums as points from where the love [of God] may freely radiate on the great Calcutta . . .

At the Dispensary the doctors and nurses are wonderful. The way they look after the people, you would think they were the princes of the country.

Dear Jacqueline, pray much and often for the little Society and for the Sisters. At present they are all preparing for different examinations, but they love their work and the poor. In the slums you can now hear the children singing.

Be brave and cheerful and pray much for,

Yours affectionately in Jesus Christ
Mother M. Teresa

During the next few years, Jacqueline went through a series of operations. The slightest movement was painful. She would need special collars and corsets even to sit up. It had become clear to her that she could never now hope to become a Missionary of Charity. Three years later, Mother Teresa wrote with excitement about a new idea that she had developed:

Missionaries of Charity
14 Creek Lane
Calcutta 14.
20 Oct 1952

My dear Miss de Decker,

I hope you are better. Very often I think of you and I unite the work with your suffering and so I have you close to me. Today I am going to tell you something which I am sure will make you very happy. You have been longing and are still deep in your heart a Missionary. Why not become spiritually bound to our Society, which you love so dearly? While we work in the slums etc., you share in the merit, the prayers and the work, with your suffering and prayers. The work here is tremendous and I need workers, it is true, but I need souls like yours to pray and suffer for the work. Would you like to become my spiritual sister and become a Missionary of Charity, in Belgium in body, but in soul in India?

She went on to add:

We are twenty-four now and about five more have applied. They all know you, for often I have spoken to them of you. If you join, you will have a great claim on their prayers. How are you? Are you still on your back? How long will you have to be like that? How Our Lord must be loving you to give you so much a part in His suffering. You are the happy one, for you are His chosen one. Be brave and cheerful and offer much for me. I pray often for you.

Yours in Jesus
M. Teresa MC

In her next letter, the first that she wrote from the new convent, Mother Teresa's ideas had crystallised:

Mother Teresa

Missionaries of Charity
14 Creek Lane
Calcutta 14
13 Jan 1953

My dear Child Jacqueline,
   I am happy that you are willing to join the suffering members of the Missionaries of Charity. The aim of our Society is to satiate the thirst of Jesus on the Cross by working for the salvation and sanctification of the poor in the slums. Who could do this better than you and the others who suffer like you. To satiate this thirst we must have a chalice, and you and the others, men, women, and children, old and young, poor and rich are all welcome to make the chalice. In reality you can do much more while on your bed of pain than I running on my feet. But you and I together can do all things in Him to strengthen us.
   There will be no vows unless some get permission from their confessor to do so. The one thing we must have in common is the spirit of our Society. Total surrender to God, loving trust and perfect cheerfulness. By this you will be known as a Missionary of Charity. Everyone and anyone who wishes to become a Missionary of Charity, a carrier of God's love, is welcome. But I want specially the paralysed, the crippled, the incurable to join. In our turn, the Sisters will each one have a Sister who prays, suffers, thinks, writes to her and so is a second self . . . I am sincerely very happy and grateful to God to have you for my second self.

God bless you my dear Sister,
Yours in Jesus
Mother Teresa

In February 1953, Mother Teresa and her Sisters moved to 54A Lower Circular Road. From here she wrote:

> Missionaries of Charity
> 54A Lower Circular Road
> Calcutta
> 15 March 1953

My dear Sister,

We have at last come to our convent. I am sure you are longing to see it. As soon as somebody takes a photo, I shall send you one.

I did not write to you but my thoughts are very often with you. When things are difficult my soul is encouraged with the thought of having you to pray and suffer for me. Then I find it easy, and the smile for the good God comes more quickly. It must be so hard for you to write and yet you do it. I need all that you can give. The Sisters feel the same for their Sisters. Just now they cannot write as they are preparing for their profession. The first ten will be professed on 12 April. They will make their vows for one year. I will make my final vows on the same day.

On 9 January 1956 she wrote a general letter to the Sick and Suffering:

> 9 Jan 1956

My dear Brothers and Sisters,

The Sisters and I wish you all a very happy New Year. May it be a year of love and joy for us all.

Please do not be displeased with us if we do not write. Our love for you all does not diminish but it grows even more fervent and one day you will be surprised to find out how close we have been to each

other. 1955 has been very fruitful. We had 1114
children in our school; 1416 in our Sunday schools;
48,313 sick were treated; 1546 dying were assisted. So
you see the fruit of your suffering is worth while. In
everything you have half share.

> God bless you all and us,
> Yours in Jesus
> M. Teresa

On 18 July 1956 she addressed her for the first time as
'Jacqueline-Teresa'. She wrote:

I wonder how disappointed you must be with my
silence. Do please forgive me as I am kept going the
whole day. Please thank in my name all those who
gave so generously. I used the money for the convent
. . . Sister Gertrude came third in her examination in
the MBBS course. Sister Francis Xavier came second in
Bengal in the DMS. In a few years we shall have our
doctors.

On 21 May 1958 she wrote a short and hurried letter:

We are now seventy-six and soon another eight will
come. They are from all over India and they all come in
a strange way. I hope some day we get some from
Europe and some other countries.
You must have heard about our leprosy work. We
have a mobile clinic for them with eight centres. I
want to start a colony for them.

The next letter was written from Agra on 10 March 1961. In
the space of one year she had opened four new houses:

My dear Jacqueline-Teresa

You must be just wondering what has happened to me. Well, I have no other explanation except that my Sisters take every possible minute from me. We are now 127 [Sisters] with new houses in Delhi, Ranchi, Agra, Jhansi, Creek Lane and Calcutta. Next month we are going to Simla.

Write and let me have all the news about yourself. In Agra we have plenty of work. In Delhi the Sisters are doing very well. We have English, German, American and Maltese novices. When will a Belgian come? You must help.

> God bless you,
> M. Teresa MC

By 1965, Jacqueline de Decker had already undergone about half of the fifty surgeries that she eventually had to endure. In a letter dated 22 April 1965, Mother Teresa said:

After so long to get news from you. Very often I think of you and because my second self is suffering so much, I am able to grow and move. You are again in bed. I think you have had as many operations as we have houses. . . . You must be doing all the getting sick and suffering because in spite of everything I am able to keep up travelling long distances by 3rd Class*. We are now 235 Sisters and we hope to have 30 new girls joining.

On 16 December 1972 Mother Teresa wrote to Jacqueline with concern:

---

* This was at that time the cheapest form of train travel in India, which has since been discontinued. There are now only 1st and 2nd Class coaches.

My dear Jacqueline-Teresa,

My thoughts and prayers are often with you. With your nearly completely crippled body full of pain you try to do for your mother all the services which even healthy persons now-a-days don't often do. It is your life of sacrifice that is my strength. Your mother is Christ in the distressing disguise and your taking care of her brings you so close to me in Nirmal Hriday, where our people long for love and care. I wish I could come to your place and take care of your mother while you have the operation.

Regarding letters, we are just eaten up, like bread, by the people. For me to keep letters going [is difficult]. I go to bed at 2 a.m. and get up at 4.40 a.m. I would not like any young sister to do the same, and so the reason for not writing.

During those years Mother Teresa was constantly on the move. In a letter of 26 July 1973 there is once again a reference to travel:

Your letter is a very great joy to me, and also strength. Because of you I am able to spend eight nights in the train and work during the day.

As the years went by, pressures of time and illness slowed Mother Teresa down. Her letters to Jacqueline, too, became less frequent. After Mother Teresa permitted a telephone to be installed in Motherhouse, Jacqueline began to rely on it increasingly. A few letters did trickle in. In a comparatively recent one, written on 13 March 1990, when she herself was quite sick, there was a glimpse of Mother Teresa's humour:

Raghu Rai

Mother Teresa at prayer.

The first photograph taken in the
chapel in Motherhouse, 1955.

Mother Teresa with one of the
first patients in the Home for the
Dying (Kalighat), Calcutta.

The first chapel of the
Missionaries of Charity, 14
Creek Lane, Calcutta, 1950.

Mother Teresa's first room, 14 Creek Lane, Calcutta.
There was very little furniture when she stayed there.

Father Celeste van Exem, Mother Teresa's spiritual adviser.

Leprosy patients constructing the settlement of Titagarh.

A view of the production centre, constructed by the leprosy patients of Titagarh.

Cured leprosy patients wearing the saris of the Missionaries of Charity at Titagarh.

Chitrabani-
EMRC

*Prince Charles on a visit to
Shishu Bhawan, Calcutta.
Mother Teresa is in the centre.*

*Mother Teresa with Jacqueline
de Decker, Rome, 1982.*

*The author with Sister Agnes,
Mother Teresa's first postulant.*

Mother Teresa greeting a child in Shishu Bhawan, Delhi.

Sisters at prayer in Motherhouse.

S. Tarafdar and Associates

MOTHER TERESA, M.C.

54A

S. Tarafdar and
Associates

*Motherhouse, 54A Lower Circular Road,
Calcutta.*

*A Sister at the entrance door,
Motherhouse. The chain hangs on the door
post just below the board.*

*A leprosy patient talking to one of the
Sisters.*

Chitrabani – EMRC

Raghu Rai

Mother Teresa with a child at Nirmala Shishu Bhawan, Calcutta.

Raghu Rai

Mother Teresa at prayer.

*With the author and his wife,
Rupika.*

*With the Princess of Wales in
Rome.*

Raghu Rai

Mother Teresa at her desk in
Kalighat.

Raghu Rai

Mother Teresa – a portrait.

With the Chairman of the Norwegian Nobel Committee, Oslo, 1979.

At a prayer service in Oslo, 1979.

The Nobel Peace Prize and Medal.

DEN NORSKE NOBELKOMITÉ

HAR OVERENSSTEMMENDE MED
REGLENE I DET AV

ALFRED NOBEL

DEN 27 NOVEMBER 1895 OPPRETTEDE
TESTAMENTE TILDELT

Mother Teresa

NOBELS FREDSPRIS FOR 1979

'A pencil in the hands of the Lord.'

Manjit Bawa

Volunteers.

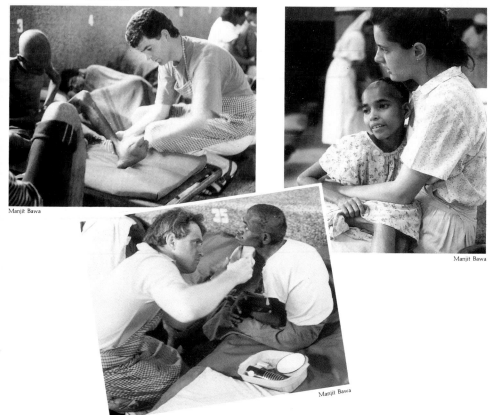

Manjit Bawa

Manjit Bawa

Manjit Bawa

Raghu Rai

Mother Teresa, Home for the Dying, Kalighat, Calcutta.

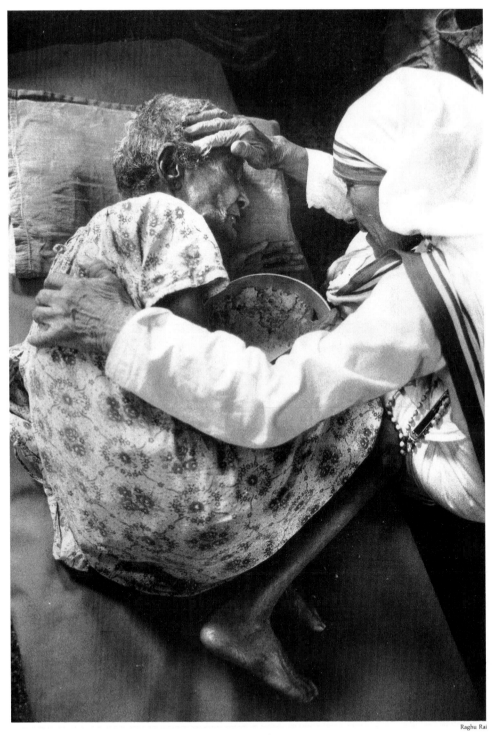

Raghu Rai

Mother Teresa with an inmate
in the Home for the Dying, Kalighat, Calcutta.

I am sorry to hear that the noise in your ear still persists and it keeps you awake all night and no pain-killers give you any relief. This is how the Lord treats His friends. Sorry to hear that the operation of your teeth and jaw bone was not successful and that you had to be operated again. The good God will surely reward you a hundred fold for offering your sufferings and operations for 1) Albania, 2) Leningrad, 3) Romania. I will ask the Lord not to shower His gifts in such quick succession as you really need to have a proper break.

God bless you,
M. Teresa MC

Mother Teresa's 'second self' has built up a chain of about 5000 current Sick and Suffering Co-Workers from as many as fifty-seven countries. This figure does not include almost 2500 Sick and Suffering who have died and been replaced by others. Sometimes two Co-Workers write to the same nun. The maximum number of such Co-Workers is about 400 in England, 300 in France, about 200 each in the US and Canada.

On my last evening in Antwerp, while I sat with Jacqueline at her desk, she read out several letters she had received that very day. There was a particularly poignant one from the United States. It said:

I am thirty years old and have been disabled with multiple sclerosis since I was twenty-two. I have been in the hospital many, many times. My neurologist says it is just a matter of time before I become wheelchair-bound and possibly bedridden. Obviously, he doesn't know that God is the Great Physician, not him.

During the time I was bedridden, I spent countless hours writing encouraging letters and praying for others. Through the last eight years I have learned that indeed God's Grace is sufficient and He has a purpose for me, even when the world's system rejects me.

I am compelled to get involved in praying for those who are physically able to do the work that I cannot. I have begun to pray for Mother Teresa.

There were other letters that Jacqueline read out. Some were written in anguish, others in hope. Each of them formed a small but important link in a long chain that was born out of a simple idea of Mother Teresa's. And how well Jacqueline had returned the compliment. When I arose to leave, she said, 'Spiritually, I have always belonged to India. I have made a request to Mother Teresa, that when I die I may be buried in a sari of the Missionaries of Charity. What I could not achieve in my lifetime, I could achieve, in a small way, in my death.'

8

· *Shishu Bhawan* ·

Early one January morning in 1975, when it was still quite dark and chilly as winter mornings in Calcutta are surprisingly wont to be, a cycle rickshaw stopped at Nirmala Shishu Bhawan on Lower Circular Road. From it stepped a woman of about thirty, carrying in her arms a child of four or five. She draped her shawl closely around the boy and hugged him fiercely, as if for the last time. For a moment or two she stood still before tugging on the chain that rang an old-fashioned bell within the house. Almost immediately, a side door was opened by a Sister and she was led into a small sparse room near the gate. There she hesitatingly narrated her tragic story.

Her son was born with many problems. From almost the first day, she and her husband had begun the round of public hospitals and clinics. Two years ago her husband had died in an accident, and she and the child were now alone. The doctors had told her that they could do no more. She worked as a washerwoman for several households, beginning her work at dawn. She had nowhere to leave the child during the day. She had even tried a nearby crèche, which she could ill afford, but they would not accept the responsibility of a sick child. Last week one of the ladies she worked for had told her about Mother Teresa, and advised her to take the child to Shishu Bhawan. Mother Teresa was her last resort.

The Sisters soon discovered that Bapi, for that was the boy's name, suffered from multiple sclerosis, a spinal disorder which prevented him from making even the simplest movement. He could not turn on his side or scratch himself. To make matters worse, he was also deaf and mute. He could only communicate with his large and expressive eyes: these would sparkle when he was happy; when he was sad, his face would redden and tears would roll down his cheeks. His way of answering questions was to open his mouth wide and sigh convulsively. Painstakingly, the Sisters learned to interpret Bapi's 'language'. They began to understand when he wanted to sit up or to lie down, to be taken to the toilet or to be moved to his wheelchair. They knew when he was happy and could anticipate his tears when he was not. It was only natural for them to become as protective of Bapi as they were of the tiniest infants in their care.

Over the years I had several glimpses of Bapi. I first saw him when he was about eight, a child with a beautiful face and long, black eyelashes. A Sister was carefully feeding him a liquid diet. About half an hour later, when I left the room, the process was still going on. I saw him again about two years later. That morning he was in the process of trying to 'talk' to the Sisters, and as he did so, his entire frame convulsed so violently that I was afraid he would fall off his wheelchair. I learned that his mother had stopped visiting; the Sisters believed that she had died. Since then I saw him two or three times a year. I saw him again soon after his fourteenth birthday. He was always in the cheerful rooms upstairs, where the Sisters kept a constant vigil on premature and very sick children. That was the last time I saw him.

In October 1991, when I visited Nirmala Shishu Bhawan to take some photographs, I did not find him in his usual place. It was then that I learned that Bapi had died. The Sisters told me that he had developed a harsh cough and fever. He refused all food. It was with great difficulty that they were able to coax him to drink a little milk. The doctors attending on him finally gave up hope. On the morning of 28 July, Bapi died. In their sorrow, the Sisters showed me several photographs of Bapi that had been taken over the years. The very last one was taken just before his body was taken to Kalighat for cremation, for Bapi was a Hindu. It showed him wreathed in marigold garlands. Around him stood the grieving Sisters and children of Nirmala Shishu Bhawan.

Every Shishu Bhawan has its share of sorrow. Yet these homes are not sad places at all. On the contrary, they are full of cheerful youngsters at play, chintzy curtains, colourful posters on the walls and floors littered with toys. The children wear a variety of clothes, the shapes and sizes of which depend on the deftness with which hand-me-downs are altered. The sound of laughter resounds constantly. One would usually find a Sister or two, assisted by some novices and a clutch of volunteers, manning the establishment. The toddlers react to a visitor in predictable ways. Some carry on without a glance, others scurry for cover behind the nearest dress or sari, while the gregarious ones come forward to be introduced to 'Uncle', to have their photographs taken and to be hugged. In marked contrast to most of Mother Teresa's homes which are spartan, the Shishu Bhawans are almost luxurious. Perhaps it is Mother Teresa's way of making up for the parental love that the children do not have.

Shishu Bhawan is a general name for the many children's homes that the Missionaries of Charity have opened in India. They are usually set up near their convents, for premature and sick children need constant care. The number of children in each Shishu Bhawan depends on the shape and the size of the building. There may be anything from twenty to 200 children, ranging from infants to seven-year-olds. In Delhi, for instance, there are two Shishu Bhawans. The older is a small bungalow which has room for about fifty cribs. In the newer building, which an industrialist built especially as a gift for Mother Teresa a few years ago, there are about 200 children from the age of two upwards. In some centres where space permits, Shishu Bhawans have small kindergarten schools. For the most part, however, the children are sent to the nearest regular school. The cost of education, including uniforms and books, is entirely met by the Missionaries of Charity.

Mother Teresa tries especially hard to establish a Shishu Bhawan in each of her leprosy centres. In the country-like atmosphere of the Shishu Bhawan at Shantinagar in West Bengal, Sister Albert encourages leprosy-afflicted parents to visit as often as they wish, but discourages them from kissing the children. When I observed that such a separation could be traumatic, especially if the treatment was lengthy, Mother Teresa told me about a woman who lived near Shantinagar. One day, she noticed a small telltale patch on her child's back. She was so alarmed that she carried the child three miles to the leprosy centre. This may not have been so unusual, except that the woman herself was severely afflicted by leprosy and had stumps for feet. 'When the patch was diagnosed to be leprosy, she pleaded for the child to be admitted to the Shishu Bhawan. She returned every day. Sometimes her hands would go near the child, wanting to hold it, to kiss it. They would fall back again. I cannot forget the deep love of that mother for her child,' Mother Teresa recounted.

Yet it is the tragic lives, like those of Bapi and Gita, that remain etched in one's memory. Gita was a child who had forgotten how to smile. I saw her standing in her crib at the Shishu Bhawan in Shantinagar. There would have been nothing unusual about this except that she was almost three, much too old for a crib. While the other children were tumbling on the floor or playing with toys, she stood with her face to the wall. All of the time that I was in the crèche with Sister Albert, she steadfastly refused to look in our direction. Sister Albert explained why. A few years ago a terrible fire broke out in the nearby town of Dumka. Several people, including the child's parents, perished. Little Gita was rescued by the firemen and rushed to the hospital. For weeks she hovered on the verge of death. In the end she survived, but her face was a mass of scars. No-one was able to locate even a distant relative. Finally, when they could no longer keep the child in the hospital, they sent her to the Missionaries of Charity at Shantinagar. Further surgery was needed to enable her to open her mouth fully and to use her fingers better. The doctors promised to perform these free of charge but said that if the child were ever to look normal again, she would require extensive plastic surgery. 'Gita is so traumatised that she cannot bear pain of any kind for a long time to come,' said Sister Albert. 'We must wait and see. We first need to help her to overcome the pain in her heart.'

There are many infants who are unable to survive premature births, attempted abortions or the aftermath of drug abuse by expectant mothers. Very often they are brought to the Sisters on the verge of death. Mother Teresa has often been asked whether it is of much use for her organisation to spend precious time and resources on children who would inevitably die within the hour. Could their efforts not be put to better use? 'I don't understand this,' she said with indignation. 'For me, even if a child dies within minutes, that child must not be allowed to die alone and uncared for. Even an infant can feel human warmth. This is why a dying child must be loved and comforted. There is a joke in Calcutta,' she continued. '"Mother Teresa talks about family planning, but she certainly does not practise it because every day she has more and more children!" Everyone in Calcutta knows that I am willing to take every single child. I have often said, "If there is an unwanted baby, don't let it die. Send it to me."'

Letters are sent periodically to all clinics and nursing homes in every city, saying that the Missionaries of Charity would welcome any child, even if the child is severely handicapped or premature. Despite these pleas and the assurance that no questions would be asked, abortion clinics are not always forthcoming. Wherever possible, destitute pregnant girls are welcomed by the Sisters to work in their centres until childbirth. 'It helps to keep them off the streets,' said a Sister. After the child is born, if the mother cannot be persuaded to keep the child, or if her circumstances or occupation do not permit her to look after it, the Missionaries of Charity take the child. This is as a matter of last resort. 'I cannot give the love a real mother can give,' says Mother Teresa, 'but I have never refused a child. Never. Not one. Each child is precious. Each is created by God.'

Although Mother Teresa does say that she can take in all the unwanted babies in the world, this is clearly not possible. As it is, the Shishu Bhawans seem to be bursting at their seams. However, this is not an entirely one-sided movement. Hundreds of children are increasingly given out for adoption in India. Boys who are too old for adoption are sent to the Boys' Homes, run by the Missionary Brothers of Charity, the Brothers' branch of the Order. Here they are educated, taught a trade and helped to obtain employment. 'If a child is not adopted, for instance, older children or a brother and sister who should not be separated, we usually get a sponsor for his or her education. We have thousands of children whose education is paid for by sponsors, in India and overseas,' said Mother Teresa.

The children, on the whole, do remarkably well. Many qualify for universities. Girls who do not show scholastic ability are found husbands. Mother Teresa is realistic enough to give to each of them a small dowry: a few saris, utensils, furniture and a little money placed in a bank account opened in their name. Without following this Hindu custom, it would be difficult to get the girls married. Mother Teresa may not be an intellectual, but no-one can accuse her of not being practical. There are innumerable girls from Shishu Bhawans who are now well settled, with happy families of their own. Those of them who live in Calcutta are frequent visitors to Motherhouse, especially on festivals and feast days. Mother Teresa is usually there to welcome and bless the families. The girls often do not know which of the many Sisters to hug first. One of the many jokes among the Sisters is that a prospective bridegroom for any of their girls had better watch out, for he is likely to inherit several score 'mothers-in-law' with his bride!

Mother Teresa's views on abortion and sterilisation have many detractors. Social scientists have often stridently pointed out to her that several countries where she works have massive population problems, and these are unlikely to go away by her simply offering to take in all unwanted children. Family planning and welfare programmes are an integral part of development, and in most of these countries facilities for sterilisation and abortion are widely available. There are many who argue that Mother Teresa should use her very considerable influence to propagate birth control. To this Mother Teresa firmly replies that she advocates 'natural family planning', involving abstention by couples, and calls for the exercise of self-control. Mother Teresa believes that this method involves 'love and respect for one another', and that this has, over the years, successfully averted thousands of births. It is interesting to note that the Annual Report for 1989 lists sixty-nine Natural Family Planning Centres. There are some who point out the serious limitations of this method, for it presupposes keeping an accurate count of the menstrual cycle. Despite being given instructions in the rhythm method and a string of beads of various colours to help keep track of the safe period, there are frequent cases of forgetfulness. For every birth averted there must probably be several that occur because of inadequate understanding of the bead method, problems of self-control and the fact that it does not always work even when followed. For impoverished families, sex is one of the few sources of pleasure, and it's free!

Natural family planning cannot, of course, be expected to apply to unwed mothers or girls forced into prostitution. Nor does Mother Teresa have a very convincing answer to the problems of the pressures on most Indian families, and indeed, in most conservative societies, when faced with the prospect of an unmarried mother in their midst. In such countries, a child born to an unmarried girl would not merely bring shame to the immediate family but disgrace to an entire village or community.

In most Asian, South American and African cities, facilities for abortion are neither widely available nor cheap, yet families that find themselves in such predicaments often do somehow obtain the means to get rid of the unborn child. There are a small number of comparatively wealthy families that manage to send their daughters away for a few months, explained as a holiday, to arrange for a discreet delivery. The child would then be sent to an organisation such as the Missionaries of Charity for intended adoption. In most cases, however, these hapless girls eventually find themselves in abortion 'clinics', where they often lie two or three to a bed in deplorably insanitary conditions. Septicaemia and secondary infection are common, and should these lead to the death of the girl, it would, more often than not, go unreported by a family already laden with shame or guilt.

None of this deters Mother Teresa. She has implicit faith in the Roman Catholic doctrine of birth control and abhors the word 'abortion'. There have been innumerable occasions, particularly on her visits to the United States and

Europe, when she has spoken up against it. In her Nobel Lecture itself, which she delivered in Oslo in 1979, she said that she believed that the greatest destroyer of peace was not war but abortion. Abortion was a 'direct war', murder committed by the mother herself. 'Many people are very concerned with the children of India, with the children of Africa where quite a number die, maybe of malnutrition, of hunger and so on, but millions are dying deliberately by the will of the mother. If a mother can kill her own child, what is left?'

During the fortieth anniversary celebrations of the United Nations, the premiere screening of a film on Mother Teresa was a gala event. At the conclusion of the film, Mother Teresa, who was present, made a brief speech. She spoke about love and sharing and the need to bring prayer back in our lives. 'We are frightened of nuclear war,' she went on to tell that select gathering of international civil servants and celebrities, 'we are frightened of this terrible new disease, AIDS, but we are not frightened to kill an innocent child. Today I feel that abortion has become the greatest destroyer of peace.'

These views made many in the audience uncomfortable, not least because the United Nations supports abortion under special circumstances, under its United Nations Fund for Population Activities (UNFPA). To others present, it seemed somewhat incongruous that Mother Teresa should speak against abortion, especially as many of the countries that she works in are vastly over-populated and that sizeable sections of the populace live in what appeared to the delegates to be appallingly unacceptable conditions. Inescapably, several in the audience concluded that Mother Teresa was a thoroughly good woman who was just a little out of touch with things. There were others who remarked that even saints should be permitted an idiosyncrasy or two!

Mother Teresa is, of course, perfectly aware that her views on abortion are not widely shared and that most governments, the press and the intelligentsia do not support them. She also knows that other religious denominations do not always take a rigid stand against abortion. She is certainly aware that there are many Catholic organisations that fail to agree with her; time and time again, polls in America and Europe have revealed that a majority of Catholics favour contraception and abortion under many circumstances. None of this has caused her to amend her beliefs in the slightest. She has often said to me, 'I feel that the poorest country is the one that has to kill the unborn child. They are afraid to feed one more child, so as to enjoy a few extra pleasures.'

In India, there is hardly a day that the Missionaries of Charity do not receive a few children at one or other of their centres. 'Often it is the police who bring the children. On other days it is unwed mothers themselves. Once in a while, a hospital or clinic telephones us requesting us to collect a baby. There are times, less often now, that we find them abandoned in the streets. Occasionally, a baby is left on our doorstep. These are usually severely physically and mentally handicapped,' said a Sister at Nirmala Shishu Bhawan. 'It is a miracle,' said Mother Teresa. 'Every day we have one or two families, even high-caste Hindu families, who come to adopt a child. According to Hindu law, an adopted child becomes a legal heir and can inherit property.'

Attitudes towards adoption have changed. 'Some years ago, people wanted only boys and were fussy about light skins and nice noses,' said a Sister with a laugh. 'People are now increasingly prepared to accept children virtually unseen, and even girls. Some years ago couples without children would arrange for one of our infants to be sent quietly into a nursing home and a few days later the wife would leave after a "delivery". People are now more open,' she said. The preference for a male child in India is largely because traditional Hindu society has always viewed a girl as *paraya dhan* (someone else's wealth), for she would marry into another family. While the middle class is beginning to accept the girl child with more confidence, it is the physically handicapped children who are difficult to place. 'Part of the reason is that we do not yet have the ways and means to help a handicapped child. But it will come soon,' said the Sister.

The practice of children being sent overseas for adoption has always had its critics. Dealing in children is not unknown, and stories of 'child running' appear regularly in the press all over the world. These stories are not always exaggerated. Wealthy people the world over are often prepared to pay enormous sums for 'perfect' children, the euphemism for white, non-handicapped infants. South America has always been a favoured source in the children's 'bazaar'. The demand for such babies is so high that some adoption agencies have difficulty meeting even a fraction of it. Some agencies place the percentage as high as fifty to one. The occasional incidents of newborn babies being stolen from public hospitals understandably causes a furore. It also results in the slowing down of foreign adoptions, or even a review of adoption policies.

There have been occasions when media reports have caused Mother Teresa to stop offering children for adoption. One of the few occasions when I saw her in absolute anguish was when a journal published a sensational story that handicapped children from Third World countries were being sent to a country in Europe, ostensibly for adoption. Instead these children were ending up as guinea pigs for medical experiments. She was so distressed that she caught the first flight from Calcutta to New Delhi. I drove her to the Embassy of the country that had been named. The Ambassador immediately received her and quickly understood her deep concern. A letter was sent to the editor of the journal, which informed him that the story was both an outrage and libellous. An apology followed, but Mother Teresa took considerable time to recover.

'The French, Swiss and Canadians are particularly generous,' said one of the Sisters. 'They are more than willing to take babies who have severe orthopaedic problems, or polio, or are thalassaemic. They don't bother whether a child is beautiful or not. Some families have natural children of their own and still take our handicapped children. If you ever visit Europe or North America, you can visit some of these families, I am sure they would be willing to meet you. You would find it interesting,' she added.

Some time later, while on a visit to Switzerland, I took the opportunity to visit some of these families. By happy coincidence, I had written to an adoption service which has been working closely with the Missionaries of Charity for many years. Jo Millar, who lives in Geneva, is the founder of the 'Diwali Adoption Service'. She helped to arrange a visit to some families who lived nearby.

We met in the cafeteria of one of the many international agencies of the UN which have made Geneva their home. 'By the way,' she said, 'I have a son working here as a chef. Perhaps you'd like to meet him.' A few minutes later, I saw the chef striding towards our table. What she neglected to tell me was that he was originally from India. It was then I learned that the Millars, themselves the parents of four 'homemade' children, had adopted the child when he was nine. Babloo's father was a porter at the railway station in Siliguri, a town about 350 miles from Calcutta. He had died of tuberculosis when the boy was seven. When the local Sisters took him in, he was so weak that he could not sit up. Now he is a member of the local football team. Two years ago he returned to Siliguri, this time as a Swiss citizen. It was a journey which his understanding parents encouraged so that he might continue to keep a sense of his roots, while he took on a European identity.

Jo Millar is hardly a missionary, but the zeal with which she places handicapped children in carefully selected, caring homes makes her an excellent instrument for Mother Teresa in Switzerland. 'I have to feel very strongly about a family before I can offer them a child. Sometimes I try as many as fifty families before I know I have the right one,' she said. This would explain why most children placed by her are cases that end happily ever after. I would have found this quite difficult to believe, had I not seen them for myself. I made my own random selection from a list submitted by the Sisters of Calcutta, and chose only families who lived near to Geneva, as my time in Switzerland was limited. During the course of my research, I discovered that there were less successful instances, but happily these were few.

The following morning, I found myself in the home of the Rudaz family in a village near Geneva. Oliver, thirty-eight, works in a computer firm and his wife, Marguerite, gave up her job to look after the family. A young couple, they live in a small, sunny house, full of toys and children. As they could have had children of their own, why did they need to adopt any? Marguerite replied, 'Blood is universal. There are many poor people in the world; that in itself is a great injustice. To make my own child would be an act of egoism.'

The Rudazes first adopted a girl from Yugoslavia. Then, two years ago, they heard about Daddu, a boy of four or five. He had been found in the streets of Raipur, a town in Central India and brought to the Sisters. Daddu suffered from acute poliomyelitis, which had affected both his legs and, less severely, his arms. Jo Millar showed them photographs of the child, as well as a medical report prepared by Nirmala Shishu Bhawan. These made it clear that Daddu had little or no chance of ever being able to walk. The Rudazes decided to adopt him. Jo Millar began to complete the lengthy formalities in India, and some months later brought the child to Geneva where the Rudazes were at the airport to receive him.

'From the moment he arrived,' said Oliver, 'he was interested in everything around him. He was especially interested in cars, and kept repeating the word *gari*, which means "car" in Hindi, to every passing vehicle.' Marguerite added, 'He was operated upon soon after his arrival, and remained in a plaster cast for two months. The doctors were surprised at his rapid progress. In the beginning they said he would always be confined to a wheelchair, but now they are confident that he will be able to support himself with the help of calipers and crutches.'

'He is a clever little boy,' said his father as he ruffled Daddu's hair. 'He loves school. Do you know, he picked up French in just two months?'

As if two children were not enough, the Rudazes went on to adopt Alexis, a boy of almost three, with slight polio, and Camille, a beautiful little girl who was afflicted with severe thalassaemia. Doctors had given her only a year to live; she arrived at the age of one and was five when I met her, no longer thalassaemic. The doctors explain that she has outgrown her mother's blood. As I looked from her to the others in the room where we sat, they seemed to me, a perfect family. I asked if they were religious. Marguerite smiled. 'I am not a religious person, and nor is Oliver,' she said. 'We hardly ever go to church.'

The families who have adopted handicapped children from India, mainly from Mother Teresa's homes, refer to themselves as 'Diwali' families. (Diwali, India's traditional festival of lights, is celebrated even in the humblest Hindu home, to commemorate the triumphant return of Lord Rama to his kingdom, bringing twelve long years of his exile to an end.)

In this tradition, I was warmly received in a neat little Swiss house in Lausanne. On the table of their sitting room was a 'Diwali' lamp, lit in welcome. This middle-aged couple, who requested anonymity, had decided to adopt a child but then had two daughters of their own in quick succession. Yet they could not shake off the idea of an adoption, and finally succumbed. They soon found that they had a wide choice of countries: Chile, Colombia, India. Somewhere along the line, they heard of a 'Diwali' family, and went to visit them. This led them to Jo Millar. 'We asked her a lot of questions. We also thought a lot about sick children. Finally we were ready.'

The child they decided on had only six months to live, unless he could be given blood transfusions every three weeks. He was a thalassaemic baby needing constant doses of the magic drug Desferal, which reduces the excess iron content of the blood. Their local doctor warned them not to get too attached to the child. 'He won't be there always,' he had cautioned, but that was several years ago. Now, he is hopeful that the child will have a normal lifespan.

To prepare for the child, the family had to make sacrifices. The father, a driver, earned a good wage, but not enough for the extensive medical expenses that their decision entailed. 'We had no money in the bank, so we sold our car. These things are not important. Life is more important. What the children give to my wife and me cannot be compared with anything material.' After a pause he added, 'Some people say we are a little mad. I tell them that we invest in children.'

A child whom Mother Teresa remembers with great affection is Prince. He was a year and a half old when he was sent to join the Ballestraz family in the mountain town of Sierre. Mr Ballestraz is a specialist in problems of the handicapped. Prince has no hips, no legs and his hands turn backwards. In this unique family, with an army of handicapped children, it mattered very little. What came across was the child's beauty, serenity and lively personality. It was as pleasurable to see him manoeuvre himself deftly up the spiral staircase to his room, as it was to watch him take his first hesitant steps. Recently, specialists had fitted his torso into a rubber 'bowl', which in turn was placed into a pair of artificial legs. This was still an experiment, but Prince was delighted to try it out and pose for my photographs. He could also move about in a battery-operated wheelchair, which was designed to look like a toy car. I was told he would soon drive himself to school.

Prince was the sixth member of the family. After three 'homemade' children, they still had enough space to construct a few more rooms. They visited an adoption agency, which offered them albums of photographs to choose from; it was rather like buying something from a mail-order catalogue. Repelled, they came away. In due course, they heard about 'Diwali'. Sabita was the first to arrive, a girl of two with psychological problems. She was followed by a seven-year-old called Maya: originally from Nepal, she was rescued by the Sisters from a hazardous life on the pavements of Calcutta. In the Shishu Bhawan, she was inseparable from little Sabita, and looked after her as an older sister might. Learning of this attachment, the Sisters advised Jo Millar to give them in adoption together. While the Ballestrazes agreed to take both the children, the Magistrate in Calcutta found Maya's papers to be incomplete and did not permit her to leave with Sabita. It took six months before he was satisfied and the girls were united, this time, as sisters.

With Sarjan, a little boy who was almost blind when he arrived, and Sapna, probably a thalidomide baby, the Ballestraz family was complete, or so they thought until they heard of Prem Kumari. This pretty thirteen-year-old was found several years ago in a mountain town in northeast India. She had no arms or legs. Unlike Sapna, hers was no accident of birth. It is rumoured that in some hideous accident, the child's hands and legs were amputated. When the Ballestrazes heard about Prem Kumari, they believed they had to have this child, even though she was already almost ten, much older than the average age for adoption. 'It came to me as a call. When I heard about that child, I felt that this was to be her home,' said Mrs Ballestraz.

From Mother Teresa, I heard about another child called Rani, who lived not far from Sierre. The Machoud family were very welcoming; they had adopted not only Rani, but also six other children. The first to come were two boys orphaned in the war in Kampuchea. Then, the Machouds decided to adopt Raj and Suraj, half-brothers, who were seven and five years old when they arrived from the mountain town of Darjeeling. With four boys in the house, they soon felt the need for a girl, and ended up with three! First came Gita, a child of six whom no-one seemed to want because she was very withdrawn and unusually dark, and last to arrive was Bindu, a three-year-old, deaf and dumb, found abandoned by the Sisters in Delhi. 'She was in a terrible state when she came,' said Mrs Machoud. 'She could not communicate if she were hungry or cold or wanted something. It would take hours to dress or feed her. She has come a long way since then.' Using sign language, the boys explained to Bindu what their mother had said, and everyone broke into uproarious laughter.

But quite clearly, it is little Rani that is the Machouds' ray of sunshine. Found as a baby in Darjeeling, she, too, is deaf. She came when she was four, but looked half that age. I saw her when she was ten, and she looked no more than six. The doctors have said that she will not grow to more than a metre in height. It does not matter; she is in a warm and loving family. Looking at this smiling child and hearing her laughter resound through the house, it is obvious that the Machoud family is the richer for her presence.

*   *   *

In the early days, Mother Teresa herself accompanied the children for adoption abroad. But travel is expensive, and Mother Teresa, always frugal, disliked having to pay her own passage. One day, not long ago, when we were on a flight together, I asked her how she managed to persuade the airlines to give her unlimited free travel. She gurgled with delight at the memory of it.

'As the work increased, I wrote many times to the Indian Government, asking them to allow me and a companion Sister a free pass. Finally, I offered to become an air hostess to pay my way, and this time, received an immediate reply. Air India agreed to give me a pass, then Indian Airlines [the domestic carrier] gave me two free passes, and now Alitalia, Pan Am and Ethiopian Airlines also give me free tickets,' she said, her eyes twinkling.

The thought of Mother Teresa as an air hostess was delectable, but it is just as well that she travels as a passenger. I can testify that, otherwise, her service would probably consist of signing autographs all the way.

I discovered the impact of Mother Teresa quite early in our acquaintance. I had not seen her for several months, as she had been on an extended visit abroad. One day I received news that she was to arrive from Rome that very evening. It was not certain how long she would stop in Delhi, so I decided to go to the airport to meet her. The Air India flight from Rome landed fifteen minutes late, and by the time Mother Teresa reached the terminal building it was almost 7.30 p.m.

'I am glad you have come,' she said, as she greeted me with a smile. 'You must make sure I catch the plane to Calcutta tonight.'

I did not think that that was possible, and pointed out that the flight to Calcutta departed from the domestic terminal. The scheduled departure was 8 p.m.; aggravatingly, the flight was on time, while Mother Teresa's luggage was not yet off the Air India plane. I was still new to this phenomenon called Mother Teresa, and had not reckoned with her determination. In any case, what she went on to say was sobering enough.

'There is a child dying in Shishu Bhawan in Calcutta. I am carrying in my luggage an experimental drug that might save the child's life. You must help me to catch the flight,' she said softly. She had pulled out her rosary from the old cloth bag she carried, and began to pray. Watching her made me considerably nervous. It was now past 7.45 p.m., and the flight to Calcutta had boarded.

Meanwhile, several people in the terminal building, aware of Mother Teresa's presence, were coming up to her, to be blessed, for autographs, and just to be near her. Yet unknown to me, the word had spread that a child lay dying in Calcutta and needed Mother Teresa desperately. I learned later that the airport staff, from senior managers to humble porters, had sped in every direction to help. Suddenly, Mother Teresa's luggage, which consisted of six cardboard cartons (one of which contained her personal effects and the rest medicines), rumbled in on the conveyer belt, the very first pieces of luggage to be brought in. As if from nowhere, someone placed a boarding card in her hand. Unknown to us, the control tower had had a word with the captain of the flight, who was just then taxiing towards the runway. The captain, a Calcutta man himself, brought the aircraft to a halt. Flight control warned air traffic of a slight change. The aircraft was now ready for Mother Teresa. Would I be so kind as to drive her to the aircraft in my car? A few minutes later, a ladder emerged through the mist, the aircraft door opened and Mother Teresa, with her boxes of medicines, boarded the flight to Calcutta.

Ten days later, Mother Teresa was in Delhi again. My first question, of course, was about the child in Shishu Bhawan. Her face wreathed in smiles, Mother Teresa told me that she had reached Calcutta just in time. The child was well on its way to recovery. 'It was a first-class miracle, wasn't it?' she asked.

9

· *Titagarh* ·

Every leprosy centre that I have ever visited, whether in India or abroad, has been a story of courage. It has required courage to establish, organise and administer them, and courage, too, on the part of the afflicted, who have often had to rebuild their fragmented lives or to begin new ones. The Gandhiji Prem Niwas ('abode of love') Leprosy Centre at Titagarh is one such monument to courage.

Mother Teresa had often spoken to me about the work being done by the Missionary Brothers of Charity in this industrial suburb of Calcutta. On one of my visits to Calcutta I asked her if I might visit the Centre, and she promptly wrote to Brother Mariadas, its Director. 'Go and see,' she said, 'our leprosy patients are very beautiful people. If they have leprosy, then that, too, is God's gift. It is His way of bringing them closer to Himself.'

The drive from Calcutta to Titagarh that early February morning took the better part of an hour. I was soon lost in the cacophony of sound and the spirit of human enterprise as we honked and lurched over the fifteen-odd miles. Images flashed by: vegetable markets and small shops, children joyfully bathing at fire hydrants, colourful saris drying in the breeze, basketweavers weaving intricate designs. We passed a statue of Jawaharlal Nehru, India's first prime minister, standing cheek-by-jowl with a small shrine dedicated to Lord Krishna, before whom a devotee was bent almost double in prayer. Further along the road was a mosque, its dome covered with tiny porcelain pieces, glinting in the sun like an oversized pearl. Soon, we came across the silent chimneys of the once famed paper mill, which had given this suburb its importance in years gone by. We stopped to ask for directions. 'Is this the lane to the leprosy home?' the driver asked a group of pedestrians. 'Yes,' said one, pointing in the direction of a yellow washed building at the end of the lane, and added in explanation, 'Mother Teresa.'

The centre at Titagarh was established by the Missionaries of Charity in 1958. It is one of over 100 such centres spread across Africa, the Middle East and Asia which the Missionaries of Charity now run. It is no coincidence that it is named after the messiah of India's freedom struggle, for Mahatma Gandhi championed the downtrodden communities, amongst whom the four million leprosy afflicted received special attention. The outpatients' hall of the Centre, where I waited a few minutes till Brother Mariadas was free, displayed several posters to remind one that 30 January, the day Gandhiji was felled by an assassin's bullet in 1948, is observed in India as anti-leprosy day. Amongst pencil sketches of Gandhiji drawn by patients was one that showed him nursing two leprosy sufferers at his ashram in Sewagram. There were more posters and diagrams, and as I was reading these, a lithe young man with a beard and gentle eyes strode purposefully towards me, his hand outstretched in welcome. Brother Mariadas led me to a tiny office with a bare floor, a simple desk and a couple of chairs. On the wall facing me was a single photograph, that of Mother Teresa with Brother Andrew, co-founder of the Brothers' branch. Below this was the legend: 'There are no lepers, only leprosy, and it is curable.'

Prem Niwas is also a testimony to Mother Teresa's determination. Not so many years ago, the site it occupies was a cluster of shanties that had sprung up on both sides of a major artery of railway lines. Here, scores of leprosy-afflicted families had been ostracised to their own sub-culture of disease, poverty and crime. So wretched was their plight that even the residents of 'normal' shanties would have nothing to do with them, so they were pushed to the very edge of town and ended up by a swamp alongside the railway tracks. Not just the townspeople, but the agents of the law, too, were afraid of contagion. The police kept away from this shanty town and turned a blind eye to the smuggling and illicit distillation of liquor that went on there, so long as the lepers kept to themselves. Within this *bustee*, violence frequently occurred and once ended in murder.

There was no-one in the town whom the lepers could turn to for medical aid. Doctors were reluctant to treat them, and no self-respecting clinic or hospital would admit them, though some desperately needed medical attention. There were whole families who were infected, and transmission of the disease was facilitated by unhygienic conditions. There was no-one to explain that leprosy was a disease that gave no forewarning. In silently attacking the nerves, it removed the protective panoply of pain and led frequently to loss of sensation in the hands and feet. Injuries that easily occurred were painless, leading to ulceration and sepsis, and neglect over long periods led to deformities and the rotting away of fingers and toes, depressed noses and loss of eyebrows.

It was inevitable, then, that some of the afflicted came to Calcutta in search of medicine. Here they learned of Mother Teresa's mobile dispensaries, one of which treated leprosy patients outside the walls of the Loreto Convent at Entally each Wednesday. Sister Collett, assisted by three young Sisters, attended to more than 100 patients each week at this mobile clinic, distributing valuable medicines and vitamins free of charge. Food packets were given to malnourished patients. It was not long before several families from Titagarh began making weekly visits to the mobile dispensary.

The Sisters soon realised that many of the patients could not afford the bus or train fare every week. Sometimes they travelled without tickets and if they were caught, they were made to get off the train at the first stop. The disease was also spreading to newborn children, and it was difficult for mothers to travel with them all the way from Titagarh. The patients went to Mother Teresa and begged her to open a clinic there.

Mother Teresa's first visit to Titagarh convinced her that there was no alternative. Within a few months, she had started a small clinic in a shed near the railway lines. A few Sisters were sent to handle the staggering caseload. It rapidly became evident that this clinic could not make even a dent in the problem. Something needed to be done urgently about the snake-infested swamps and the insanitary living conditions of the patients. There was no drainage, no drinking water, no sewage, no electricity, not even a proper roof over their heads to protect them from the torrential monsoon rains and the chill of the early January mornings. Recognising that this task was more suitable for men, Mother Teresa handed over this arduous work to the Missionaries of Charity Brothers.

However, when Brother Christo Das and his young assistant, Brother Mariadas, tried to improve living conditions, their attempts were thwarted by *goondas*, or gang leaders, who were involved in illegal activities. The camp soon became divided between those in favour of change and those against, resulting in considerable tension. Stones were thrown at the Brothers and the young men and women working alongside them.

As a first step, the pro-changers began to build a brand new housing block. The construction, which took a few months, generated increasing excitement. By the time it was ready, the last of the resistance was broken. Gang leaders fled the scene, and all traces of rancour and suspicion vanished with them. From then on, everyone pitched in, men, women, even children. They first constructed two large tanks in the swamp, using the excavated earth to fill in the remainder of the marsh. Then the construction of the main buildings began in earnest; first more housing blocks, then an enormously long and narrow barrack-like building with green doors and windows, which today is the rehabilitation and production centre. A hospital followed, with separate wings for men and women, a cafeteria, and an assortment of smaller structures, until these stretched from the Titagarh railway station almost to the Kardah railway station, a mile down the track.

Brother Mariadas led me across the railway tracks to the Rehabilitation Centre. There is no bridge or underpass; we simply looked on both sides of the track to see whether a train was about to pass, and crossed. At the entrance to the Centre, I noticed a small board that acknowledged the efforts of the patients in the construction of the building. Although when we entered I could see the main building, I must confess that I was unprepared for its enormous length – it seemed to stretch and stretch! On both sides of the hall stood dozens of looms on which leprosy patients were weaving the uniform white saris with their familiar blue borders. Last year almost 4,000 saris found their way from this Centre to every outpost of the Missionaries of Charity in India and overseas. On the floor sat several women working *charkhas*, the Hindi word for spinning wheel. I was reminded that the *charkha* had not so long ago been fashioned by Gandhiji into his principal weapon against foreign economic influence. He had persuaded the country to forgo expensive imported cloth and to wear, instead, the simplest of cotton, spun on the humble *charkha* by the poorest of the poor. As the movement spread like wildfire, the *charkha* not only began to provide employment to millions, it also became the symbol of India's freedom movement. The patients, who sat spinning on the floor, their heads covered by their saris, possessed the quiet dignity that conquest over disease or hardship often brings.

From the Centre to the hospital, we approached well-scrubbed floors and a strong smell of antiseptic. The hundred-odd beds were occupied by patients from all over India. Treatment, inclusive of medicines, surgery, hospitalisation and even food, was entirely free. Many expensive drugs were gifts from overseas benefactors; when supplies ran out, these had to be purchased locally, for any break in treatment could lead to other complications and become counter-productive.

The family quarters were hives of activity. In several cottages, I encountered people whose deformities were extreme, but this did not inhibit them from spinning yarn or engaging in household chores. I noticed an elderly man, with stumps for arms and no fingers at all, adroitly working at a sewing machine, which he operated by special foot pedals. Meanwhile, Brother Mariadas was being pulled in every direction by children, who had just got back from schools in town. 'Brother, Brother,' they shouted in unison, pulling his arms. He told me the name of each child as he tweaked a nose here, pulled an ear there. He introduced me to several other people, among them, a grandmotherly figure with a shock of white hair. 'Sambari here,' he said, 'was among those who pelted stones at us. She was later to become the leader of the women's construction team, and is one of the pillars of our community.' Sambari showed me around her neat little house with considerable pride, her little patch of garden a blaze of sunflowers and huge purple dahlias. It was difficult to imagine that the ground on which we stood had once been a swamp.

Finally, before I left, I somewhat hesitantly asked Brother Mariadas if I could see the home where the Brothers themselves lived. Eschewing the pleasure of riding pillion on his bicycle, I persuaded him to drive with me in my car, which was just as well, as they live three miles away. Over a welcome mug of tea, he told me a little of their routine:

'We rise at four-thirty in the morning and from five-thirty to seven, we meditate and pray. A priest says mass at six. For half an hour after mass we clean the house ourselves. We have no helper. From eight to past one, and again for three hours in the afternoon, we work at Prem Niwas. Sometimes we are able to rest a little, but it depends on the number of patients on a given day. At six-thirty we say our evening prayers, followed by supper. We pray again at eight-thirty at night.' I asked him what he owned in his life of poverty. Like the Sisters, who have two saris and a third for special occasions, the Brothers have two plain cotton shirts and two pairs of cotton trousers, with a third set for 'special occasions'. He reminded me that their vows were the same as those of the Sisters. Perhaps reacting to my expression when I saw his hard wooden bed and his worldly possessions tidily placed on the thin cotton mattress, he smiled and, quoting Mother Teresa, said, 'To understand the poor, you must stand under the poor.'

A few months later, I had occasion to recall that remark. It was when I decided to visit Shantinagar. Mother Teresa had often spoken about this 'abode of peace,' her voice brimming with enthusiasm when she described this centre for the leprosy-afflicted. Shantinagar is set in over thirty-four acres of what was once jungle, located near the border of the neighbouring state of Bihar. To get there one has to travel four hours by train from Calcutta to the town of Asansol, 150 miles away. Shantinagar is a further fifteen miles.

'I will send a Brother with you,' said Mother Teresa. At that precise moment, who should come up the stairs to see her but Brother Mariadas. Seeing that we greeted each other like old friends, Mother Teresa promptly asked him whether he would accompany me, and happily he agreed.

We arranged to meet very early the next morning at Howrah railway station, as the train to Asansol, the Black Diamond Express, was scheduled to leave at 6.10 a.m. Realising that he would have come from Titagarh, I asked, when we met, where he had slept the night. 'At the station,' he said with a smile. But as I had the tickets with me, I enquired how he could have gained entry into the Second Class waiting room, which provided a few beds. Brother Mariadas replied, 'My vow of poverty does not permit me to spend money on a hotel or even a bed in a waiting room.' With a growing sense of unease I asked him what he had done. 'I slept on the platform,' he said. 'I reached Calcutta close to midnight. It was far too late to disturb the Brothers in our Calcutta home at Hooghly, so I decided to spend the night at the railway station.' Finding the floor cold that January night, he found some boxes used by the shoeshine boys and, putting four together, improvised a bed, where he spent a fitful night. While I wrestled with my thoughts as the train steamed on its way to the heart of the coal country, Brother Mariadas fell sound asleep.

As the train slid slowly into Asansol station, Brother Mariadas, suddenly wide awake, shook me out of my reverie. Before he could suggest any outlandish mode of travel to cover the distance to Shantinagar, I promptly hired a taxi on the excuse of saving time, for we had to make the return journey that evening. Initially, the taxi driver was puzzled when we asked to be driven to Shantinagar. In a conversation that involved the use of Bengali, Hindi, English and a great deal of gesticulation, we succeeded in communicating our objective. 'Why couldn't you say "Lepers' Home" in the first place?' enquired the taxi driver. But surely, he must recall the name 'Shantinagar', I asked. After all, he must have ferried several people there over the years. 'I have only been there once in the last ten years,' he said. 'No-one in his right mind would wish to visit a lepers' home.'

Titagarh

Sometime, somewhere that afternoon, Ramu, for that was the taxi driver's name, changed his mind. Bored in the isolation of his taxi, curiosity and perhaps hunger got the better of him. At first he refused the Sisters' offer of lunch, probably believing that he might find a small roadside eating house. Finding none in the immediate vicinity, he finally went into the kitchen, where the Sisters fed him as generously as they had fed us immediately upon our arrival, parboiled rice of the cheapest kind found in Bengal, some *dal* and a little salad. There was fish, too, fresh from the lake, which Ramu said was delicious. He confessed that his family and friends would be appalled to know that he had visited, let alone eaten, in a leprosy institution, but that afternoon he had learnt an elementary lesson: that leprosy is easily curable if detected early, and that contagion is no longer a dread.

The afternoon's images were strung together by Sister Albert's joyful laughter, which pealed time and again like some melodious temple bell. She explained that the West Bengal Government had given Mother Teresa thirty-four acres of land in 1961, on a thirty-year lease at a token payment of one rupee per year. It was truly a gift from the State's Chief Minister, one of India's most redoubtable politicians and a deeply committed Communist. As is well-known in Calcutta, he is never able to say 'no' to this diminutive nun and her band of Sisters, because whatever they ask for is never for themselves and only for those dregs of humanity whom we so often pass without actually seeing.

'Shantinagar,' said Sister Albert, 'is a miracle.' In Mother Teresa's lexicon, 'miracles' are created almost at the drop of a hat, and they use the word happily several times a day, when things get done to their satisfaction. Shantinagar was also hard work. 'In 1961, it was a large uncultivated area like a jungle,' said Sister Albert. To begin with, there was no money to create Mother Teresa's dream of a self-sufficient home and treatment centre for the leprosy-afflicted.

Then a 'miracle' occurred. Pope Paul VI visited India as a guest of the Government in 1965. During his State visit, a 1964 Lincoln Continental limousine was specially flown out for his use in India, as a gift from the American people. In it he rode to bless multitudes of the faithful; it also took him to Mother Teresa's Home for the Dying in Calcutta's Kalighat. So touched was he by the work of the Missionaries of Charity which he witnessed that, before leaving India, he gave the limousine to Mother Teresa. Nothing if not practical, Mother Teresa promptly raffled it, and obtained far more money than she would have had she advertised its sale through newspapers, such was the publicity that the event attracted. The money she received went towards the building of the main hospital block in Shantinagar. Additional funds were raised by children in Germany. Some years ago, I asked Mother Teresa how she got the idea of a lottery in the first place. Looking this near-atheist in the eye, and in a tone that spoke volumes, she said, 'If you pray, you too will get these ideas.'

In 1968, Sister Francis Xavier, a garrulous Yugoslav nun, armed with a pioneering spirit and ably assisted by some young Sisters, arrived to tame the wilderness. And how well they succeeded! Blessed with plentiful water from the nearby Mekhand Dam, Shantinagar soon abounded with flowers and flowering shrubs. Fruit trees were planted: not just fruit trees, but a whole orchard of mango trees, interspersed with wheat and vegetables. A large pond was stocked with fish, and today is teeming with this supply of protein so badly needed by the malnourished. And all this was accomplished before the first arrivals, so that they would be somewhat self-sufficient from the start.

Within two years the essential buildings were up: the rehabilitation centre, cottages for leprosy patients, which they built themselves, and a hospital. From the beginning, Mother Teresa's idea was that the leprosy families should be as independent as possible. She wanted to create an oasis where the leprosy-afflicted of all faiths and denominations could come for medical advice and guidance, and where they could gain at least partial use of their limbs. It was important to teach them how to care for their deformities, and to create a place where the elderly could live out their remaining lives in peace and dignity. The new arrivals were taught to make bricks and then to construct their own dwellings according to a simple design which merged with the architecture of the countryside. A Shishu Bhawan followed, to house children to protect them from infectious parents. Next came a small hospital with a reconstructive surgery unit equipped with prosthetic and orthotic appliances and other inputs. The residents grew their own rice, set up a small poultry farm, wove baskets and cultivated the orchard. The village elders were encouraged to establish a system of local government, and elected their leaders.

Nothing was allowed to go unutilised, not even animal waste. Adjoining the livestock pens is a plant (called a gobar gas plant) which converts waste into an odourless, colourless gas that is piped into the kitchen and community centres – far more practical than an irregular supply of cooking gas from the nearest town. I was not surprised to see hundreds of coconut trees, as the milk is rich in phosphorus while the fibrous husks are used to make inexpensive coarse matting. The young teak trees I saw would provide for the construction needs of many 'homes' in the years to come. On the farm, at the lake, in the kitchen, everywhere we went that afternoon, non-infectious patients, with and without deformities, were at work on community projects with a true sense of belonging. 'Several of the patients, even those with deformities, have a far greater commitment than any outside help we can ever hope to hire,' said Sister Albert.

The statistics for 1990, proudly displayed by Sister Albert, are impressive indeed: 17,613 leprosy patients and 4,362 general cases were treated at the outdoor clinic last year; 966 leprosy patients were admitted to hospital, and 449 underwent surgery. 785 pairs of special shoes were made at the rehabilitation centre, and thirty-five patients received prosthetic appliances. 135 children were admitted to the Shishu Bhawan, and thirty-eight were discharged. 2000 individuals were given rations each month, and 400 persons received cooked food each day. Not a penny was charged. Once a fortnight, three doctors, none of whom share the Sisters' faith, drive in from nearby Asansol to perform reconstructive surgeries free of cost.

Just off the paved brick path, which is rather grandiloquently called the Pope Paul Avenue, is the boys' dormitory. Amidst neatly-made beds and pop posters on the walls, about twenty boys, having just returned from school, were in the midst of recreation. A boy of about ten came running up to Sister Albert. After we shook hands and he had moved out of earshot, she said, 'Shapun was found some years ago near the railway tracks, an emaciated little chap, sitting beside the body of his dead father. No-one could explain the cause of his father's death. Shapun was found by some railway mechanics, and they brought the child to us. He is doing very well in school,' she added proudly, 'and is always first in his class.'

There was an energetic young man in the dormitory whom I mistook for a Brother, as he seemed to be in charge of the smaller boys. 'How was your computer class today, Santosh?' asked Sister Albert of this Bengali boy, who was receiving special tuition at a private school in a neighbouring town. 'You'll soon be making a lot of money, so we'd better get you married to a nice girl,' teased Sister Albert. 'I'm not getting married,' said Santosh. 'And I am not leaving home,' he growled. On our way to visit the cottages on the Estate,

Sister Albert told me about the cataclysmic event that had just occurred in young Santosh's life. The child had been found abandoned, literally at the doorstep of the Centre, when he was two. The Sisters had brought him up, and theirs was the only love he had ever known, this his only home. Two weeks ago, Santosh's world changed dramatically. A couple deformed by leprosy came to meet the Sisters, and claimed that Santosh was their child. After all these years they had come to 'take him home'. For the Sisters, it was first necessary to obtain proof that they were, indeed, the parents. After this had been established beyond doubt, they had to prepare Santosh to accept this sea-change in his life. When the time came to unite Santosh with his parents, he was called into the parlour. There, for the first time after sixteen years, he saw his parents, who were beggars, almost totally deformed by leprosy! Santosh was completely bewildered by the events that had engulfed him. Sister Albert explained to me, 'We are trying to bring Santosh around, to make him accept and understand the tragedy that befell his parents when they were affected by leprosy. They were both excommunicated from their families, they had no means of retaining employment, and had drifted into begging on the streets. They had no wish to expose their only child to the disease. So they sent him away, not because they loved him too little, but because they loved him too well.' The Sisters hope that Santosh will accept the situation and will be reunited with his parents soon.

All of a sudden, the afternoon's harmony was shattered by a tall, well-built man who was shouting and advancing menacingly towards us, waving a stick in one hand, his other arm in plaster. 'I will not be kept here against my will,' he shouted at a Sister a little distance away. 'I am not a prisoner. I wish to leave immediately.'

Sister Albert's composure and smile did not desert her. 'Why don't you stay a few more days till your plaster is removed? Then you can leave. In any case, your brother won't be back till next Tuesday,' she answered. 'What brother?' he screamed. 'My brother is dead as far as I am concerned. I want to leave now,' he declared. Tension crackled in the air. For a moment it seemed as if the stick might come down on the head of the Sister near him. For a few seconds everything froze. Suddenly, palpably, his anger drained away. He turned around, threw away the stick, and walked back towards the hospital.

Sister Albert said sadly, 'Pramod's pain is sometimes too great for him to bear. His wife ran away with another man, leaving him and abandoning the children. He has not been able to forgive or to forget. His brother is a good man who loves and cares for him. He is presently taking care of Pramod's children too. He was the one who brought Pramod here for surgery. Pramod will soon regain the use of his fingers, but the pain in the heart will take a long time to heal.'

It was soon time to leave, to say goodbye to the Sisters and to Santosh, who had quietly followed us around all afternoon. Sister Albert placed the Visitor's Book before me, and asked me to write a few words. Leafing through some earlier entries, I chanced upon the sentiments expressed by a group of ladies who had visited Shantinagar the month before:

'We thoroughly appreciate the sincere,
selfless and dedicated work done by
all the Sisters of Shantinagar. We seek
the blessings of Mother Teresa.'

Eastern Railway Women's Organisation
28 January 1990

Today, the world has an estimated 12,000,000 leprosy cases, concentrated largely in Asia, Africa, South America and the Middle East. Inexplicably, leprosy vanished in Europe in the sixteenth century. India alone has as many as 4,000,000 cases. Leprosy is not a killer disease. However, from Biblical times until a few decades ago, there was no effective cure, which led to a dread of the disfigurement and social rejection that came in its wake. It was only in the last decade that an important breakthrough was achieved in the form of a multi-drug regimen, which has revitalised national eradication programmes in countries where leprosy is endemic. The treatment is effective only if the disease is detected at the early stages, that is, before deformity sets in, and requires close supervision and regularity. Government programmes aided by voluntary effort have helped to establish and man hospitals and detection and treatment centres. As a result, hundreds of thousands of patients have been cured in recent years. Nonetheless, ignorance and poverty continue to claim victims, particularly malnourished slum children, who are the most susceptible. Government effort is not completely effective, as in many countries eradication programmes lack funds and technical personnel, and equally, voluntary effort, although often deeply committed, is not nearly enough.

The leprosy-afflicted constitute a very special place in Mother Teresa's world of destitutes. There is hardly a country in the developing world where she has not set up at least one leprosy station. In some countries there are several. She prefers to establish these Centres outside city limits, partly because leprosy clusters are not encouraged within municipalities and partly because, being some distance away, there is less occasion for the patients to travel into the city to beg for alms.

Mother Teresa's battle against the stigma attached to the leprosy-afflicted has not always been smooth. She has had to endure hardships and humiliations. Once there used to be a leprosy hospital in Calcutta called the Gobra Hospital, located on the outskirts of the city. But, as the city spread and engulfed it, residents and developers alike put pressure on the government to close it down or to relocate it. No one wanted a leprosy hospital in their midst. Mother Teresa went repeatedly to the then Chief Minister of West Bengal, Dr B. C. Roy, and begged him not to close the hospital. Despite the esteem in which Dr Roy held her – some of his family members were amongst Mother Teresa's most ardent workers and supporters – she failed, and the Gobra Hospital was closed down. It was then the only institution of its kind in the city, and its closure was a great blow to those who had no other place to go to for treatment. Another incident occurred when Mother Teresa tried to set up a leprosy clinic elsewhere in the city. She located a suitable plot, but on one of her visits she found that the local councillor was waiting to 'welcome' her at the head of an angry crowd of local residents. No sooner did Mother alight from her van than she was greeted by a barrage of stones. Mother Teresa's response was perfectly practical. 'I don't think God wants us to open a clinic here,' she said. 'Let us pray and find out what He does want.'

Inspiration came in the form of an ambulance which had been donated by American benefactors. Mother Teresa decided to convert this into the first of her mobile clinics. At about the same time, a renowned skin and leprosy specialist, Dr Sen, completed his tenure at a well-known hospital. Not knowing what to do with his time, and impressed with the selfless work of the Missionaries of Charity, he asked Mother Teresa to utilise his services as she thought fit. He said he would accept no salary. One complemented the other, and in September 1957, the first mobile leprosy clinic was launched by Archbishop Perier. When I visited the clinic parked outside the Entally Convent recently, I discovered, from the meticulous records maintained by the Sisters, that over 1,000 patients were registered at that one stop alone.

Some years ago, I had accompanied Mother Teresa on one of her visits to her Delhi Centre, which had been set up on the twelve acres of wilderness presented to her by the Lieutenant Governor of Delhi seventeen years before. The buildings were cheerful enough: a simple surgical theatre and dormitories, mainly for 'burnt out' cases and destitutes. It was operation day. Each Wednesday a young surgeon, Dr. Chadha assisted by two trained Sisters of the Missionaries of Charity, gave freely of his time to perform as many as a dozen reconstructive and other surgeries. These simple operations often enabled the patients to get back the use of a finger and a thumb, thus enabling them at least to lift objects. During the tea break, I was able to chat with the doctor for a few minutes. I learned from him that his family considered him quite odd. Why, they constantly wondered, would a young graduate from one of the best medical schools in the country, who could easily afford to set up a lucrative private surgery, wish to give of his time voluntarily to Mother Teresa's home for the leprosy destitute? He wasn't even a Christian, they argued. He said, with a disarming smile, 'I tell them I am a little mad. But, seriously, having received the best from my country, I have to "pay back" as well.'

The cheerful buildings, the flowers and the vegetable gardens could not mask the human tragedy that leprosy had brought in its wake. Jehangir, a middle-aged young man from the state of Bihar, said to me, 'I have returned home only once these last nine years. I stole into my home like a thief. I could not let the village see me. My father wept. My wife would not come near me. My two little daughters hugged and kissed me. They had not learned fear yet. I long to go back, but I must let them lead normal lives. If the village gets to know I have leprosy, who will marry my daughters?'

The need to lead 'normal' lives also led to the casting out of Kalu almost fifty years ago. He has never returned to his village. As far as his brothers are concerned, Kalu is 'dead'. He speaks of his life to anyone prepared to listen.

*   *   *

Kalu, for that is his nickname, is about seventy years old. He has only stumps for limbs. At first glance he is head and torso alone, propped up in a child's handcart against a supporting wall. From a distance he looks like an infant with a wizened head. Despite life's unending adversities, Kalu is usually cheerful. But not today, I can see that from afar. Today, I must accompany him yet again on his journey of pain and humiliation. Kalu was once a respected member of a reasonably well-to-do farming family in South India. He was one of four brothers. He was still a young man when he noticed a patch on his back. He showed it to a doctor in a nearby town, who diagnosed leprosy. Kalu could not believe what he had heard. Filled with horror, he rushed instinctively to the temple to beseech Lord Vishnu to spare him. What sin, Lord, had he committed in which previous incarnation, that so severe a punishment was being meted on him? He lay prostrate before the Lord as his body was wracked with sobs.

God, he believed, soon revealed himself in the form of a soothsayer, who sold him a 'special' medicine that would cure him in a matter of weeks. From soothsayer to astrologer, to an old woman who sold him magic potions, he went secretly to distant towns, where no-one might recognise him, in search of a cure. He did not reveal his secret to his brothers, or to any of his friends in his village. Nor did he return to the doctor, who had initially diagnosed the disease, for fear that he would be forced to reveal his true identity. For two years, he hid the terrible truth until one day, inevitably, a tell-tale patch appeared on his right hand. The discovery was met with horror. It was clear to his family that this was a divine visitation for sins committed. They remembered all too well the last case of leprosy in their village, a few years earlier, which had caused the village elders to banish the offending family. They remembered, too, that that entire family was rendered outcast, and the difficulties the family went through to arrange marriages for their two daughters. If the truth about Kalu were to be known, they would lose their status in the village. Who would marry their daughters? The shame would kill them. The brothers took a decision to isolate Kalu in a small shed at the bottom of the fields. It was a lonely spot, and no-one would know for a few days. When Kalu refused to comply – for he was part owner of the twenty acres of land the brothers jointly farmed – he was trussed up like a chicken and taken there in the dead of night. His brothers chained him to the floor, and threw some food for him into a metal bowl.

Unable to bear the humiliation, one night he broke the chain and ran away, never to return. For months he wandered like a sick animal, sometimes to this town, sometimes to that, begging for food at bus stops, railway stations and outside temples. He was arrested twice and put in special prisons for lepers. Medical treatment was irregular and infrequent. In a matter of a few years, nerve damage overtook his once beautifully shaped fingers until one horror-filled afternoon, his by now benumbed and ulcerated hands were amputated in some anonymous jail hospital, it no longer mattered where. Sick at heart, more dead than alive, he found his way to Delhi. There he learnt of Mother Teresa's home for leprosy patients. That was five years ago. Now he is among friends, and is usually cheerful. After years of living like an animal, Kalu has once again found a little dignity and some peace.

*   *   *

In the women's dormitory, Mother Teresa stopped to console a small figure that lay huddled on a bed. Once the matron of one of the country's leading private schools, she lies now, a wretched bundle covered with sores. She hid her leprosy for several years, and took no treatment. Inevitably, nerve damage set in, and with it the familiar cycle of disfigurement and deformity. She soon became an embarrassment to her sons. One of them brought her to Mother Teresa's home. I learned that the older one has not visited her even once since she was brought here. The younger son came to visit her on Christmas Day the past two years. Would he come this Christmas? she asked Mother Teresa in anguish.

Perhaps Mother Teresa had this case in her mind when she addressed a gathering of dignitaries, senior civil servants, foreign diplomats and, amidst them, a dozen children of leprosy patients. Mother Teresa was releasing my Report on leprosy which she, herself, had inspired. She opened the meeting with a prayer, after which she spoke briefly. For the sake of brevity, I am only reproducing the opening and closing words of her address – the full text is in the Appendix:

'Leprosy is not a punishment, it can be a very beautiful gift of God if we make good use of it. Through it, we can learn to love the unloved, the unwanted; not only just to give them things but to make them feel that they, too, are useful, that they, too, can do something because they feel they are loved and wanted, that they can share the joy of loving.

'If you can remove fear, you will have done a lot. It is a big thing. I think this book is going to bring confidence to many people and remove the fear that we have had all these years; to make them really feel that God has done something beautiful for them, that they also can stand like ordinary people and do ordinary work and lead an ordinary life.'

10

· *Kalighat* ·

Only devout Hindus or the most intrepid tourists make their way to Kalighat in South Calcutta. It is here, near the famed temple to the Goddess Kali, that the Hindus bring their dead to be cremated on the banks of the River Hooghly, into which flows the Ganga, itself the object of veneration. Legend has it that the right toe of the Goddess fell from the heavens at that particular spot, and a temple was erected to sanctify it. Medieval texts refer to it as one of the fifty-one most sacred places for Hindus. Several hundred worshippers throng the temple each day, some to fulfil a vow, others to pray for safety before a long journey, and others to seek a cure for diseases. They come for ceremonies associated with life's journey: the naming ceremonies of infants, hair cropping for children, the initiation rites of the sacred thread for adolescents, marriages, and finally, funeral purificatory rites, conducted on the burning *ghats* near the temple.

On one's first visit to the area, one might find it difficult to locate Mother Teresa's home for dying destitutes, as Kalighat is one of the most congested areas in an overcrowded city. The temple opens onto a narrow lane, and around it have sprung up scores of small shops and stalls selling numerous items essential for worship. Marigold flowers, incense, and vessels to hold them, as well as images and pictures of the deities, jostle with other more mundane merchandise of daily life. The roads and lanes are crowded with people, among them mendicants in saffron, with their foreheads emblazoned with vermilion *tilaks*, beggars holding tin plates, the odd cow making its leisurely progress, and the occasional group of tourists. To this must be added the many varieties of vehicular traffic, buses and cars, rickshaws and handcarts, that contribute to the verve and confusion of a Calcutta bazaar. Just as the eye begins to focus on the fluted domes of the temple, a funeral procession with its pall bearers chanting ancient Vedic hymns captures one's attention, while in the distance, the mist of funeral pyres and the fragrance of incense are a constant reminder of a stoic acceptance of death amidst life.

More often than not, it is the familiar white saris bordered in blue, bending down to carry a stretcher, that provide the first indication that one is near to Nirmal Hriday. (In Bengali, this means the Place of Immaculate Heart. The Missionaries of Charity are dedicated to the Immaculate Heart of Mary.) There is no front door, just a small entrance to what was once the pilgrims' hall. There are actually two halls, one for men and another for women, divided by a reception area.

I vividly remember my first visit to Nirmal Hriday several years ago. Just before I entered, initial curiosity gave way to fear, even a feeling of repugnance. Why had I ventured so far, I wondered. I decided to make my escape as soon as I could. But, to my surprise, I remained there for hours, until the Sisters finally nudged me to leave because it was time for their evening prayers. Since that occasion, no visit that I have made to Calcutta has ever been complete without some hours spent at Nirmal Hriday, interchangeable to me with its location, Kalighat.

I entered a hall crammed with low stretcher beds, placed row upon row on an antiseptic, scrubbed floor. To my right, there was the reception area with some work tables, and nearby there were a couple of patients on stretchers. These, I discovered later, were the very sick on whom the Sisters might keep a special eye as they went about their ministering. There must have been a hundred emaciated bodies, each lying in a bed with a number painted on the wall behind it. Even more striking than the shafts of light that streamed in from the skylights was the stillness. There was hardly a sound above the rustle of the saris or the ministering of some treatment, in contrast to the noisy and polluted street, a few feet away. I found myself whispering, and when my camera bag fell inadvertently, with a clatter, it was like some hideous profanity. There was a marked absence of religious decoration, but I noticed a board that proclaimed Kalighat to be 'Mother's first love', which I believe to be the case.

I recently asked Mother Teresa whether she would have wished to play her final innings in Kalighat, had she been allowed to retire in September 1990. She replied, not with any great conviction, I felt, that it did not matter, since God was everywhere. Yet, I do believe that it is to this Home for the Dying in Kalighat that Mother Teresa would have liked to return. To the young faces old before their time, the cart and rickshaw pullers dying of diseases too advanced to cure, to the women, mentally disturbed, and to Pagola, an occupant of twenty years, who is invariably the first to wave to Mother Teresa whenever she visits.

Although the entrance to Nirmal Hriday is always open, a stranger, entering, feels intrusive. This is not a place to stand and stare, or to sit and watch the world go by. It is not even a hospital where one might have the defined role of a visitor. As I stood feeling unconscionably healthy, a man was brought in and left propped against the entrance wall. A Sister went rapidly to him. Someone was needed to carry him in. My offer was accepted with a smile. As I settled the man on to a pallet and helped the Sister fasten the glucose drip, I felt less uncomfortable.

By the time I stepped into the women's ward, slightly larger than the men's and suffused with the same quiet, my mind had adjusted itself to the surroundings. The gaunt faces beneath closely cropped heads and the young faces on emaciated bodies had began to assume form and substance. An old woman who was lying on her side mistook me for a doctor, and called me to sit by her. I did so. She told me her name was Jehanara Begum and that she lived in a mosque near the Convent Road. She had no-one left: whether they had died or had abandoned her, she did not say. Nor did she explain how her legs were a mass of sores. She held on to my hand. 'I feel very weak,' she said, 'as if I have no blood left.' She also complained that it was not the pain from the bandaged sores that troubled her, but that she disliked being bathed each day. 'Doctor,' she cajoled in Hindi, 'tell the Sisters that bathing me each day is bad for my skin. And doctor,' she continued, 'can you get me two lemons? I can't eat food without lemon.'

Nirmal Hriday, like the school in the Motijhil slum, 'began on the ground'. When Mother Teresa started to walk about Calcutta, she came across scores of shelterless people who lived on pavements and in the streets. Some families had managed to build shacks with waste building material; others made roofs out of pieces of cloth or thatch. Many were not so fortunate. They eked out their days by begging outside temples and at traffic intersections. At night, they slept on the pavements. Already malnourished, the onslaught of illness was inevitable. Tuberculosis was rife among them. Sanatorium beds were few and far between, and often had to be obtained through influence. The general hospitals were overcrowded and could do little for them in their advanced stages of illness. So they died where they lived, on the pavements. When information about a dead body reached the municipality, it would send a van or a cart to pick up the offending corpse. A single line in a register would record the obituary: name unknown, age unknown, religion unknown.

Mother Teresa has often spoken in her public speeches about the woman she helped in those early months when she began her work outside the Campbell Hospital (later renamed the Nilaratan Sarkar Hospital). She saw what appeared to be a bundle of rags lying on the pavement. When Mother Teresa and a companion Sister went closer, they found a middle-aged woman, barely conscious. Half her face had been eaten away by rats and ants. Lifting her, they carried her to the hospital. The hospital refused to accept her, saying that they had no unoccupied bed. In any case, the woman was dying, and there was nothing they could do for her. When asked where she might take the dying woman, the hospital suggested that Mother Teresa place her back where she had found her. Close to despair, Mother Teresa refused to budge. 'In the end, because I insisted, they took her in,' said Mother Teresa. They gave the woman a mattress on the floor. She died a few hours later. 'It was then that I decided to find a place for the dying and take care of them myself.'

In the past, the Sisters came upon people on the threshold of death almost every day. One rainy day, Sister Agnes and Mother Teresa encountered a woman lying on the footpath, her hand buried in the mud. When they lifted her, the skin of the hand simply peeled off. How long she had been lying there, ironically near the same Campbell Hospital, they could not tell. The Hospital authorities, knowing by now how adamant Mother Teresa could be, admitted the woman without much fuss.

'When Mother Teresa began her work in the slums,' said Sister Agnes, 'we often found people dying or sometimes dead. On occasion we took them to the nearest hospital, but beds were not always available. Sometimes the patients were in a pitiful condition, and we had nowhere to take them.'

Mother Teresa rented two rooms for five rupees each in the Motijhil slum. One became the school room, the other, her first Home for the Dying. In this space, which was eight feet square, she began looking after people the hospitals had refused. The experiment was doomed to failure. It was with difficulty that two or three patients could be crammed on to the floor, with hardly any space for Mother Teresa to minister to them. One night, inevitably, one of the sick died, and the next morning, the others fled.

Undeterred, Mother Teresa went to the Municipality, where she was directed to the Chief Medical Officer, Dr Ahmad. She told him that the city hospitals had problems in accepting the dying. Where, then, was she to take them? 'I asked only for a place,' she said, 'the rest, I would do myself.' The officer had the foresight to recognise that this earnest, middle-aged nun was offering to perform a function that belonged essentially to the local government. Obviously it was not in the Municipality's interest for the poor to continue to die on public roads. Dr Ahmad took Mother Teresa to the city's most famous temple at Kalighat. Adjoining the temple, he showed her two halls which had been constructed several years ago by a Hindu benefactor for pilgrims who wanted to stay overnight. Dr Ahmad had received complaints that the halls were being misused, and probably thought that by offering them to Mother Teresa, he would kill two birds with one stone.

Dr Ahmad certainly could not have anticipated that there would be any opposition to this move, but antagonism there was. 'It was local,' said Father van Exem, 'not general, otherwise it surely would have been reported in the newspapers. People did not want the dying to come there actually to die.'

Rumours circulated that those who died were ministered the last rites and then buried as Christians. Dr Ahmad and a senior police officer decided to see things for themselves. As they entered Nirmal Hriday, they saw Mother Teresa hunched over a figure whose face was a large, gaping wound. So intense was her concentration that they were able to observe her for several minutes before she saw them. With the help of a tweezer, she was pulling maggots from the raw flesh. The stench of the wound was so foul that most people would have hesitated even to enter the room. They heard her say to the patient, 'You say a prayer in your religion, and I will say a prayer as I know it. Together we will say this prayer and it will be something beautiful for God.'

When Mother Teresa saw the officials, she offered to show them her work. The police officer, his eyes filled with tears, said, 'There is no need, Mother.' Turning to the crowd outside he said, 'Yes, I will send this woman away, but only after you have persuaded your mothers and sisters to come here to do the work that she is doing. This woman is a saint.'

Despite this intervention, there continued to be simmering discontent. The idea of a place for the dying, so close to a venerated Hindu shrine, upset the temple priests. Furthermore, the Brahmin priests were shocked that the precincts of the Kali temple had been handed over to a Christian missionary. They petitioned the municipal authorities several times to discontinue the arrangement. These petitions remained unattended. Then one day, a strange incident occurred, that brought this opposition to an end. A young temple priest, not quite thirty, began to vomit blood. He was diagnosed to be in an advanced stage of tuberculosis, and no hospital was prepared to admit such a hopeless case as it would mean depriving a curable patient of a bed. Sick in body and heart, the priest was finally brought to Nirmal Hriday. Mother Teresa gave him a special corner to himself, where she nursed him. He was angry and felt humiliated, but with each passing day, he slowly began to accept his situation. By the time he died, rage had given way to tranquillity. Meanwhile, the temple priests, who had been unable, or unwilling, to help their brother, observed the care that he received. Nor did they fail to notice that, when he died, far from being given a Christian burial, Mother Teresa sent his body to be cremated by Hindu rites.

There are many religious and social organisations of all sizes and denominations in and around Calcutta, that provide succour to the poor and ailing. Yet none actually take in those destitutes who can find neither home nor hospital to die in. For the Hindu mind, unshakeable in its belief in the transmigration of souls, the ailing body is beside the point. It is merely to be cast off to free the soul to continue its cycle of birth, death and rebirth in its pursuit of salvation. Mother Teresa and her Missionary Sisters, however, feel that it is important to touch these broken bodies and unattended souls with their compassion. Yet one would entirely miss the point if one failed to grasp that, for them, each of the occupants of the stretcher beds in Nirmal Hriday is the sick, abandoned or dying Christ. Without this unshakeable conviction, they would be as unable to do this work as anyone else. It is this that is fundamental to the philosophy of the Missionaries of Charity, not the conversion of souls nor giving the bodies a Christian burial, which, unless especially indicated or requested, would be considered by Mother Teresa to be a sacrilege.

Soon after the incident of the priest, local antagonism diminished. The people of Calcutta also began to recognise three things. The first was that the Sisters were fulfilling a need. Some of the people who were brought there were beggars from outside the temple, or local rickshaw pullers, amongst whom tuberculosis was rampant. When they were admitted, they not only received medical attention, but also love, from total strangers. Secondly, the last rites were performed according to the deceased's faith. Where patients were brought in unconscious, and therefore unable to disclose their faith, a simple method was followed. Muslim males could be identified by their being circumcised, and the local *Anjuman* contacted, to collect their bodies. In other cases, an identification mark or a tattoo sometimes helped to reveal their faith. When there was no indication, the body was (and is) sent for cremation by Hindu rites. The third factor that people grew to acknowledge, was that the Sisters were obviously as poor as anyone else in the city. Of course, they were better fed and cleanly clothed, but in their self-avowed poverty, they were at one with those who came through these doors.

From 22 August 1952, when Mother Teresa opened Nirmal Hriday, there is an exact record of the number of cases admitted. A register lists the names of those who survived and those who died. In the case of a person who died before recovering consciousness, there is only the name of a street, or a road, for example: 'Male, Convent Road'. There were occasions when a person may have recovered and left, only to be readmitted later to die. For the most part, however, the register meticulously maintains details about the inmates.

Glancing through the earlier volumes, it is interesting to note that in the 1940s and 1950s, nearly all those who were admitted succumbed to their illnesses. In the 1960s and 1970s, the mortality rate was roughly half those admitted. In the last ten years or so, only a fifth died. The number of daily admissions now varies from two to ten. In September 1991, I noted that 177 people had been admitted, 106 discharged, and 35 had died. At random, I opened an earlier page. September 1987: 165 had been admitted, 117 discharged and 28, or about a sixth, had died. Perhaps this is because people are now better fed, housed and clothed. Medical facilities, too, have vastly improved and are more widely available. Inescapably, this is also because Mother Teresa has shaken the city's conscience, to the extent that no-one is any longer allowed to die on the streets. Someone, somewhere, takes the trouble to dial the telephone number

102; an ambulance does go there, and the destitute is taken to hospital. If the hospital refuses admission, the ambulance takes the case to Nirmal Hriday. The police, too, bring to Nirmal Hriday those whom the hospitals are unable or reluctant to accept. Meanwhile, the Sisters continue to look for the dying as they walk through the city.

'One of the small problems we face,' said a Sister, 'is to distinguish between "street cases" and "family cases". "Street cases" are the destitutes, the abandoned. They have no-one to look after them. No family, no relatives, no-one who loves them enough to wish to keep them. "Family cases" are those where families are unable or unwilling to take care of their members. We always remember Mother's words: I prefer you to make a mistake in kindness than to work miracles in unkindness; and try never to refuse anyone who is sick. We have only 105 beds, but on some days we have as many as 130 patients. Frequently, patients volunteer their own beds. We have seen patients giving up their pallets for someone whom they see as suffering more than they are. A richer man may have thought, "Let me stay on a few days more." The poor think differently. "I have suffered. There is another whose suffering is greater than my own. Let him have a little of the comfort that I have had." The Sisters also try never to reject anyone in abject poverty, the hungry or starving. Many of these people suffer from tuberculosis. They are mainly rickshaw pullers, cart pullers and others who carry loads in the market place. They often come here and say, "I have fallen ill. I have nowhere to lie down. The market is so crowded. It is only at night that I get a little corner to sleep in. I have nowhere to go. Could you not keep me for a few days?"'

I asked Sister Suma how she looked serene, even happy, in these halls where she saw death at such close quarters. The emaciated bodies with their resigned eyes, these lives of deprivation and inequity, did they not make her wish for a change in her constituency, perhaps looking after children, instead? Her first few days had made her sad, she said, especially when a young person died. She frequently ran to the chapel, lest someone should see her weep. She would pray late into the night and beg for grace. Now, after several months of deep prayer, she was better able to give of her strength and compassion.

'Now, I no longer feel afraid [of death]. We tell them [the dying] that they are going to face God. Every person has an origin in God, and in every human being, God dwells. For me, my God is Jesus. For a Hindu, he may be Shiva or Vishnu or Brahma. For a Muslim, Allah. If a person lies unconscious, I always request another person, perhaps a Sister or Brother or a volunteer, to sit next to the dying person and hold his or her hand, to ask pardon for the sins he or she had committed, or make an act of love or faith for God. Sometimes when this is whispered in the ears of those near death, tears roll down their cheeks. Most people you see here are not afraid of death. When I prepare someone whom I feel we have not been able to save, he often says, "That is what I came here for." Last month I remember an old lady who said to me, "Sister, I am suffering so much pain. Does He not see what I am going through? I now have only one desire left, to cross over to the other side." She died a few days later. There are many who tell us, "There is no better place to die than here."

'Yet when a young life goes, it saddens me. Last Sunday, a young boy was brought in. He told me that he had been spitting blood. I immediately put him on a saline drip to stop the bleeding. When I made him more comfortable, I went across to the other hall to attend to an urgent case. I was back in a few minutes, but the boy was not on his bed. I could not find him anywhere. I even ran out on to the street. Finally I located him in the rear toilet. He had lost blood profusely and had collapsed. I think he had been vomiting blood for several days before he came here. I brought him back to his bed. He died within fifteen minutes. Maybe if he had come sooner, we could have saved his life. He was only twenty. I did not let anyone see my tears, but at the same time, I thought that perhaps it was better for him to have reached God sooner than to continue to struggle in this world the way that he must have done.'

While Sister was talking to me, I could see a flurry of activity in a corner of the men's ward. A Sister and two volunteers with masks across their faces were applying some treatment. As we got closer, I stopped short. Sitting up, holding his leg, was an old man. His left foot was raw flesh, which the Sister and the volunteers were cleaning with spirit. His face was contorted with pain, yet he made no sound. 'He was knocked down on the road, and a car ran over his foot. He lay there until someone brought him to us. He is very brave, as you can see. Life's struggles enable the poor to accept much tribulation, which is one of the reasons why the poor are often such good people.'

As we moved away, I stopped at a surprisingly young and healthy face, wondering what he was doing in this sea of the sick and terminally ill. The Sister laughed. 'He is one of our own children from Shishu Bhawan. Now he lives at Boys' Town, with the older children. One day, we discovered that he had contracted tuberculosis, and so he was brought here. He has to complete one last injection. He hates to lie in bed, and follows us around like a puppy. But he must rest, so I have to be very strict with him,' said Sister Suma, while Mundu did not quite know whether to smile or scowl.

Sister Suma led me to an old man sitting up on his pallet, and affectionately ruffled his hair. 'Jagdish has nowhere to go. He begs near the temple and has stayed here several times. Sometimes I see Jagdish in the street. He shows me what he has earned during the day. I tell him that if it is not enough for his dinner, he can always come home.'

Kalighat

All the while that I spoke to Sister, I watched the other Sisters and the volunteers going about their work, tending to the needs of the patients. A drip to be adjusted here, a vein to be found there, the floor to be constantly scrubbed. A young Bengali boy, who was working for an honours course at Calcutta University, was going from pallet to pallet, giving a shave to those men who needed it. It was not just providing a shave, but giving them a feeling of wellbeing. On bed seventeen there was a man lying on his back with his legs folded up at his knees. He looked both twenty and seventy at the same time. Sitting by his side was a young man from Sweden, his golden hair cascading to his shoulders, gently massaging his legs. When I returned half an hour later I found the patient with his eyes closed, his hand held firmly by the young man, as his life slipped away.

Each time that I have entered Kalighat and observed the dozen or so volunteers hard at work, I have invariably remembered what Mother Teresa said about them when I first accompanied her there. 'Look at our volunteers working here. They come from all over the world. They work [in their respective countries] to earn money, and then they come here to serve others. They, themselves, pay for everything, because we give them nothing. They often stay two or three months.' To be constantly on their hands and knees scrubbing the floors, changing bed clothes, mopping urine-soaked beds, feeding or holding sick people in the Home for the Dying, in a city they may not have otherwise visited, was this a part of their *bhagya*, their fate?

'Why am I here?' asked Eamon Butler rhetorically. 'This is a question I have asked myself every day for these past six weeks. I could be home in Ireland, enjoying a social life with the money I make. It is difficult to explain this in a few words.' For several minutes I watched this thirty-one-year-old carpenter help make an old man comfortable. He had given him a shave and changed his bedclothes. The man then soiled his bed, and Butler cleaned and changed him again. He could not have been gentler. 'I first saw Mother Teresa on a chat show on TV. The man interviewing her was close to tears. It spurred me to buy a ticket to Calcutta. I took all my shots and got my visa. Four days before the flight, I chickened out and cancelled the whole thing.' Four years later, he finally made it. 'When I arrived, Sister Joseph Michael asked me to come to Kalighat. A shiver went down my spine. I had never worked with dying people. Sister asked me to go for half a day and see.

'As soon as I walked in, I felt a special grace which has helped me to cope with what I saw. Within a week, I was able to hold dying people, wash the dead, something I could never had dreamt of. Now I have seen death in a different light – as a rebirth, as life after, as "going home", as the "final stuff". The body goes, the soul and peace remain. I have found myself at peace with death. And I have seen some wonderful things about life as well. What human beings are, how people on the streets care for one another, the way they care here in Kalighat, and the love of the Sisters. The frustration for a lot of us Co-Workers is to return to a world full of materialism. I say to myself that I will allow the pain and suffering of this poverty to penetrate me so deeply that I will want to change.'

Much the same sentiment was expressed by other Co-Workers. Teresa is a qualified nurse from Ireland. She is in her early thirties, and has been working in Kalighat for ten weeks. 'In another three months, I will return to the society from which I have come, with all its materialism. But Kalighat has altered me for good. Our own contribution is very, very small compared to what Kalighat is giving us. It is an insight into life and death. One of the first things you notice here is the presence of God.'

Mary Cox, fiftyish, from England's stockbroker belt, also wanted specially to work for a few weeks in Kalighat. 'It's the place which I believe is closest to Mother Teresa's heart,' she said. 'But the first morning here, I was physically sick and I didn't think I would be able to cope. I was better the next day. Over a period of time you see the smile of God coming through. In England we have poverty, but it is a spiritual poverty, a loneliness not so evident in Kalighat. Here you see terrible deprivation on the one hand, and tremendous life and love and joy coming through the smiles of some of these people, despite their suffering. It makes us very humble that they can express this joy out of their nothingness. Here you touch the body of Christ in a very special way. What I will find difficult is to go back and keep this vision in my mind and my heart, living as I will do again, in comfort. It must change you. It must do. We are on a pilgrimage in life, and we have to keep on changing.'

By definition, volunteers came for short periods. It is the Sisters who are the backbone of Kalighat. Theirs seemed to me to be an incredibly difficult service. To begin with, it is necessary to be physically strong, as the work involves being nurse, porter and doctor rolled into one, often working eighteen hours at a time, six days a week. It is an endless succession of medication, washing, feeding and cleaning, or simply sitting by to listen to a request, a prayer or a complaint. To sheer physical strength, add compassion and a sense of humour. 'He got a ticket straight to St Peter,' or, 'She went smilingly, she died such a beautiful death,' is a frequent refrain. Despite it being difficult work, all the Missionaries of Charity must be prepared to work with the dying. The irony is that most of them actually plead to be sent to Kalighat. Since this is simply not possible, most must make do with short stints before being sent elsewhere.

It was early evening by the time Sister Suma led me to the women's hall. It was curious how little had changed since my last visit, and yet, in a sense, everything had. When I was last here I had spent time talking with Dalim Das, once a governess with a wealthy family. Dalim was dying of cancer. The disease appeared to have invaded her entire body. She had lost her hair, probably the after-effects of chemotherapy. Sister whispered to me that sometimes her pain was so intense, she screamed for the end to come. Yet all the while she spoke with me, she never made a sound nor expressed any sadness or regret. Her 'indisposition' might have been a slight headache that would go away soon. I was, after all, a stranger, and well-bred ex-governesses did not discuss their ailments in public. She spoke about the years gone by, when she accompanied her wards to Europe, and that made me forget that we were in the Home of the Dying. We might instead have been sipping tea at the Grand Hotel in Chowringhee Street. It was only as our conversation drew to an end, and we both realised that we were unlikely to meet again, that she made a personal admission. She told me that she had fought her cancer for nine years armed only with willpower and prayer; she was a Hindu, but she prayed not only to the vast pantheon of Hindu Gods and God-desses, but to Jesus Christ and Allah besides. For the end of her litany, Dalim reserved a very special prayer, one that she herself composed. It was a little prayer to Mother Teresa. She prayed for her *moksha*, her salvation, that she might escape the cycle of birth and death, with all the pain that accompanied life, and go home finally to God. Sometimes this prayer would assume form and substance, and Dalim Das would find Mother Teresa herself sitting by her side, holding her hand or stroking her brow.

Today, Dalim Das' pallet was occupied by Snehlata, who was suffering from both cancer and tuberculosis. Last week, a Sister found a few biscuits under Snehlata's pillow. 'These are for my children,' she had explained. 'When my sister visits me on Sunday, I shall send these with her.' She had saved her own share of biscuits for her children, for she had nothing else to give them. Sister Suma said to her, 'Snehlata, enjoy your biscuits. I promise you that when your sister comes, I shall send biscuits for your children.' Snehlata shook her head in reply, and Sister did not insist. She understood that Snehlata's act of love would be incomplete without the sacrifice of giving the only thing she could. When her sister came, and Snehlata sent with her the eight biscuits she had saved, it was, as Mother Teresa later described when I told her about the incident, 'giving until it hurt'. Later, the Sisters discovered that the children were not even Snehlata's own. Her husband had rejected her for another woman, and these children were by his second wife.

As we walked past bed number twenty-six, its frail occupant reached out and kissed the Sister's hand. Her name, said the Sister, was Hasina. She laughed and wept alternately. A beggar on Ripon Street, she had a perch under a large shady tree near a busy intersection. Pedestrians and commuters needed to board their buses or change them at this point. Hasina was a favourite amongst the 'regulars', and her little aluminium bowl would fill up quite nicely by the evening. On a very good day, she sometimes made ten rupees. Then disaster struck. A series of strikes in the city disrupted normal life and prevented Hasina from reaching her usual spot. It took a week for the city to get back to normal. When Hasina hurried back, she found that her place had been occupied by a whole family that had spread themselves out over the entire intersection. There was no place for Hasina. Frantic, she tried other spots. Nothing worked. Her anxiety mounted because her own family expected her to contribute her share of her pitiful earnings. Finally, when she was unable to do so, they shut her out of their house. The Sisters found her dying on the street. After about ten days of forced feeding, she recovered. Her children had been informed, but they had not cared to visit her. Each time someone entered the hall, she looked up, hoping it might be her family.

The next afternoon, as we returned from a visit to Tita-garh, I asked Mother Teresa about Kalighat. 'Over the years, we have rescued over 54,000 people from the streets, about half of whom have died a beautiful death.' How could death be beautiful? I asked. Naturally we feel lonely without a loved one, she had explained, but death meant 'going home'. After a pause, she added softly, 'Those who die with us die in peace. For me, that is the greatest development of human life, to die in peace and in dignity, for that is for eternity.' I asked her if she recollected any specially poignant case such as that of the dying priest. She said, 'One day, I picked up a man from an open drain. His body was full of sores. I took him to our Home (Nirmal Hriday). We cleaned and bathed him, and tended to his sores. All the while he made no complaint and there was no fear on his face. All that he said to me was, "I have lived all my life like an animal on the streets, but now I am going to die like an angel!" He gave me a smile and, within three hours of my bringing him in, he died.'

I remembered that Mother Teresa had told me some years ago that she had found a woman lying in a garbage dump, delirious with fever. It was not her fever, nor that she was dying that was breaking her heart. It was the fact that her own son had abandoned her there. Mother Teresa took her to Kalighat and washed and cleaned her. She asked the woman to forgive her son. It took a long while for Mother Teresa to persuade her, but in the end, she did forgive him. As she lay in Mother Teresa's arms, finally at peace with herself, she smiled for the first time, and then she died. Her last words to Mother Teresa were, 'Thank you.' Mother Teresa remembers it to be one of the most beautiful smiles that she has ever received.

11

· 'The Most Powerful Woman in the World' ·

It was 1981. Mother Teresa had just returned from a mission to Ethiopia. A terrible drought in the northern part of that country threatened hundreds of thousands of lives. She had carried a few hundred kilos of medicine and food from Calcutta, but that was a tiny drop in a vast ocean of need. Although there were many international relief agencies helping the beleaguered Ethiopian Government, there appeared to be more confusion and less co-ordination. The poor state of the roads also made it difficult to get supplies to the scores of villages in the interior where they were most desperately needed.

Even after she returned to Calcutta, her concern did not lessen. Together with her Sisters, she prayed (and even fasted) that further tragedy be averted. Finally, as an inspiration, she wrote a letter to the President of the United States. It was about a week later that she received a telephone call from the White House. President Reagan himself came on the line. He thanked her for her letter and assured her on behalf of the American people and himself that he would do everything possible to see that help arrived quickly where it was most urgently needed. He was as good as his word. Not only did the US Government rush in food and medicine, but co-operation with other relief agencies improved significantly. 'After that, thank God, the supplies started to flow, and helicopters reached food to the villages.' It was then that I had remarked for the first time, half-teasingly but with an undercurrent of seriousness, that she was the most powerful woman in the world. In an unaffected way, she had replied with a smile, 'I wish I was. Then I would bring peace to the whole world.'

Without any constituency save that of the least powerful and the poorest, Mother Teresa's entrée into the halls of power is as effortless as her visits to the meanest slums. At home in Calcutta, she can and does walk into the office of the influential Chief Minister of West Bengal 'at any time'. That he has never been known to refuse her anything is well-known in Calcutta. When once asked what he, the head of a Marxist government and an atheist, had in common with Mother Teresa, for whom God was everything, he is said to have replied, 'We both share a love for the poor.' When he was hospitalised for a heart ailment some years ago, she visited him in the nursing home and led her Sisters in prayers for his recovery.

Both Prime Minister Indira Gandhi and her son Rajiv, when he became Prime Minister, saw her whenever she wished. She enjoyed a particularly close relationship with Indira Gandhi. Whenever she wrote to her, Mother Teresa invariably received an immediate reply. Indira Gandhi once wrote: 'To meet her is to feel utterly humble, to sense the power of tenderness, the strength of love.' Although there were differences regarding the sterilisation programme adopted by the government during the Emergency – Mother Teresa had written and spoken against it – when Indira Gandhi was humbled in the 1977 general election and subsequently hounded out of power, Mother Teresa went to see her. When asked why she bothered, she replied publicly, 'She is my friend,' a remark she repeated to me more than once. Mother Teresa's feelings had, of course, nothing to do with politics.

It is not in India alone that all doors are open to Mother Teresa. Wherever she may find herself, should she feel the need to call on a city father or the country's chief executive, she is usually received immediately. Everyone knows that she does not go for herself, but for problems concerning the poor, or on account of some difficulties that her Sisters might face. President Mitterand of France, Prime Minister Major of the United Kingdom, President Reagan and now President Bush of the United States, the King of Belgium, the King of Spain – the list of members of the world's most exclusive club who consider her to be their friend is endless. Of course, being seen with Mother Teresa is good for one's image. And there have been occasions when heads of state and government have confided in her in times of stress. Being at the top is usually very lonely, and those at the pinnacle often do not have many people with whom they can share their problems of conscience.

Father van Exem told me of an amusing story that concerned her encounter with the former President of Pakistan, General Zia-ul-Haq. In response to an invitation from the local bishop, Mother Teresa decided to visit Pakistan. She applied for a visa on her Indian passport from the Pakistan Embassy in New Delhi. Not only was she given a visa; she was invited by General Zia-ul-Haq himself to visit any part of the country. To facilitate this, he even placed his own plane at her disposal. He generously invited her to open convents whenever she wished. There was, however, one condition. She could bring nuns from any part of the world except India! 'I don't think Mother Teresa took that seriously, because there are several Indian nuns in the Mission's establishments in Pakistan,' said Father van Exem.

It was calamity that took her post-haste to India's other neighbour, Bangladesh. Early in May 1991, when I was visiting Mother Teresa in Calcutta, a devastating cyclone hit the coastal areas of Bangladesh. It brought tragedy in its wake, and 300,000 people are estimated to have died. Mother Teresa was recovering from a heart problem and had only just been discharged from hospital. In spite of her doctor's advice, she decided that it was necessary for her to go. Accompanied by two of her Sisters, she quickly packed some boxes of essential drugs.

I know that she barely had time to inform her Sisters in Dacca of her arrival. Certainly no-one else knew of her visit. Yet shortly after her arrival, the international media focused on the ailing nun visiting scenes of devastation. She was accompanied throughout by the Prime Minister of Bangladesh, Begum Khaleda Zia. When their helicopter had to make an emergency landing because of rough weather, the story was carried by all the networks. When she returned to Calcutta, she said to me, 'I am glad I went. The misery and tragedy of human suffering was terrible to see. The greatest need now is to send food and medicine and something with which to clean the water. My Sisters are right there where help is needed.' Natural calamities, as Third World countries are all too sadly aware, are often events of peripheral interest to the West. Watching various networks focus on Mother Teresa, it was quite apparent that her presence at the scenes of devastation helped to generate an immediate and widespread response.

One of her more interesting encounters was with the Ethiopian court just before the coup that toppled Emperor Haile Selassie. In 1973, Mother Teresa had been able to open a mission in Ethiopia with considerable difficulty. It was only a meeting with Emperor Haile Selassie's daughter, which had not been easy to arrange, that paved the way for an audience with the Emperor. Mother Teresa had been cautioned not to be over-optimistic, as many organisations, religious and social, had attempted to begin work in Ethiopia without success. Mother Teresa soon realised, in her practical way, that the Emperor alone could decide. The actual audience was preceded by a session with the Palace Chamberlain which went as follows:

'What do you want from the Government?'
'Nothing,' answered Mother. 'I have only come to offer my Sisters to work among the poor suffering people.'

'What will the Sisters do?'
'We will give whole-hearted free service to the poorest of the poor.'

'What qualifications do they have?'
'We try to bring tender love and compassion for the unwanted and the unloved.'

'I see you have a different approach. Do you preach to the people, trying to convert them?'
'Our works of love reveal to the suffering poor the love of God for them.'

When Mother Teresa was finally ushered into the Emperor's presence, his response was unexpected. He spoke only a few words:

'I have heard about the good work you do. I am very happy you have come. Yes, let your Sisters come to Ethiopia.'

Barely a year later, on 12 September 1974, the eighty-one-year-old Emperor was deposed in a military coup and imprisoned in Addis Ababa with his entire family. The conditions in the jail were so appalling that it evoked protests. Many heads of state in Africa, Europe and elsewhere wrote to the Revolutionary government, urging humane treatment to the erstwhile royal family. Haile Selassie himself died in detention. Mother Teresa was to tell me that she was the only person allowed to visit them in prison, and later was able to help towards their release.

Quite understandably, her relations with the Head of the Catholic Church, Pope John Paul II, are very good. She invariably refers to him as 'Holy Father' and looks upon him as a real father. She admires his simplicity. She deeply appreciated his offering a place to the Missionaries of Charity in the Vatican, where they have set up a soup kitchen for the destitute of Rome. Not only does it serve as an acknowledgement of the presence of the poor, it has helped to demystify the aura of the Vatican as an oasis of great splendour and wealth. Whether the fact that both are Slavs – he is Polish and she a Yugoslav Albanian – has contributed to their mutual understanding and respect is a matter of conjecture. The Pope certainly holds her in great regard, and admires her for her outspoken defence of the Church's traditional values.

On 22 January 1992, I was privileged to meet the Pope in the Vatican, a meeting arranged by Mother Teresa herself. I was led into a small private chamber, where I spent a few minutes alone with him. At that very time, Mother Teresa lay critically ill in a California hospital. The Pope was praying for her recovery, and looked forward to her stopping in Rome on her way back to Calcutta. He recalled his own visit to Calcutta in early February 1986. He had driven straight from the airport to Kalighat. There he went from person to person, not only giving each his blessings, but actually serving them with food and water. He told me how moving the experience had been, and recalled it vividly.

We spoke about the premises that he had given to Mother Teresa in the Vatican, adjoining the very chamber in which we sat. 'How could I refuse?' he said, when Mother Teresa had made the request. He was happy to have done so, and every Christmas, and whenever else he was able, he went to the House to serve the poor himself.

Before I left, I said that the only person whose advice Mother Teresa might heed in slowing down her punishing pace was his. He laughed and said, 'When it comes to her work, she does not listen even to me, but I will try.'

Not all her intercessions are successful. Many a time she has written letters or spoken to authorities about issues about which she has felt strongly. Such is the personal regard in which she is held, she almost always receives an immediate reply or explanation. But this is not always followed by action. On some issues, government or local policies, or even opposition from the people, dictate otherwise. Sometimes the issues involved are beyond her reach. Even there, if she feels strongly she does intervene without involving herself with the politics of the issue. At the point of conflict between Iraq and the USA, Mother Teresa addressed a joint letter on 2 January 1991 to both Presidents. She wrote: 'In the short term there may be winners and losers in this war that we all dread, but that never can and never will justify the suffering, pain and loss of life which your weapons will cause.'* One of the unexpected results was that when the war ended she received a reply from the Health Minister of Iraq, inviting her Sisters to Iraq to help the orphaned and disabled.

At a time when people crave recognition and many work single-mindedly towards obtaining it, it is ironic that a woman who stands as a curious contradiction to everything this age holds dear keeps no count of the awards that have been heaped upon her. Apparently, some years ago the Sisters did attempt to compile a list, but it was incomplete. In any case, it was soon rendered out of date because, in that year alone, Mother Teresa was conferred over twenty

* The entire text of this letter is in Appendix III.

honours, large and small. The Sisters gave up. Not long ago, I asked Sister Priscilla (who keeps the general statistics) to give me whatever information she had. She sighed and finally offered me a record, which she said was the best she could manage. It was two years old. The implication was clear: if I considered a list of honours to be important, I would have to research and prepare it myself! This did not prove to be an easy task. Even the tentative record that I managed to produce ran into many pages. At the end of the exercise, I was left in little doubt that Mother Teresa deserved an entry in the Guinness Book of Records on this count alone!

For a woman who never went to university, Mother Teresa holds a string of honorary doctorates conferred on her by some of the most prestigious universities. They range from an honorary degree in Divinity from the University of Cambridge, to that of Humane Letters from the University of San Diego. Harvard University awarded her their honorary doctorate amidst an unprecedented standing ovation. She holds an honorary doctorate of Law from the University of Madras, and another from the Vishva Bharati University of Shantiniketan in West Bengal, an institution founded by Rabindranath Tagore. Not to be outstripped by universities, a number of American cities have presented her with their keys, among them Miami, Scranton (Pennsylvania), Toledo (Ohio), New York, Washington, Newark (New Jersey), San Francisco and San José. Innumerable magazines have nominated her 'Woman of the Year' in their annual polls. For three straight years, the readership of *Good Housekeeping* magazine edged out Jackie Kennedy, Madonna and Queen Elizabeth to vote her as their 'Most Admired Woman', an extraordinary tribute to a wrinkled old lady in a sari that costs about a dollar, from the readership of a magazine whose pages are filled with designer clothes, fashionable houses and advertisements that promote a frenzied quest for an eternally smooth skin. She went on to adorn postage stamps in Sweden and in India. Holland, not to be outdone, has named a tulip after her.

However, the first recognition of her work, fourteen years after she began it, came from her adopted country. On 26 January 1962, in the customary list of honours announced on India's Republic Day, was the name of Mother Teresa, who had been nominated for the Padma Shri (the Order of the Lotus). This was the first time that a person not born an Indian was given this distinguished award. She was invited to go to New Delhi to receive it from the President. Her first impulse was reluctance, prompted by the conviction that she had done nothing to deserve it. It was the Archbishop of Calcutta who advised her to accept, as a recognition of the poor. In September that year, she was ushered into the chandeliered Durbar Hall of the magnificent Presidential Palace, the Rashtrapati Bhavan. Earlier, eschewing the offer of a limousine to drive her from the Convent, she drove past the resplendent President's bodyguard and cavalry in the ambulance-cum-general purpose van of her Delhi mission.

Mrs Pandit, a former Indian High Commissioner to London and sister of Prime Minister Nehru, was present that morning. She gave a vivid account of the ceremony. 'The sari-clad nun, a picture of humility, walked up to the dais. She took the award as if she was taking a sick child or a dying man in her arms. The hall went mad. There were tears in the eyes of the President. Later, when we were going home, I asked my brother, "Wasn't that a moving thing?" He said, "I don't know how you felt, but I had great difficulty in restraining my tears."'

Upon her return to Calcutta, Mother Teresa was to install the beribboned medal around the neck of a small statue of the Virgin, placed in a glass case at Nirmal Hriday in Kalighat. Not for a moment was she lulled into believing that it was she who was deserving. To this day, this first of innumerable honours adorns the statue of the one whom Mother Teresa believes is deserving of praise.

The timing of the Ramon Magsaysay Award from the Philippines, which came a few months later, was particularly opportune. It was in 1960 that Mother Teresa had been permitted, for the first time, to set up establishments outside the Archdiocese of Calcutta. She was especially keen to start an institution for leprosy sufferers in Agra, the city of the Taj Mahal. On the very day that she had informed her Sisters that she would have to postpone the project for want of funds, the announcement of the Award and the 50,000 rupees that came with it seemed to be divine intervention. Similarly, the US $21,500 that accompanied the first International Pope John XXIII Prize (1971), went into the much-needed development of the leprosy settlement at Shantinagar. Close on the heels of this came the Joseph Kennedy Jr Foundation Award. The Foundation's purpose was research into the causes and treatment of mental retardation. At a ceremony held in Washington, where the Kennedy clan was present in full force, Mother Teresa received the award, which carried US $15,000 with it. With this she founded a home for crippled, spastic and mentally retarded children in Dum Dum, Calcutta. Appropriately, she named it the Nirmala Kennedy Centre.

The highest award that can be given by the British Monarch, the Order of Merit, was conferred on Mother Teresa by Queen Elizabeth on 24 November 1983. Instituted in 1902, and limited to twenty-four members, its investiture is the personal prerogative of the Queen. The actual presentation was made some months later, during the Queen's visit to India for the Commonwealth Heads of Government meeting in 1984. It was in the gardens of the Rashtrapati Bhavan, where the Queen was staying, that the medal was presented by one of the world's wealthiest persons to one who could claim to possess but three saris. After the simple ceremony, they spoke to each other alone for a few minutes. In the course of researching this book, I asked Mother Teresa what they spoke about. 'Her son,' she replied. 'Son?' I enquired, 'which son? She has three.' 'Oh,' said Mother Teresa, 'I thought she had only one. She spoke about Prince Charles, and told me how much he admired our work. He had visited Nirmala Shishu Bhawan in Calcutta some years before.' On that occasion, he had also joined her in a prayer in their simple chapel.

Princess Diana, too, was eager to meet Mother Teresa and see the work of the Missionaries of Charity. A visit to the Mission was arranged during her official visit to India with Prince Charles in February 1992. She was unable to see Mother Teresa, because the nun (who had miraculously survived a severe cardiac attack while she was visiting one of the Mission's houses in Tijuana, Mexico) had suffered a relapse in Rome, en route to Calcutta. The Princess reflected her deep concern by making an unscheduled stop to see her in Rome on her way back to London.

The first member of the Royal Family to meet Mother Teresa was Prince Philip. The occasion was when she was invited to receive the first Templeton Prize for Progress in Religion, in London on 25 April 1973. Prince Philip had agreed to present the award. On that occasion he spoke about 'a tremendous power that had entered Mother Teresa'. He observed that she had shown by her life what people could do when faith is strong. 'By any standard, what she has done is good, and the world today is desperately in need of this sort of goodness, this sort of practical compassion.' The Templeton Prize exceeded even the Nobel Price in value. Its purpose was 'to stimulate the knowledge of God on the part of mankind everywhere'. From 2,000 nominations received from eighty countries, nine judges drawn from the major world religions had selected Mother Teresa. The citation stated that 'she has been instrumental in widening and deepening man's knowledge and love of God, and thereby furthering the quest for the quality of life that mirrors the divine.' Four years later, in 1977, Prince Philip, this time as Chancellor of Cambridge University, conferred on her the University's honorary degree of Divinity. As is well-known, this University had been the theological centre of the Reformation after the separation of the Church of England from Rome. Perhaps for this reason, Mother Teresa travelled especially to England to receive the degree. Here, in an unusually long speech, she spoke about the Eucharist. Earlier, in his own introductory remarks, Prince Philip remarked with dry wit that 'the Reverend Mother, whom we are delighted to see among us, would reply, if you inquired about her career, that it was of no importance.' The assembly burst into cheers.

'I am unworthy,' was her first reaction when she was told that she had been named as the recipient of the ultimate accolade, the Nobel Prize for Peace. She sent word to the organisers that she would accept the award 'in the name of the poor', which the Norwegian Nobel Committee acknowledged. Many people had been disappointed by some of the preceding selections of the Committee, for not all were doves of peace. It seemed to them that the Peace Award needed to be restored to the tradition of Albert Luthuli, Fridtjof Nansen, Albert Schweitzer and Martin Luther King Jr. The choice of Mother Teresa came as much-needed reassurance that politics was not the only way to pursue peace. There were many who believed that it was Mother Teresa who had, with her acceptance, enhanced the Award.

Accompanied by her first two postulants, Sisters Agnes and Gertrude, Mother Teresa arrived in Oslo on 9 December 1979. If anyone had not heard of her before, the four days she spent in Oslo changed all that. From the time she arrived to the time she left, she was subject to the most relentless media attention. Hundreds of photographers, TV crews and journalists had especially converged on Oslo to cover her every step. Even today, long years after the event, she shudders at the thought. 'For that publicity alone, I should go straight to heaven,' she has often said.

On 10 December 1979, in the presence of the King of Norway, diplomats and high officials, as well as the enormous press battery, the Nobel Prize (£90,000) was awarded to this slightly bent, sari-clad woman in the Aula Magna of the University of Oslo. The Chairman of the Norwegian Nobel Committee, Professor John Sannes, spoke movingly when he said:

'The hallmark of her work has been respect for the individual and the individual's worth and dignity. The loneliest and the most wretched, the dying destitute, the abandoned lepers, have been received by her and her Sisters with warm compassion devoid of condescension, based on this reverence for Christ in Man. . . . In her eyes the person who, in the accepted sense, is the recipient, is also the giver and the one who gives the most. Giving – giving something of oneself – is what confers real joy, and the person who is allowed to give is the one who receives the most precious gift. Where others see clients or customers, she sees fellow-workers, a relationship based not on the expectation of gratitude on the one part, but on mutual understanding and respect, and a warm human and enriching contact. . . . This is the life of Mother Teresa and her Sisters – a life of strict poverty and long days and nights of toil, a life that affords little room for other joys but the most precious.'

Sannes concluded: 'There would be no better way of describing the intentions that have motivated the decision of the Norwegian Nobel Committee than the comment of the President of the World Bank, Robert S. McNamara, when he declared, "Mother Teresa deserves Nobel's Peace Prize because she promotes peace in the most fundamental manner by her confirmation of the inviolability of human dignity.'''

Mother Teresa's acceptance speech was prefaced, in her usual manner, by a prayer, copies of which had already been placed on every seat. At her request, 800 voices joined her in the intonation of St Francis of Assisi's immortal prayer for peace. Then, in her unaffected way, Mother Teresa offered to the glittering audience in black tie and formal dress, a vision of the poor, their unselfishness and spirit of sharing. She told them about a woman she had rescued from the streets. She was dying. Mother Teresa took her to the Home for the Dying in Kalighat and told the Sisters that she, herself, would take care of her. 'I did for her all that my love can do. I put her in bed, and there was such a beautiful smile on her face. She took hold of my hand, and she said one word only, "Thank you" – and she died.'

She continued: 'I could not help examining my conscience before her, and I asked what would I say if I was in her place. And my answer was very simple. I would have tried to draw a little attention to myself. I would have said, "I am hungry, that I am dying, I am cold, I am in pain," or something, but she gave much, much more. She gave me her grateful love.'

She also spoke about the poverty of the West: 'Around the world, not only in the poor countries, I found the poverty of the West so much more difficult to remove. When I pick up a person from the street, hungry, I give him a plate of rice, a piece of bread, I have satisfied, I have removed that hunger. But a person that is shut out, that feels unwanted, unloved, terrified, the person that has been thrown out from society – that poverty is so hurtful, and so much, that I find it very difficult. Our Sisters are working amongst that kind of people in the West.'

Mother Teresa convinced the organisers of the Nobel Committee to cancel the customary awards banquet and, instead, offer the money saved for those who really needed a meal. Almost as much as the presentation of the award itself, this gesture captured the imagination of people. There was an outpouring of emotion, which brought in its wake considerably more than was saved from foregoing the banquet. Ordinary people all over Norway, Sweden and elsewhere in Europe, including little children who gave of their pocket money, collected another £36,000. When added to the sum of £3,000 saved from the cancellation of the banquet, this amounted to almost half the award money. Asked how she proposed to utilise the prize money, she remarked with a laugh, 'I have already spent the money in my mind.'

Upon her return to Calcutta, she found bands and receptions awaiting her. After Rabindranath Tagore, who received the Nobel Prize for Literature in 1913, Mother Teresa was the second Indian to receive an award from the Nobel Foundation. 'Joy swept Calcutta,' headlined the Calcutta *Statesman*, which had followed her activities from the very start of her work. Mother Teresa's response to the deluge of letters, telegrams and telephone calls, not to mention the media which had parked itself outside Motherhouse, was typical. She disappeared into strict retreat for a month. By the time she emerged, the photographers and journalists had dispersed.

But no sooner did she emerge than came the announcement that India had conferred on her its highest honour, the Bharat Ratna. Only seventeen distinguished citizens had received this award before. Like the Padma Shri she had received in 1962, this was also the first time that someone not born an Indian had been conferred the Bharat Ratna.

Over the years, I have attended a number of ceremonies where Mother Teresa has been the guest of honour or where she has received some commendation. At first I thought that her restlessness on these occasions was on account of fatigue. I gradually realised that she was actually uncomfortable. Whenever I have had occasion to drive her to such an event, she would invariably say a little prayer in the chapel before she set out, or murmur a prayer in the car. She once told me that she prayed for inspiration before she spoke. Father van Exem confided to me that she sometimes got tired of the number of invitations she received from churchmen. She even told the Pope, 'Holy Father, so many cardinals and bishops ask me to come to meetings and to speak. I cannot, it is too much for me. I have to be busy with my congregation, with my Sisters. They are all over the world now. I am sick, I am old. Give me an order that when a Cardinal or a Bishop wants me to come, that I can tell them that the Holy Father has forbidden me to go.' The Pope answered with a smile, 'I shall think about it.' 'He is still thinking,' said Father van Exem with a chuckle.

It was this discomfort that I noticed, when I sat with her in the wings of the packed auditorium where she was about to be given yet another award, this time from the hands of India's Prime Minister, Narasimha Rao. She looked around the hall and said, 'This publicity, these lights, this also is a form of humiliation. I accept this, as I did the Nobel Prize, only as a recognition of the poor.' Halfway through the lengthy ceremony of customary speeches, she asked to be excused because she had to catch a flight to Calcutta. On the way to the airport, she remembered that she had left behind the award on the dais. She asked me to collect it for her. I asked her what she planned to do with it. 'Sell it,' she said matter-of-factly. 'I am sure the Organisers won't mind. I think I will be able to get 10,000 rupees for it. It will come in useful for buying medicines for our leprosy patients in Titagarh.'

It is no coincidence that Mother Teresa had named the Leprosy Centre in Titagarh 'Gandhiji Prem Niwas' after the Mahatma. Mother Teresa had never met Mahatma Gandhi, but she recognised a kindred soul in him, for both shared the spirit of renunciation and compassion. He was a Hindu who sought to strengthen India's fundamental values and cultural ethos, and in doing so enveloped all faiths. Far from being an old-fashioned evangelist, Mother Teresa's life and work have demonstrated the breadth of her Catholicism. While the Mahatma was a man spurred by impulses that went beyond politics, Mother Teresa eschews politics completely. Yet they both understood well the power of symbolism. She gave up her convent habit for a coarse sari woven by leprous hands, and he wore a handspun dhoti, not elegantly draped down to his feet, but as a loincloth. Both had the same purpose: to identify with the very poorest by becoming as poor as they.

No nun in the history of the Church had ever attempted such an unorthodox way before. Despite hardships, she converted her poverty into freedom and created from her nothingness a powerful instrument for religious and social action. Gandhiji, meanwhile, had created *satyagraha*, a nonviolent striving after truth. He called it an argument of suffering, voluntarily undergone. Knowing that he was unable to match the might of Empire by conventional means, he developed 'nonviolence' as his weapon. With it he inspired his followers to accept even physical torment without resistance, until the perpetrator was shamed into ceasing. In this, both Gandhi and Mother Teresa came to recognise the power of innocent suffering.

Neither lacked physical courage. At the height of the fiercest communal carnage, Gandhi rushed into the heart of the worst-affected areas to bring about an end to the killings. By his own example he turned the blows of police *lathis* and detention in prison, once demeaning, into badges of moral and emotional commitment. Mother Teresa also believes that her own life is of no importance. She has often been amongst the first to reach areas affected by a cyclone, earthquake, flood or war. Arriving in Beirut in August 1982, when the conflict there was at its height, Mother Teresa learned that a number of mentally ill children were trapped without food and water in West Beirut, where the shelling was heaviest. Ignoring the warnings of the local authorities, including church leaders, that it would be suicide to proceed, Mother Teresa and her Sisters went in a Red Cross van to rescue the children. Miraculously, the snipers held their fire, enabling them to achieve the rescue operation.

Many years earlier, when she started the Home for the Dying, there was an uproar from the priests in the Kali temple and the local people. They went to the police to complain that a foreign lady was converting the poor to Christianity. There were threats; angry young men brick-batted the entrance to Nirmal Hriday. One day, when several stones came hurtling through the windows, Mother Teresa stepped out to confront the group. With her hands outstretched, she approached the mob. She said, 'Kill me if you want to, but do not disturb those inside. Let them die in peace.' For several long moments tensions crackled in the air. Then a hush descended and the agitators turned away.

Both Gandhi and Mother Teresa share a curious combination of religious conservatism and radical empiricism. At heart, Gandhi always remained deeply conservative. Mother Teresa, too, has remained faithful to the official interpretation of the Catholic doctrine, particularly on abortion and family planning. All too often she has been criticised as the 'last obedient woman' of the church, an anachronism in the face of the winds of liberalism. Some years ago, a well-known feminist described Mother Teresa as a 'religious imperialist'. The story made headlines around the world. It was a pity that she had not studied Mother Teresa more closely. For, without diluting her faith, Mother Teresa has adapted it to permit her to transcend the barriers of religion. When the Bharatiya Vidya Bhavan, a much respected Indian organisation set up for the regeneration of Indian culture and values, conferred on Mother Teresa its highest honour, they spoke of her as 'a quiet but courageous crusader who, in a God-inspired moment, launched a mission of mercy and compassion, reaching out to alleviate the suffering of millions the world over – the nameless, voiceless, homeless, depressed and dispossessed, whom Mahatma Gandhi christened the "*daridra narayans*".' Its President concluded with the words: 'She is one of those rare souls who has transcended all barriers of race, religion, creed and nation. She aspires for no kingdom, no honour, not even salvation or *moksha*. She is a true *Vaishnavajana* – minstrel of God – wholly dedicated to the removal of *peeda paraayi* (the pain of others), in the manner of Mahatma Gandhi.'

· *Epilogue* ·

Mother Teresa has often told me that she has never read a single book about herself or her work. I never needed to ask why. Even if she had wished to, she would not allow herself the luxury of being deflected from the 'real work', even for a few hours. I was always conscious of the amount of time, sometimes as much as an hour, that she spared on many occasions to answer my questions or explain her beliefs. Knowing that she would make up for lost time by working late into the night, I tried to make these sessions as brief as possible. I soon realised that the best time to talk to her was when we travelled together, so I tried to accompany her on as many trips as possible.

One afternoon, while we sat in the parlour of Mother-house, I told her that I had written the Prologue and would like to read her a few paragraphs. Before she could say 'no', I began. Now, an essential trait of Mother Teresa is that once she undertakes something, or talks to someone, she gives that work or person her undivided attention. Listening intently, she nodded a few times in emphatic approval. Finally, she said in her simple way, 'Very good, very good. Get it published everywhere!'

It was then I mentioned to her, that while I did not wish to burden her with the rest, it would help considerably if she would designate someone to provide me with information or settle my doubts when she was away. Her organisation was growing at such a fast pace that statistics, names and places were constantly in danger of becoming dated. Besides, as a Hindu, there were occasional aspects of her faith where my understanding was incomplete or inadequate. Mother Teresa nodded again and, after a moment's thought, suggested Sister Joseph Michael. However, she enjoined me not to take up too much of her time, as, being one of her four Councillors-General, Sister Michael already had her hands full. In the course of the last eighteen months, this Sister, with her gentle smile, made time for me, often at short notice. She gave me letters of introduction to the Superiors in the Mission houses I wished to visit, without which they would not have answered my questions.

It was Sister Joseph Michael who asked me whether I had met Father van Exem, and when I said that I had not even heard of him, she arranged a meeting. No-one but Father van Exem could have made Mother Teresa's early years – especially the years when the Mission was just a gleam in her eye – come alive so vividly. No visit to Calcutta was complete without long talks with him. His prodigious memory, gentle manners and sense of humour were powerful magnets that made him a major reference point for me. Many times our conversation would begin thus: 'Did I tell you what happened that afternoon?' He could as easily have been referring to an event of the previous week as to one which took place forty or more years ago. He would then proceed to unfold some new revelation about Mother Teresa or her work, or recount an amusing anecdote about his own days as a priest in Calcutta. In the course of these talks, Father van Exem pointed the way to milestones in Mother Teresa's life which I might otherwise have missed. Sometimes he referred me to people with whom he thought it would be useful to speak.

The last time I met Mother Teresa before entrusting this book to my publisher was on 2 May 1992. She was busy that day in a meeting with her Regional Superiors, who had gathered from all over India. She came out of the meeting briefly, to tell me that I could see her after her evening prayers. I decided instead to attend the service. Observing her for the better part of an hour, I found it difficult to believe that, only a short time ago, she lay critically ill in a California hospital. Clearly, St Peter was not ready. I remember her telling me how once, soon after starting her work, she developed a very high fever. In a delirious state, she went before St Peter. He told her to return home, for there were no slums in heaven. She became angry and replied that she would fill heaven with her people from the slums. This is why, whenever someone in Kalighat dies a particularly 'beautiful' death, the Sisters say: 'Oh, he went smilingly. He got a ticket straight to St Peter.'

To watch Mother Teresa in prayer is an extraordinary experience, for she is completely at one with her God. No-one, nothing else matters at the time. When she bends double to touch her head to the ground in obeisance, her surrender is complete. As I watch her, I can't help but ask myself, for the thousandth time, how one even begins to explain her in everyday terms. She is not a genius. She has a good mind, but is very ordinary in many ways. Of course, she works very hard, and is practical and effective. She never went to university, nor had the time to read much, other than the scriptures. How then, can one explain the monumental achievements for which she is responsible? There is no direct relationship between the number of Missionaries and the strength and influence that they exert. The number of people who are alive today because of this woman's vision – the hungry, the ill and destitute, the victims of famine and disaster, both divine and manmade, whose plight she has directly alleviated and upon whom she has focused attention would run into hundreds of thousands, even millions. In addition, are the number of people that she has inspired.

Epilogue

People who have never met Mother Teresa, who have simply read about her in a book or a magazine, have been inspired to do something themselves. As she kneels before the altar, what alternative do I have but to consider the mysterious spiritual God-Divine factor? As if explaining my lingering doubts, she once said, 'I am an instrument, a little pencil in the hands of the Lord. Even today, God shows His humility by making use of instruments as weak and imperfect as we are.' She was not just saying it, she really believed it. How else can one explain her remarkable achievements?

The prayers are over. The last of the worshippers has left. It is dusk. Mother Teresa joins me on the little bench on the bridge outside the chapel. I ask her what changes she believes her work has brought to the people of her adopted city. 'We have come a long way,' she replied. 'The people of Calcutta have come to know and love the poor. No-one is left to die on the road. Someone, somewhere will pick up the man and bring him to us. I have seen children pick up and take old people from the street to Kalighat. People of all faiths come to share in the work. They say, "Mother Teresa, we want to help." They are willing to touch the poor, no? That is the beauty of the work. It is the same everywhere else.'

Her work has expanded throughout the world, and yet it is difficult to imagine her belonging anywhere other than Calcutta. Her life and that of the city have come to be inextricably bound, one nurturing the other, each strangely incomplete without the other. Millions around the world know her as 'Mother Teresa of Calcutta'. It is almost as if it were a title. For the people of Calcutta, she is one of its presiding deities, certainly its conscience keeper. The Governor of West Bengal once told me that whenever he meets Mother Teresa, he asks himself, 'What have I done to serve humanity?' Like thousands of others, he too feels humbled by her presence.

Keep the joy of loving
God in your heart
and share this joy with
all you meet
especially your family.
God bless you
M Teresa m c

It is no wonder, then, that the people of the State call her the 'Mother of Bengal'.

'Ma, Ma,' – suddenly there is a shout at the door downstairs. A Sister comes to tell Mother Teresa that it is a beggar, insisting that she come down. He says he must speak only to Mother Teresa. She goes down. I follow her. The beggar has not come for food or alms. Instead he has come to make her a gift of his day's earnings. There are a few coins in a metal bowl, perhaps a rupee or two at most. For a moment, Mother Teresa seems undecided. If she takes it, he will go without food that night. If she refuses, she will hurt his feelings. She decides to accept. He kisses her hand with joy. When we returned to the bench, she looked at me and said, 'He gave me everything that he had. He probably won't eat tonight. I value this gift much more than I value the Nobel Prize and all the other awards that I have received.'

I prepare now to take my leave. The manuscript is finally ready. When I think back on the five years it has taken me to write this book, I realise that, not once, did she refuse me anything. She made no imposition, no demand, not even the whiff of a suggestion. She only gave. It has been the culmination of an experience that has enriched and strengthened me. For I have had the inestimable value of her advice, her blessings and her prayers. The last time we met, she said to me, 'I have never given to anyone else this kind of opportunity. Whatever you do, do it for the glory of God and the good of the people. Achha, take care of yourself and your wife and daughters. And, before I forget, give these prayers from me to the girls.'

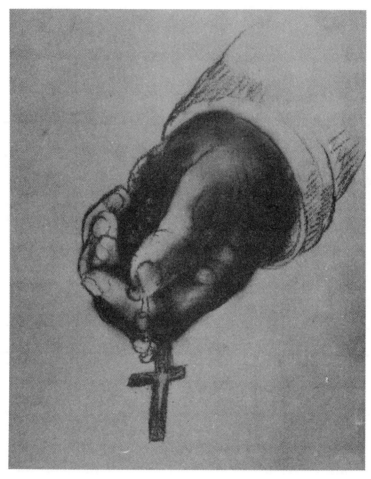

Drawing of Mother Teresa's hand by Manjit Bawa, 1992.

Appendix I

A Conversation With Mother Teresa

Question Mother, as you look over your life, would you
    say that it has been one of happiness?
*Mother Teresa The happiness that no-one can take from me. There
    has never been a doubt or any unhappiness.*

Question Are the Sisters from all over India? Are their
    parents happy?
*Mother Teresa The Sisters are from all over India; their parents
    are very happy to give God their own child, it is a big thing.
    It has to be a sacrifice also, a very big sacrifice. No, there is
    no sadness, but a sacrifice. Sacrifice does not cause sadness,
    especially when you give up to God.*

Question But sacrifice is a difficult thing.
*Mother Teresa No. When you give it to God, there is a greater
    love. These girls want to give their best. They make to God
    a total surrender. They give up their position, their house,
    their parents, their future, dedicating it also to God through
    the poorest of the poor.*

Question Over all these years that you have been
    separated from your own family . . .
*Mother Teresa Where? They have all gone to heaven. There is
    nobody on earth.*

Question But over the years, despite the sacrifice, there is
    the human bond.

Mother Teresa Of course. Naturally, that, nobody can separate. The beautiful thing is that you give it to God and that is very important. 'If you want to give, my disciple, take up the cross,' Jesus says. Very simple, there is no difficulty.

Question Does your Order expect total obedience?

Mother Teresa Total obedience, wholehearted service, complete poverty and undivided love for Christ. Since the Sisters are going to bind themselves by their vows, they must know what these are going to mean. The vow of obedience means that we have to do God's will in everything. The vow of poverty is very strict in our Congregation. We take the vow of chastity, our hearts entirely dedicated to Christ. Finally we take a unique fourth vow – that of giving wholehearted free service to the poor. We cannot work for the rich, nor can we accept any money for our work.

Question How is it that all the Sisters look so happy?

Mother Teresa We want the poor to feel loved. We cannot go to them with sad faces. God loves a cheerful giver. He gives most who gives with joy.

Question What happens if any of the Sisters feel they have made a mistake [in joining]?

Mother Teresa They are free to go. But once they have made vows, if they want to go, they can ask permission. Very few have left. It is quite extraordinary that most of our Sisters have been so faithful.

Question What about doubts in day-to-day matters, for example, about how work should be structured? Can they come to you?

Mother Teresa We are a normal family, only with big numbers. But we are a normal family, we share everything together, that makes the difference, I think.

Question In the midst of great faith can there be doubt, for instance in performing a task?

Mother Teresa It depends for whom you are doing the task. A mother has no doubt when she serves her child. Because she loves. It changes everything in her life. The same thing for us. If we are really in love with Christ, this doubt does not come. Maybe a longing comes to do better, but not doubt. I wouldn't call it a doubt. Doubt disturbs.

Question Most of us have doubts. Are we doing the right thing?

Mother Teresa No, that's not a doubt. You want to do greater good for the child. You want to do something better. That's not doubt. Doubt takes away your freedom.

Question When one is face to face with someone who is physically maimed, suffering from leprosy, crawling with maggots, then having to touch such a person might cause a doubt.

Mother Teresa That's fear, that's not doubt.

Question How is that overcome?

Mother Teresa First of all with prayer, but if you really love that person then it will be easier for you to accept that person and it will be with love and kindness. For that is an opportunity for you to put your love for God in living action. For love begins at home. And for us in our Scriptures it is very clearly said. What Jesus said was, 'Whatever you do to the least of my brethren, you do it to me.' If you give a glass of water in my name, you give it to me. I was hungry. I was naked. I was lonely. Faith is a gift of God, which comes through prayer. The fruit of silence is prayer, the fruit of prayer is faith and the fruit of faith is love, the fruit of love is service and the fruit of service is peace. So it is a whole connection.

Question From where do you get your strength?

Mother Teresa The Mass is the spiritual food that sustains me. I could not pass a single day or hour in my life without it. In the Eucharist, I see Christ in the appearance of bread. In the slums, I see Christ in the distressing disguise of the poor – in the broken bodies, in the children, in the dying. That is why this work becomes possible.

Question I want to ask you a question which many people who know that I have worked with you in a small way often ask. They say you stand for peace, they also say, whether you like it or not, that you are the world's most powerful woman.

Mother Teresa (interrupts) Do they? I wish I was. Then I will bring peace in the world (laughs).

Question You can pick up a telephone and reach a President or a Prime Minister because you speak in the name of peace.

Mother Teresa In the name of Christ. Without Him I could do nothing.

Question Whereas you work to bring about peace, why is it you do not work, they ask, to lessen war?

Mother Teresa If you are working for peace, that peace lessens war. But I won't mix in politics. War is the fruit of politics, and so I don't involve myself, that's all. If I get stuck in politics, I will stop loving. Because I will have to stand by one, not by all. This is the difference.

Question Mother, when you go into situations like riots, don't you feel fear?

Mother Teresa Fear for what?

Question Fear for (hesitation) . . .

Mother Teresa Fear for going to God! (laughs).

Question Or fear for your Sisters?

Mother Teresa No, we have given our lives to God. (Pause) Once we were going to go to Sudan with food, to Southern Sudan. We have our Sisters in Northern Sudan. There was danger of shooting, and the Government did not want us to go. Five of us signed [a declaration] that we were ready to die if the plane was shot down. The next day when we were to leave, [the rebels] said, 'We will shoot the plane.' The pilot refused to go. Otherwise we would have certainly gone.

Question In the early days, did you have many obstacles? I read about a case when you wanted to start a leprosy colony in Titagarh, local people opposed it because people are afraid of leprosy.

Mother Teresa But once they saw, they understood. Even outside India, sometimes we have that opposition, but once they see the work, they understand. You see, when the people come in touch with the poor they realise how beautiful they are.

Question Aren't you spreading yourself too thin, channelling your missions and opening houses in so many countries?

Mother Teresa Because we are Missionaries of Charity, and a missionary is a person who has to go and spread the good news it makes no difference. Today in India, tomorrow in Europe, anywhere the voice of God calls you. And a missionary is a person who is sent to become a carrier of God's love. That's why we are Missionaries of Charity. Double. Like somebody said to me, 'You are spoiling the poor by giving everything to them.' Then I said, 'Nobody has spoiled us more than God Himself.' Because He is also giving. And another person said to me, 'Why do you give them the fish to eat? Why don't you give them a rod to catch the fish?' So I replied, 'My people, when I pick them up, they can't even stand. They are either sick or hungry. So I take them. Once they are all right, they don't come to me anymore, for they can stand on their own!'

Question What about the Suffering Co-Workers?
Mother Teresa Yes, the Suffering Co-Workers are sick persons

who adopt one of our Sisters. If you are sick, and you have got me and you offer all your pain and all your suffering for me, you offer that to God for me, for the work I do. And I offer the work, and my love of God for you. I help you and you help me. And we become second selves to each other. It is a tremendous gift. You cannot go out to work, so I do the working and you do the suffering. I have a person who does that for me, she has had so many operations already. She offers every operation for me, while I go running about the place for her. She is in terrible pain but she offers everything for me. We have an understanding that we share everything together. That is the bond. She, with suffering, I, with work and prayers. Beautiful. Every Sister has a sick person praying for her.

Question So you get extra strength, and you give that to your work.
Mother Teresa Yes, yes, and they get extra strength from our prayers, from our work, from the sacrifices we make. Beautiful.

Question And the other Co-Workers?
Mother Teresa We have family of almost 400,000 Co-Workers in the world, who come and share the work with the Sisters. I give them the opportunity to touch the poor and the lonely. Loneliness is worse in many ways than physical poverty. Many people of all faiths come to me, not merely to give a donation, but to do work with their hands. Then we have doctors, Medical Co-Workers who come in the dispensaries and they take care of the sick; Youth Co-Workers who spread the love for the poor among the youth, love for purity, love for prayer, they share that among the youth. Youth, they are looking for a challenge. Sometimes they are misled. Lots of them are really longing for God. Look at all the volunteers from all over the world. They come to serve here for two or three months. They work during the whole year to earn

*money, because we give them nothing, so they have to pay
for everything.*

Question An interesting thing I have always observed in
Kalighat is that there are many people there, maybe
a hundred, some close to death, but no-one seems
afraid of death.

*Mother Teresa You feel the presence of God there, and they feel
the love they get. Like one of them said, 'I've lived like an
animal in the street but I will die like an angel,' with love
and care. They die content. 23,000 have died there.*

Question What is their greatest enemy, is it rejection?

*Mother Teresa Poverty. They don't have anything. They have
no-one. They have nothing. They are street cases. We don't
take anyone else, only the sick and dying destitutes; they have
to be from the street. We don't take house cases. In Prem
Dān maybe some of our slum cases are there, but in Kalighat
we don't take anybody else. Prem Dān, have you been there?
You should go there.*

Question You once said to me that the greatest fear a
human being can face is the fear of humiliation.

*Mother Teresa The surest way to be one with God is to accept
humiliation.*

Question Have you encountered humiliation?

Mother Teresa Oh, yes, plenty. This publicity is also humiliation.

Question Is it humiliation, or is it the acceptance of your
work for the poor?

*Mother Teresa Humiliation, because we know we have nothing
ourselves. You see what God has done. I think God is wanting
to show His greatness by using nothingness.*

Question So all these awards that you have received, the
Nobel Prize for instance?

Mother Teresa I don't even remember the number. They are

nothing. Of the Nobel Prize, I said I will accept it if you give it for the glory of God and in the name of the poor. I do not accept awards in my name. I am nothing.

Question You did not allow the traditional banquet to take place after the Nobel investiture?
Mother Teresa No. Instead they gave me the money for it. So we had a big dinner for 2,000 poor people on Christmas Day with that money. That was much better. In Delhi, they gave me a reception and they prepared dinner. I made them all go to Nirmal Hriday, and they fed the people. All the Ministers and the big people went there and fed our people.

Question Do the leprosy patients continue to be the most rejected people?
Mother Teresa Not now. Because we have medicine. And if they come in time we can cure them. But being unwanted is the most terrible disease that human beings can experience. The only cure can lie in willing hands to serve and hearts to go on loving them.

Question And are they able to go back into society?
Mother Teresa Yes, yes. If they come in time. Everywhere we have land to rehabilitate them. In India, we have quite a number of homes: in Delhi, Lucknow, Ranchi, Asansol, Calcutta, many places. The Government has given big amounts of land, we buy the material and give it to the leprosy family. They often build their own houses. In many countries people give us land or a house. Like in Nicaragua, someone gave us a house; in Budapest, someone gave us a house.

Question You have been working in Calcutta for so many years. Has this work changed people's perceptions?
Mother Teresa It has brought many people to love each other better, and that's more important.

Question Are there fewer destitute people now than when you started?

Mother Teresa I don't know. (Laughs) I could not tell you that. But those who die with us, die in peace. For me that is the greatest development of the human life, to die in peace and in dignity, for that's for eternity.

Question I want to ask you a difficult question. You have built up a very large network, and that network is associated with you.

Mother Teresa (Interrupts) How? It is associated with the whole Society, the whole Congregation.

Question Yes, but since you are its foundress, you are synonymous with the Missionaries of Charity.

Mother Teresa That is all right. But only together, with the Sisters.

Question With you as organisational head.

Mother Teresa That's right. It has to be like that. In your family you are the one. That is the same with us. That is the recognition that has to be given, otherwise there would be confusion.

Question But Mother, after you have gone. . . .

Mother Teresa Let me go first. (We laugh) Just as God has found me, He will find somebody else. The work is God's work, and He will see to it.

Question Mother, why are you going up and down the stairs so much [she has a heart problem]? I am sure this is against the doctor's advice.

Mother Teresa (With a laugh) There is no time to think of it.

Question I saw a picture of you in a magazine. You were being shown around the White House in Washington, and you looked as if you were overwhelmed.

Mother Teresa

Mother Teresa I was thinking there was so much room. I feel like taking all my poor people, and filling houses. Seeing the emptiness, I always feel like wanting to fill it. (Laughs)

Question With all this difficult work, how do you still manage a sense of humour?

Mother Teresa But the work is very, very beautiful, you know. We have no reason to be unhappy. We are doing it with Jesus, for Jesus, to Jesus. We are really contemplatives in the heart of the world. Jesus said, whatever you do to the least of my brethren, you do to me. If you give a glass of water in my name, you give it to me. If you receive a little child in my name, you receive me. That is why I want to receive all these unborn children. God's own image is in every single child, no matter what that child is, disabled or beautiful or ugly – it's God's beautiful image created for greater things – to love and be loved. That is why you and I and all of us must insist to preserve the gift of God, for it is something very beautiful. That little one who is unwanted and unloved, who has come into the world already unwanted, what a terrible suffering that is! Today it is the greatest disease, to be unwanted, unloved, just left alone, a throwaway of society.

Question Mother, you told me a beautiful story once, about a woman of Calcutta who shared her rice.

Mother Teresa Yes, I remember. I was not surprised that she gave. This is natural. Poor people are always sharing. But I was surprised that she knew that her neighbours were hungry. People often hide, especially people who have seen better days. Like, a man came here one day. He had been better off before. He had come down in life. He came here one day. He said, 'Mother Teresa, I cannot eat that food that is being given there.' Then I said to him, 'I am eating it every day.' And he looked at me and said, 'You are eating it?' and I said, 'Yes.' Then he said, 'I will eat also.' My eating it gave him courage to accept the humiliation. If I could not have said that, maybe he would have remained hard and bitter inside, and not accepted anything. But when he knew that I was with him he was encouraged . . .

Question Is poverty your strength?

Mother Teresa We do not accept anything, neither church maintenance, nor salary, nor anything for the work we do, all over the world. Every Missionary of Charity is the poorest of the poor. That is why we can do anything. Whatever is given to the poor is the same for us. We wear the kind of clothes they wear. But ours is a choice. We choose that way. To be able to understand the poor, we must know what is poverty. Otherwise we will speak another language, no? We won't be able to come close to that mother who is anxious for her child. We completely depend on providence. We are like the trees, like the flowers. But we are more important to Him than the flowers or the grass. He takes care of them, he takes much greater care of us. That is the beautiful part of the Congregation.

Question What makes you sad?

Mother Teresa When I see people suffer, it makes me sad. The physical suffering of it.

Question How to you view your achievements?

Mother Teresa There is no answer to that. We must not spoil God's work. We don't work for glory or for money. The Sisters are consecrated people. It's a consecrated love. It is all for Jesus. We work for God. Achha, I must run now.

Appendix II

Speech delivered by Mother Teresa on 18 October 1988, on the occasion of the release of the author's book on leprosy

Let us all pray together:

Make us worthy, Lord,
to serve our fellow men throughout the world
who live and die in poverty and hunger.

Give them, through our hands, this day their daily bread;
and by our understanding love, give peace and Joy.

Lord, make me a channel of Thy peace, that,
where there is hatred, I may bring love;
where there is wrong, I may bring the spirit of
    forgiveness;
where there is discord, I may bring harmony;
where there is error, I may bring truth;
where there is doubt, I may bring faith;
where there is despair, I may bring hope;
where there are shadows, I may bring light;
where there is sadness, I may bring joy.

Lord, grant that I may seek rather to comfort
    than to be comforted;
to understand than to be understood;
to love than to be loved;
for it is by forgetting self that one finds;

it is by forgiving that one is forgiven;
it is by dying that one awakens to eternal life.
Amen.

'Leprosy is not a punishment, it can be a very beautiful gift of God if we make good use of it. Through it, we can learn to love the unloved, the unwanted; not only just to give them things but to make them feel that they, too, are useful, that they, too, can do something because they feel they are loved and wanted, that they can share the joy of loving.

'We take care of thousands of leprosy patients; altogether between India, Africa and the Middle East, we take care of 158,000 leprosy patients. Every Christmas, we have a special meal for them. I remember [on one such occasion] a very badly disabled man was sitting near me. When I said that leprosy is not a punishment he started pulling my sari and said, "Say that again, say that again." It touched his heart because he felt, "I am loved, I am wanted." This is what our leprosy brothers and sisters need from us. It is true we need to give them medicines, we do need to do all that. It is a natural thing, but the most wonderful thing is to make them wanted, to make them feel loved.

'Governments have been very good to me everywhere, in the Middle East, in Africa and in India. Especially in India, in giving me land to rehabilitate them. Here in Delhi, we have a beautiful place in Seemapuri, where we take the very badly affected ones from the street. You don't see as many on the streets of Delhi as they were before. We try to get whole families together. In some places we buy building materials so that they can build their own houses. We pay them for building their own houses. They have their own shops, their own little schools and their land, and so they feel they are somebody.

'I think this is the greatest cure, to make them feel that they, too, are chosen ones. And I must say, that we have many people who have offered their services. Doctors are coming to do the operations for disabled people. As you know, a child born of a leprosy family is not a leper. So in every rehabilitation centre, we have a children's home, and as soon as a child is born, before the mother can kiss a child, we take the child away with us. They can come and see, but they cannot kiss the child until the child is able to stand. Many of the children [of our leprosy patients] have now grown up, some are studying, they are working, they are married and have settled down in life, without a sign of the disease. A new energy has come into their lives. They know "I can be all right". Thank God people take them back to work, once we can prove that they are no longer infectious.

'In Titagarh, near Calcutta, they are weaving all our saris [worn by the Missionaries of Charity], they make all our bedsheets and other such things for our homes. An energy has come into their lives, because they, too, are useful, now they, too, can do something because they feel loved and wanted, and can share the joy of loving.

'God has been very good to us in giving us these beautiful opportunities. It is wonderful to see families together, living together, bringing them back together, giving them the joy of living.

'We need to remove our fears. There is one beautiful thing I want you all to do. We have a mobile clinic in Delhi. Put leprosy patients in touch with the Sisters, so that they can get medicines straightaway. That is the greatest love you can show, to get them in touch with any of the people or organisations who are doing this work for leprosy patients, or with our Sisters. And here if any of you wish to visit our homes in Seemapuri, you are welcome.

'Let us encourage leprosy patients to go in time and get treatment in time. If a patient comes to us, we don't touch him until he brings the whole family. We examine the whole family, and decide who has to be put on medicine and so on. It is a beautiful way of showing great love. Let us remember that He wants us to love one another as He loves each one of us. And when we die and go home back to God, again it will be the same thing: "I was hungry, you gave me to eat. I was naked, you clothed me. I was homeless, you took me in, you did all this to me."

'And where does this love begin? In our own home, with our own family, with our own neighbour in need, in our own town, in our own country. So let us pray together. We need to bring back prayer. We are Hindu families, we are joint families, we are praying families. It is important for families to stay together and to pray together.

'In the West, there is loneliness which I call the leprosy of the West. In many ways it is worse than our poor in Calcutta. In Calcutta the poor, they share. I know of a family of six that was starving when our Sisters found them. They gave the woman some rice. But first, she divided it into two portions and gave half to another family that was also starving. I was not surprised that she gave. I was surprised that she *knew*.

'In Yemen, which is an entirely Muslim country, I asked one of the rich people to build a Masjid there. People needed a place to pray. I said to him: "They are all your Muslim brothers and sisters. They need to have a place where they can meet God."

'If you can remove fear, you will have done a lot. It is a big thing. I think this book is going to bring confidence to many people and remove the fear that we have had all these years; to make them really feel that God has done something beautiful for them, that they also can stand like ordinary people and do ordinary work and lead ordinary lives.

'So let us thank God for giving us the beautiful chance to be together, to pray together for our poor brothers and sisters. Thank God that you and that your families are healthy and able to enjoy life, and pray to God for our leprosy patients.'

Appendix III

54A, A.J.C. Bose Road,
Calcutta – 16

2nd January, 1991

Dear President George Bush and President Saddam Hussein

I come to you with tears in my eyes and God's love in my heart to plead to you for the poor and those who will become poor if the war that we all dread and fear happens. I beg you with my whole heart to work for, to labour for God's peace and to be reconciled with one another.

You both have your cases to make and your people to care for but first please listen to the One who came into the world to teach us peace. You have the power and the strength to destroy God's presence and image, His men, His women, and His children. Please listen to the will of God. God has created us to be loved by His love and not to be destroyed by our hatred.

In the short term there may be winners and losers in this war that we all dread but that never can nor never will justify the suffering, pain and loss of life which your weapons will cause.

I come to you in the name of God, the God that we all love and share, to beg for the innocent ones, our poor of the world and those who will become poor because of war. They are the ones who will suffer most because they have no means of escape. I plead on bended knee for them. They will suffer and when they do we will be the ones who are guilty for not having done all in our power to protect and love them. I plead to you for those who will be left orphaned, widowed, and left alone because their parents, husbands, brothers and children have been killed. *I beg you please save them.* I plead for those who will be left with disability and disfigurement. They are God's children. I plead for those who will be left with no home, no food and no love. Please think of them as being your children. Finally I plead for those who will have the most precious thing that God can give us, Life, taken away from them. I beg you to save our brothers and sisters, yours and ours, because they are given to us by God to love and to cherish. It is not for us to destroy what God has given to us. Please, please let your mind and your will become the mind and will of God. You have the power to bring war into the world or to build peace. PLEASE CHOOSE THE WAY OF PEACE.

I, my sisters and our poor are praying for you so much. The whole world is praying that you will open your hearts in love to God. You may win the war but what will the cost be on people who are broken, disabled and lost?

I appeal to you – to your love, your love of God and your fellowmen. In the name of God and in the name of those you will make poor do not destroy life and peace. Let the love and peace triumph and let your name be remembered for the good you have done, the joy you have spread and the love you have shared.

Please pray for me and my sisters as we try to love and serve the poor because they belong to God and are loved in His eyes so we and our poor are praying for you. We pray that you will love and nourish what God has so lovingly entrusted into your care.

May God bless you now and always.

God bless you
lee Teresa me

· *Index* ·

aborigines (Australia), 79
abortion, 119–24, 190
Addis Ababa, 177
adoption, 73, 120, 122, 124–32
Africa, 100, 122, 123, 212
Agnes, Sister (Subashini Das),
    53–7, 62, 71, 86, 159, 184
Agra, 78, 110, 111, 182
Ahmad, Dr, 160
AIDS: and fourth vow of
    Missionaries of Charity, 61;
    homes for sufferers, xv, xvi, 77;
    MT on, 123; visiting patients,
    67, 72
Air India, 132, 133
Albania, 1, 79, 113
Albert, Sister, 118, 119, 143,
    145–8
alcoholics, houses for, xvi, 77, 79,
    93, 94
Alitalia, 132
Ambala, 78
Amravati, 78
Andrew, Brother (Ian Travers-
    Ball), 88–91, 93, 94, 136
Antoine, Father van, 90
Antwerp, 100, 104, 113
Apostolic Nuncio, Delhi, 26
Armenia, 81
Asansol, 22, 89, 90, 141, 142, 206

Asia, 100, 122
Australia, 79

Baithak Khana Church, 21, 46, 54,
    55
Ball, Mother Teresa, 29
Ballestraz family (of Sierre),
    129–31
Bangladesh, 79, 175–6
Bapi (of Calcutta), 115–17, 118
baptism, 73
Barber, Monsignor Eric, 62
Basu, Jyoti, 85
Bauduin, King of Belgium, 85, 175
Begum, Jehanara, 158
Beirut, 189–90
Bengal: Chief Minister of, 68, 174;
    and Great Famine, 17–18; MT
    applies to Loreto order in, 5; MT
    as 'Mother of Bengal', 197; MT
    hears of Loreto nuns in, 4; MT
    remains in province for thirty
    years, 13; and partition, 18
Bernai, Dranafile (MT's mother),
    1; advice to MT, 5; influence on
    MT, 2–3; MT and Father van
    Exem write to, 27–8; sees MT
    for last time, 5
Bernard, Mother *see* Francis
    Xavier, Sister

Bhagalpur, 78
Bharatiya Vidya Bhavan, 190–1
Bharoti, Sister, 82, 83
Birmingham, 96
Birth control, 121, 122; *see also* family planning, natural
Blaikie, Anne, 98–9
Bojaxhiu, Age (MT's sister), 1, 5
Bojaxhiu, Lazar (MT's brother), 1, 2, 4
Bojaxhiu, Mary Teresa *see* Teresa, Mother
Bojaxhiu, Nicholas (MT's father), 1–2, 3
Bombay, 78
Boys' Homes, 120
Boys' Town, 166
Brazil, 79, 93
Breen, Sister Marie-Thérèse, 7, 8, 11–12, 15, 27
Brothers *see* Missionary Brothers of Charity
Budapest, 206
Burma, 17
Burundi, 79, 94
Bush, George, xxii, 175, 217
Butler, Eamon, 167–8

Calcutta: as capital of British Raj, 6; Co-Workers originate in, 98–9; de Decker's plans to work in, 103; effect of MT's work in slums of, xiii; and Great Famine, 17–18; independence, 18; leprosy centre in, 206; MT arrives in, 6; MT returns from Patna to, 30, 31, 37; MT's first patient on streets of, xiv; new house in, 111; partition, 18–19; respect for Sisters, 66; during Second World War, 13, 17; sharing by poor of, 208, 214;

Shishu Bhawan, 65, 90–2, 98, 115–17, 124; news of Vatican decree spreads in, 27; weather in, 37, 115
Calcutta, Archbishop of, 181
Calcutta *Statesman, The,* 58, 98, 187
Cambridge, University of, 180, 184
Campbell Hospital (later Nilaratan Sarkar Hospital), 41, 159
Canada, Co-Workers in, 113
Cape Town, 81
Casa Dono di Maria, Vatican, 82–3
catechism classes, xvi, 13, 22, 77
Catholic action groups, 77
Cenacle, Mother du, 11, 13, 14, 27, 28
Central America, 100
charkhas (spinning wheels), 139
Charles, Prince of Wales, 183
Charu Ma, 49
children: abandoned, xv, xvi, xxiii, 59, 66, 77, 131, 147; and adoption, 73, 120, 122, 124–32; and attempted abortion, 119; crippled, 77; and dowry, 120–1; education of, xv, xvi, 120, *see also* schools; handicapped, 92; homeless, 92, 93; mentally retarded, 77, 93; and parental drug abuse, 119; premature birth of, 119; unwanted, 119–20, 121; welfare of, 77
Chile, 129
Chittagong, East Pakistan, 13
cholera, 41
Cocorote, Venezuela, 78, 79
Collett, Sister, 137
Colombia, 129
Come-and-Sees, 71–2, 94
Co-Workers: bulk purchases by, 100; Constitution, 101; and Gandhi, 97; in London, 96–7;

MT's idea of, 97–8; publicity, 99; returning to the world of materialism, 168; Sick and Suffering, 101–2, 104, 107–8, 113, 203–4
Co-Workers Newsletter, 99, 100
Cox, Mary, 168–9
crèches, 66, 77, 119
Creek Lane: described, 45–6, 50; and grants, 40; move to Motherhouse, 62–3; MT moves in, 46–9, 54; need for larger premises, 61; new house in, 111
cremation, 73, 117, 162, 163
Creusen, Father Joseph, 23

Dacca, 176
Dampremy, 22
Darjeeling, 6–7, 78, 131
Das, Brother Christo, 138
Das, Dalim, 169–70
Das, Subashini *see* Agnes, Sister
de Decker, Jacqueline, 102–14
Delhi, 111; hospitals, xi–xii; leprosy in, xii–xiii, 151, 153–4, 206, 212, 213; MT on Sisters in, 111; MT's 'ashram' in, xvi; Nehru opens home in, 78; Shishu Bhawans, 75, 117–18
Dengal, Mother, 67
Desferal, 129
destitutes, 206; and fourth vow of Missionaries of Charity, 61; homes for, xv, 59, 77; leprosy and, 74, 149, 151; MT's resolve to help, 51–2; *see also* Home for the Dying, Kalighat
Dhapa, Calcutta, 61, 74, 93
Diana, Princess of Wales, 183
disaster relief, 83
dispensaries, 77, 106; established, xv, 28, 37, 40–2; and leprosy,

93, 137; Motherhouse teams for, 66; Sisters run, 57
Diwali, 128
Diwali Adoption Service, 126–31
Dominican Republic, 93
Dorothy, Sister, 56
drug abusers: houses for, xvi, 79, 93, 94; and pregnancy, 119
Dum Dum, 92, 182
Dumka, 119
dying, houses for, xv, 37, 59; *see also* Home for the Dying, Kalighat

East Calcutta, 46
East Pakistan, 18, 46
Eastern Europe, 79, 80
El Salvador, 93
Elise (doctor-in-charge at Patna), 32
Elizabeth II, Queen, 182–3
'Emaques, Sister', 71
Emergency, the, xviii
England: Co-Workers in, 98–9, 113; new houses opened in, 79
Ethiopia, 79, 173, 176–8
Ethiopian Airlines, 132
exclaustration, indent of, 22, 24–6
Exem, Father Celeste van: as MT's spiritual confessor, xxi–xxii, 1, 57–8; on MT's family, 1–2; in retirement, 8–9; meets MT for first time (1944), 9; on MT's call to leave Loreto and start own work, 19–21; and events leading to Vatican decree, 21–6; blesses MT's saris, 27, 28, 32; writes to MT's mother, 27–8; MT requests to return to Calcutta from Patna, 31–2; arranges for MT to stay with Little Sisters of the Poor, 32; and 'book' of MT's work, 35–6; arranges for MT to stay

Exem, Father Celeste van – *cont.*
with Gomes, 46; at Creek Lane,
49; and MT's religion, 53;
announcement for *musti bhikkha*,
56; writes Constitution of
Missionaries of Charity, 59;
reads Decree of Erection, 60–1;
and acquisition of Motherhouse,
62; explains rule of nuns
travelling in pairs, 66; and MT's
wish to step down, 86; and
Brothers, 89–90, 92; local
opposition to Home for the
Dying, 160; on MT's encounter
with Zia-ul-Haq, 175; and MT's
invitations from churchmen,
188; character, 193; points way
to milestones in MT's life, 193

Faculty of Theology, 22
family: of leprosy sufferers, 213;
Missionaries of Charity sever
links with own, 70; MT on, xx;
MT on her own, 1–2; MT
separated from her, xxi, 20, 199;
visiting, 77
family planning, natural, 77, 119,
121, 190; *see also* birth control
feeding programme, 56, 77
France, 93, 113
Francesca, Sister, 12–13, 14
Francis of Assisi, St, xviii, 101, 186
Francis Xavier, Sister (Mother
Bernard), 29, 110, 144
Fumascni-Biondi, Cardinal Petrus,
58

Gabrić, Father, 90
Gandhi, Indira, 75, 174
Gandhi, Mahatma Mohandas
Karamchand, 18, 97, 136, 139,
188–91

Gandhi, Rajiv, 174
Gandhiji Prem Niwas Leprosy
Centre, Titagarh *see* Titagarh
Guatemala, 93
Gaza Strip, 79
General Chapter, 84, 85, 86
Geneva, 126, 127
Geoff, Brother, 91–2, 94–5
Germany, 144
Gertrude, Mother General of
Loreto, 21, 24–5, 42
Gertrude, Sister (Magdalena
Gomes), 13, 55, 184
Gita (at Shantinagar), 118–19
Goa, 78
Gobra Hospital, Calcutta, 149–50
Gomes, Alfred, 46
Gomes, Mabel, 50, 51
Gomes, Magdalena (later Sister
Gertrude), 13, 54–5
Gomes, Michael, 20, 45, 46, 48–53,
55–7, 61, 98
Good Housekeeping, 180–1
Gorbachov, Mikhail, xxii, 79
Great Famine (1942–43), 17–18,
20

Haile Selassie, Emperor, 176–8
Haiti, 93, 94
Harvard University, 180
Hasina (at Kalighat), 171
Hazaribagh coal mining area,
Bihar state, 91
Henry, Father Julien, 19, 22–3, 34,
46, 50, 56, 61
Holland, 181
Holy Congregation, Rome, 25
Home for the Dying (Nirmal
Hriday), Kalighat, xiv–vi, xxiv,
52, 66, 69, 73, 98, 117, 144,
155–72, 178, 181, 186, 190, 194,
195, 205

Hong Kong, 93
Hooghly, 142
Howrah railway station, Calcutta, 52, 53, 87, 92, 142
Hussein, Saddam, xxii, 217

India: and adoption, 120, 124, 129; Co-Workers in, 98; first Loreto Sisters sent to, 29; great respect for holiness, 66; independence, 18, 24, 73; MT hears of Jesuit mission to Bengal, 4; MT sets sail for (1928), 6; MT's regular visits to Missions in, 68; partition, 18; Pope Paul VI visits, 144; preference for a male child, 125; and South Africa, 81; statistics of leprosy, 149
Indian National Congress, 18
Institute of Mary, 26n
International Association of Co-Workers of Mother Teresa *see* Co-Workers
International Speakers of the Co-Workers, 100
Iraq, MT opens centres in, xxii, 179
Irwin, Mother Borgia, 6
Islam, Dr, 62

Jagdish (at Kalighat), 166
Jambrenkovic, Father, 3–4
Jansen, Father John Baptist, 23
Japan: Brothers in, 93; MT opens home in, 79; in Second World War, 17
Jesuits, 4, 59, 90, 91, 103
Jhansi, 78, 111
Jinnah, Mohammed Ali, 18
John Paul II, Pope, 81–2, 178–9, 188
Jordan, 79

Joseph Kennedy Jr Foundation, 182
Joseph Michael, Sister, 8, 49, 168, 193
Juan Carlos, King of Spain, 175

Kalighat, 155–6, 160; *see also* Home for the Dying, Kalighat
Kalu (leprosy patient), 151–3
Kennedy, Jackie, 180
Kennedy family, 182
Kerala, 102
Kidderpore, 91
King, Martin Luther, Jr, 184
Kipling, Rudyard, 19
Knox, Archbishop (Papa Nuncio, New Delhi), 78
Korea, 93

Lausanne, 128
Legion of Mary, 56
Leningrad, 113
leprosy sufferers: abandoned, xxiii, 40; battle against stigma attached to, 149–54, 203; and Brothers, 93; centres, xii–xiii, xv, 59, 66, 77, 110, 206; children of, 213; and fourth vow of Missionaries of Charity, 61; and Gandhi's Co-Workers, 97; medicines, 75, 206; mobile clinics, 150, 213; MT speaks on (Delhi, 1987), xviii, xx, 154, 211–15; statistics, 148–9, 212; treatment, xvi; visiting, 74
Letnice, Lady of, 3
Lieutenant Governor of Delhi: allows author time off, xviii; and leprosy centre, xii–xiii, 151; and MT's Delhi hospital appeal xi–xii
Links', 99

Little Sisters of the Poor: MT shares companionship of, 48; MT stays with, 32, 46; MT travels to Motijhil from Convent, 34–5
Liverpool, 96
London, 79, 95–7, 101
Loreto Abbey, Rathfarnam, Ireland: first Loreto Sisters sent to India, 29; Mother General at, 21, 24–5; MT at, 5, 6; Sister Breen at, 11; Sister Rozario at, 14
Loreto College, 11
Loreto Convent, Entally: described, 10; and leprosy patients, 137, 150; Mother Provincial pleads for MT's return to, 44; MT applies to, 5; MT called to leave and start own work, 19; MT continues contacts with, 28–9; MT first hears, 4; MT leaves, xv, 19–20, 27, 54; MT's ex-students in Taltolla, 32; MT's years as a Loreto nun, xxi; during Second World War, 17; Sister Breen at, 11–12; written script on MT, 9, 10
Loreto Novitiate, Darjeeling, 6–7, 11
Loreto Sisters: descended from Institute of Mary, 26n; MT given four, 28–9
Los Angeles, 93
Louvain, Catholic University of, 102
Luciana (volunteer), 82
Lucknow, 206
Luthuli, Albert, 184

Machoud family, 131
McNamara, Robert S., 185–6
Madagascar, 93
Madonna, 180
Madras, 102, 103
Madras, University of, 180
Major, John, 175
Manchester, 96
Mansatala Row, Calcutta, 91, 92
Margaret Mary, Sister, 56
Mariadas, Brother, 135, 136, 138–42
Medical Mission Sisters, Patna, 27, 30–2, 35, 43, 103
Mekhand Dam, 144
meningitis, 41
mentally retarded, 74, 93
Miami, 160
Middle East, 212
Migros (Swiss supermarket chain), 76
Millar, Jo, 126–30
Missionaries of Charity, Order of the: forbidden to accept refreshments, xii, xiii, 66–7; vows, xiv, 60–1, 200; institutional ventures, xv; as multinational organisation, xvi, 45, 63; training, xvi, 70, 72; MT on work in field of leprosy, xx; MT's close connections with, xxii, 207; spreads to more than 100 countries, 14, 63, 203; Loreto past pupils as, 29; MT moves into Creek Lane, 46–9; Constitution, 51, 58–60, 70, 74, 84, 85; first postulant, 54–5; number of young women join MT, 56, 71, 72; second postulant, 54–5; and decision to accept the group as a congregation, 57–8; MT's underlying concept of the congregation, 59–60, 162; further members of the Order, 61; a cheerful nature important, 70; freedom to leave, 71–2, 200;

donations to, 75; range of activities, 77; opening of new houses, 77–9, 81–3; as a congregation of pontifical right, 79; organisation, 83–4; General Chapter, 84, 85; and Co-Workers, 96, 99; and Shishu Bhavans, 117–20; and adoption, 122, 124, 126; Pope Paul VI touched by work of, 144; Dr Sen impressed by selfless work of, 150; dedicated to Immaculate Heart of Mary, 156; and wish to work at Kalighat, 169; sacrifice of, 199, and doubts, 200–10; poverty of, 208

Missionary Brothers of Charity, 87–95, 120, 135, 136, 138–42

Mitterand, François, 175

Motherhouse, xxi, 30, 112, 192; daily routine, 65–9; described, 63, 64–5; and family visits, 121; life without luxuries in, 69–70; move to, 62–3; MT's work at, xvi, 68–9; office in, xvi, 68–9, 75; press besieges, 187

Motijhil slum, Calcutta, 19, 51; MT first visits, 33–4; MT travels from Little Sisters of the Poor Convent to, 34–5; MT's first Home for the Dying in, 160; MT's group welcomed, 57; MT's medical help to, xv; MT's school in (Nirmal Hriday), xv, 34–40, 42, 43, 158, 160; *The Statesman* advertisement, 58

Murphy, Sister (Mistress of Novices), 7

Muslim League, 18

Nabo Jeevan, Howrah, Calcutta, 92

Nairobi, 81

Nansen, Fridtjof, 184

Natural Family Planning Centres, 121

Nehru, Jawaharlal, 78, 135, 181

Netherlands *see* Holland

New Delhi, 6, 81

New York, 79, 180

Newark (New Jersey), 180

Nicaise, Father, 38

Nicaragua, 206

night shelters, 77

Nilaratan Sarkar Hospital (previously Campbell Hospital), 159

Nirmala, Sister, 86

Nirmal Hriday, Delhi, xi, xviii, 206

Nirmal Hriday, Kalighat *see* Home for the Dying, Kalighat

Nirmal Hriday, Motighil *see under* Motighil

Nirmala Kennedy Centre, Dum Dum, Calcutta, 182

Nirmala Shishu Bhawan, Calcutta, 182

Nirmala Shishu Bhawan, Calcutta, 65, 90–2, 98, 115–17, 127, 183

Northern Ireland, 79

Norway, 187

Norway, King of, 185

Nurpur, 93

nursery classes, 66

Oslo, 184, 185

Pagola (patient at Kalighat), 157

Pakistan, 18, 175

Pan Am, 132

Panama, 79

Pandit, Mrs, 181

Papua New Guinea, 79

Paris, 94

Patna, 78; *see also* Medical Mission Sisters, Patna

Paul VI, Pope, 144

Perier, Archbishop of Calcutta: and acquisition of Mother house, 62; and 'book' of MT's work, 35, 36; and decision to accept MT's group as a congregation, 57–8; and Decree of Erection, 60; grants permission for MT's return from Patna, 32; launches first mobile leprosy clinic, 150; and MT's call to work directly with the poor, 21–6; and opening of new houses, 77–8; opposes new ideas, 89; supports MT for rest of his life, 59; and Venezuela, 78–9

Peru, 94

Philip, Prince, Duke of Edinburgh, 183, 184

Philippines, 79, 93, 182

plague, 41

poliomyelitis, 126, 127–8

Portugal, 79

Prem Dān, Calcutta, 74, 205

Priscilla, Sister, 180

prison visiting, xvi, 77

prostitution, 122

Punjab, 18

Raipur, 127

Raj Bhavan, 11, 18n

Ranchi, 78, 111, 206

Rao, Narasimha, 188

Rashtrapati Bhavan, 181

Rathfarnam *see* Loreto Abbey, Rathfarnam

Reagan, Ronald, 173, 175

rehabilitation centres, 77

Riccardo (volunteer), 82–3

Romania, 76, 113

Rome: houses opened in, 79, 81; MT becomes ill in, 85; Princess Diana visits MT in, 183; visiting AIDS sufferers in, 67, 72

Roy, Dr B. C., 58, 150

Roy, Miss (Inspectress of Schools), 40

Rozario (O'Reilly), Sister, 14, 27, 28–9, 34, 41

Rudaz family, 127–8

Sabitri, 40

Sacred Heart, Church of the, Skopje, 2, 3

St Joseph's Cathedral, Trivandrum, 102

St Joseph's Home, 33

St Mary's School, Calcutta: average day at, 12; described, 10; MT looked after by ex-cook of, 49; MT made principal, 13, 14; MT sent to teach at, 8; MT's love of teaching at, 11; during Second World War, 17; and slum teaching, 35, 37, 43; Sodality at, 19, 22, 28, 34

St Teresa's Church, 22

St Teresa's parish school, Calcutta, 34, 41

St Teresa's Primary School, 13, 28

St Xavier's College, 8

Salvator Mundi hospital, Rome, 85

San Diego University of, 180

San Francisco, 180

San José, 180

Sanders, Father, 22

Sannes, Professor John, 185–6

Santosh (at Shantinagar), 146–7, 148

satyagraha, 189

schools: in Darjeeling, 7; established, xv; MT's family at, 2; MT's Sisters receive free education at Loreto, 28; and Shishu Bhawans, 118; and slum children, xvi; Sunday, 77, 110

Schweitzer, Albert, 184

Scranton (Pennsylvania), 160

Sealdah, 37, 87

secularisation, indent of, 24, 25

Seemapuri, 212, 213

Sen, Dr, 150

Sewagram, 136

Shantinagar, West Bengal: leprosy centre, 78, 118, 141–8, 182; Shishu Bhawan, 118, 145, 146

Shishu Bhawans, xxiii, 73, 115–21; and adoption, 73, 120, 124; and Brothers, 90, 91; in Calcutta (Nirmala), 65, 90–2, 98, 115–17, 124, 166; in Delhi, 75, 117–18; and leprosy centres, 118; Shantinagar, 118, 145, 146; and unwanted children, 119–20, 124

'shut-ins', xvi, xx, 97, 100

Sicily, 79

Sick and Suffering Co-Workers, 101–2, 104, 107–8, 113, 203–4

Sierre, 129, 131

Siliguri, 126

Simla, 7, 111

Skopje, xxi, 1, 5

Snehlata (at Kalighat), 170–1

Sodality of the Blessed Virgin Mary, 3–4, 5, 19, 22, 28, 34

soup kitchens, 82–3, 94, 97, 178

South Africa, 79, 81

South America, 100, 122, 125

Southworth, John, 98–9

Soviet Union: houses opened in, 79, 81; refuses to allow MT to open a convent, xxii, 79

sponsors, 120

Stephanie, Sister, 32

sterilisation, 121

Sudan, 202–3

Suma, Sister, 166, 169, 170–1

Sweden, 181, 187

Switzerland, 126–31

Tagore, Rabindranath, 160, 187

Taiwan, 93, 94

Taltolla suburb, Calcutta, 33

Teresa, Mother, of Calcutta (Mary Teresa Bojaxhiu): and Delhi hospitals, xi–xii; requests leprosy centre, xii–xiii; appearance, xiii, 4, 32, 35, 69; Indian citizenship, xiii; at Loreto Convent, xv, xxi, 8–15, 17–20; school in Motijhil, xv, 34–40; work at Motherhouse, xvi, 65, 68–9; speaks on leprosy, xviii, xx, 154, 211–15; family of, xxi, 1–5, 20; attitude to biographies, xxi; honours, xxii, 2, 75, 78, 102, 179–88, 190–1, 197, 205–6; power of, xxii–xxiii, xxiv, 83–4, 173–9; and Shishu Bhawans, xxiii, 75, 115, 117–21, 124, 133; birth, 1; education, 2; mother's influence, 2, 3; death of father, 3; first feels desire to become a nun, 3; early contact with Sodality, 3–4; receives her call, 4–5; learnt English at Rathfarnam, 5, 6; at Loreto Novitiate, 6–7; first vows (1931), 7, 10; choice of name, 7–8; sent to teach at St Mary's School, 8; Sister Breem on, 11–12; takes Final Vows, 13; and partition, 18; called to work directly with poor, 19–21, 59, 60; transferred

Teresa, Mother, of Calcutta – *cont.*
to Asansol, 22; events leading to
Vatican decree, 22–6; medical
training, 27; 'book' of her work,
35–6, 50; first rude shock over
begging, 39; opens first
dispensary, 40–2; opens school
at Tiljala, 42; doubts about her
activities, 44, 57; moves into
Gomes house, 46–9; and
Kalighat, 52, 98, 157–63, 167–72,
181, 186, 190, 195, 205; joined by
St Mary's ex-students, 54, 56;
underlying concept of the
congregation, 59–60; move to
bigger premises, 61–3; work
routine, 68–9; and training of
novices, 70; 'Sister Emaques'
episode, 71; principle of going
on to the streets, 73–4; and
institutions, 74; and Titagarh,
74, 135, 136, 138, 203; declines
offer of regular income, 74;
forbids fundraising, 75; and
'sacrifice money', 75–6, 77;
opens first house outside
Calcutta, 78; tries to step down
from office, 85–6; illness, 85,
176, 178, 183, 194, 207; and
Brothers, 88–91, 135; and
Co-Workers, 97–102, 204; visits
England, 99; and de Decker/Sick
and Suffering Co-Workers,
102–14; and Shantinagar leprosy
centre, 118, 141, 143–5; and
family planning, 121, 122, 190;
and abortion, 121–4, 190; and
sterilisation, 121; Nobel Lecture
(1979), 123; and adoption,
124–9, 131, 132; battle against
stigma attached to leprosy,
149–50; visits Delhi leprosy
centre, 151, 154; and Ethiopia,
173–4, 176–8; and Indira
Gandhi, 174–5; and Bangladesh,
175–6; and John Paul II, 178;
joint letter to Presidents of Iraq
and USA, 179, 217–19;
unsuccessful intercessions, 179;
compared with Mahatma
Gandhi, 188–91; at prayer,
194–5; as the conscience of
Calcutta, 195; source of
strength, 201–2; on Suffering
Co-Workers, 203–4
character: charisma, xviii, 72;
charity, 15; courage, 189–91;
dedication, 15; enthusiasm, xxii;
faith, xiv, xv, xxii, xxiv, 37, 44,
190; gentleness, 11; grace, xiii,
xxii; humility, xiv, xxii, xxiii, 15;
inspiration, xxii; obedience, 15,
21, 25, 190, 200; organisation, 4;
perception, xiii; practicality, xiii,
43; punctuality, 14; selflessness,
14; sense of humour, 11, 15, 38,
76, 112–13, 207; simplicity, 11,
15, 21, 192; unsentimentality,
xiii
Teresa of Ávilla, St, 8
tetanus, 41
thalassaemia, 126, 128, 129
thalidomide, 130
Thérèse of Lisieux, St (Thérèse
Martin), 7
Tijuana, Mexico, 183
Tiljala slum, Calcutta, 36, 42
Titagarh, 74, 93, 135, 141, 188, 203,
213
Toledo (Ohio), 180
Travers-Ball, Ian *see* Andrew,
Brother
tuberculosis, 40, 41, 50, 56, 66, 75,
93, 158, 161, 162, 166

Index

United Nations, 123, 126

United Nations Fund for Population Activities (UNFPA), 123

United States of America: conflict with Iraq, 179; Co-Workers in, 99, 113; and Ethiopia, 173; honours to MT, 180; new houses opened in, 79

untouchability, 97

unwed mothers, 77, 122, 124

Vatican: agrees to MT's request to be allowed to stand down, 85–6; decree, 26, 28; house in, 81–2, 178–9; and indent of exclaustration, 25; Missionaries placed directly under, 79; MT's need for authority to work directly with the poor, 21–2; recognises Co-Workers, 102; suppresses Institute of Mary's activities, 26n

Venezuela: first house overseas opened in (1965), 13, 78–9; more houses opened in, 79

Venice, Yugoslavia, 1

Venturella (volunteer), 82

Vietnam, 93

Vincent, Archibishop Albert, 89

Vishva Bharati University of Shantiniketan, 180

vocational training, 92

volunteers (at Kalighat), 167–9

Ward, Mary, 26

Washington, 180

West Africa, 100

West Bengal, 18

Yemen, 79, 214

Yugoslavia, 1; Jesuits from, 4, 59

Zagreb, 5

Zia, Begum Khaleda, 176

Zia-ul-Haq, General, 175